Curtis Frye
Popular computer book author and expert in privacy-enhancing technologies

Microsoft®

Home Networking

Take charge of your home network—
faster, smarter, *better*!

PUBLISHED BY
Microsoft Press
A Division of Microsoft Corporation
One Microsoft Way
Redmond, Washington 98052-6399

Library of Congress Cataloging-in-Publication Data
Frye, Curtis, 1968-
Faster Smarter Home Networking / Curtis Frye.
p. cm.
Includes index.
ISBN 0-7356-1869-0
1. Home computer networks. I. Title.

TK5105.75 .F79 2002
004.6'8--dc21 2002033844

Printed and bound in the United States of America.

1 2 3 4 5 6 7 8 9 QWE 8 7 6 5 4 3

Distributed in Canada by H.B. Fenn and Company Ltd.

A CIP catalogue record for this book is available from the British Library.

Microsoft Press books are available through booksellers and distributors worldwide. For further information about international editions, contact your local Microsoft Corporation office or contact Microsoft Press International directly at fax (425) 936-7329. Visit our Web site at www.microsoft.com/mspress. Send comments to *mspinput@microsoft.com.*

Acquisitions Editor: Martin DelRe
Project Editor: Jenny Moss Benson
Series Editor: Kristen Weatherby

Body Part No. X08-95131

Table of Contents

For my family.

Acknowledgments

Getting a book ready for the printer is very much akin to getting a kindergarten into space. I don't think it's an exaggeration to say that the only way we finished *Faster Smarter Home Networking* on time was through the tireless work of project editor Jenny Moss Benson. She provided much needed feedback on my writing, kept the process moving, and was there to prop me up when I hit the inevitable lull halfway through the first draft. This is the second time I've worked with Jenny, and I look forward to the next! Technical editor Chris Russo kept me on the straight and narrow, copy editor Lisa Wehrle made sure I made sense and avoided the passive voice, and Tempe Goodhue from nSight provided valuable feedback from what she called a "pre-beginner" standpoint that ensured I didn't make undue assumptions. The art and design team from nSight also did a great job, especially Patty Fagan, who created the art and composed the book. Thanks to them all!

I'd also like to thank my acquisitions editor, Martin DelRe, for trusting me with this project and for lending his expertise during an epic phone call when we put the finishing touches on the book outline. As always, thanks also go out to my indefatigable agent, Neil Salkind of StudioB, for all of his hard work and to David and Sherry Rogelberg, the founders of StudioB, who took me on lo those many years ago.

Introduction

This Book Could Be for You

Have you ever used a floppy disk to transfer a file from one computer to another, waited until late at night for a family member to finish using the computer with the high-speed Internet connection so you could do your homework or important research for a fantasy sports league, or wished you could print a document on the laser printer in the next room instead of on the color ink jet printer connected to the computer you're using? If you have, this book is definitely for you.

Creating a home network is a lot like setting up your own private Internet. Just as you can use your Internet connection to surf the World Wide Web and download interesting files, you can create a home network so your reports, homework, and vacation pictures are available from anywhere in your home!

Finally, this book is most definitely for you if you're building or remodeling a house and would like information on how to run network cables through your walls. There are a bunch of little things you can do to make your life easier when you install the cables for a wired network, and I've done my best to cover the tricks of the trade that will help you on your way to better networking.

An Overview of the Book

I've devoted Chapters 1 and 2 to the "vision thing." I describe networks in general and then go into more detail about how home networks let you do things you can do only with much difficulty, if at all, when your computers aren't connected. The overview in Chapter 1 includes a brief history of networks and how they're constructed, but I've also gone into some more detail about what you can do with a network. As I alluded to in this section's introduction, home networks are remarkably flexible. In Chapter 2, I describe the technologies behind home networks, whether you want to build a network where your computers are connected by wires or to link your computers using wireless networking technologies. I should note that the price difference between wired and wireless networking equipment has dropped dramatically, so you may find that the easier installation and greater flexibility of wireless networking technologies are more than worth the extra dollars you'd spend to set up a network where you don't have to put each of your computers on a leash.

I continue to get more specific about what goes into creating a network in Chapter 3, where I discuss the hardware that either goes into or connects to your computer as part of your network. If you currently have Internet access, you certainly have a modem and an account with an Internet service provider, but your computer might not have some of the other hardware you need to connect your computers in a home network. But not to worry! I'll show you what you need to buy and what you don't need to buy. I'll also walk you through the process of setting up an Internet connection, in case you're getting onto the Internet for the first time, and I'll tell you how to troubleshoot your Internet connection if it doesn't seem to work properly.

Chapter 4 is where the rubber really meets the road. I start out with some advice on how to best run the wires for a wired network. I'll give some of that advice away right now and tell you that you can hide your wires effectively by running them through closets and along baseboards, but there's a lot more to it than that. I've gone into some detail about what tools you'll need and how you can run the wires without threatening your sanity, but the best advice I could ever give you is to plan every step of the way. If you know how your house is laid out from floor to floor, you can find unique solutions for your situation that I could never anticipate.

And then there's the actual network setup, which I cover in detail throughout the rest of Chapter 4. I've developed six scenarios that cover the most common home network patterns, so whether you want to go wired or wireless, with a high-speed Internet connection or with no connection at all, you can find the information you need to create your network. I did say earlier that the chapters in this book stand by themselves, but in the spirit of planning everything, I do recommend you read the network scenarios so you get a feel for exactly what it is you're planning. Even if you're an old hand at computers and have no trouble installing the networking hardware needed to bring your network to life, it couldn't hurt to read through the scenarios and fix in your mind precisely what you want your network to look like when you're done.

Once you've got your network up and running, you should definitely read Chapters 5 and 6, where I discuss ways you can make your network and the individual computers on your network more secure. The first thing I do in Chapter 5 is describe the types of threats you're likely to face when you're connected to the Internet. Whether you are concerned about folks trying to find out your passwords by posing as technical support workers or need to guard against other users trying to hack into your computer from somewhere else on the Internet, I'll show you everything you need to know to keep them at bay. In Chapter 6

I talk about creating accounts on your computers to control how folks in your household can use your machines.

Once you've got your computers secured, you can take the time to share your files with other users on your network. In Chapter 7, I'll show you how to share your files, to restrict access to any folders you don't want to make fully available, and to reach out across the network to find the files you want. In other words, if doesn't matter which computer on the network you're using...if the file you want is in a shared folder, you can reach out and get it. Sharing printers is no problem, either. In Chapter 8, I'll show you how to add a printer to your network and make it available for anyone to use. Or not—it's your choice whether to share a printer, require anyone who wants to use it to enter a password, or to remove it from your network entirely.

Chapters 9 and 10 get into some of the fun stuff you can do with a home network. In Chapter 9, I show you how to use the Microsoft .NET Messenger programs to send instant messages over the Internet, and also to enhance those sessions with voice or, if your systems allow it, video! You can also use the advanced networking capabilities of Microsoft Windows XP to provide remote assistance to folks from anywhere on the Internet. For readers who like to play games, or who would like to get into playing networked games, Chapter 10 is a feast of information on how to set up your network for gaming, how to update your games, and how to configure your games so they run well over your network.

The last two chapters in the book are a bit more cut and dried than the gaming and network communication chapters, but they're very important. Chapter 11 shows you how to maintain your network so it continues to run effectively. Network maintenance isn't a reactive thing—you need to update your virus scanners, download new software to power your hardware, and install the newest operating system updates so your computer will be secured against attack. You should also back up your data as often as you can—once a month is probably enough, but once a week is much, much better. If something does go wrong with your network, you can always turn to Chapter 12 for troubleshooting information.

And don't forget the back of the book! An appendix compares the features of the latest Microsoft operating systems; if you need to make a decision about what system will meet your needs best, the tables in this appendix will help you to find your way. There's also a glossary. You can find definitions for all of the new terms in the book there, plus definitions for a few words I didn't use that you may encounter elsewhere.

Reader Aids

The majority of the book is taken up with explanatory text and the procedures you'll follow to create and customize your home networks, but if this is your first time investigating home networks, you'll undoubtedly encounter a fair number of new terms, not to mention new pieces of equipment. I've used a number of different reader aids to set apart important information in the text. In some cases I've defined terms, in others I've expanded on a point in the text to give you some context for my ramblings, and in still others I've warned you about potential problems you may face or mistakes I've made (so you don't have to make them, too).

Here are the different types of reader aids you'll find in *Faster Smarter Home Networking*:

- **Lingo** A definition of a technical term that appears italicized in the paragraph text.
- **Tip** Additional techniques or insights that help you understand a task and move through it more effectively.
- **Note** Additional, useful information on a topic that doesn't fit into the main discussion.
- **Caution** A warning of potential problems or preventative measures you can take to avoid a sticky situation.
- **See Also** A cross-reference to related material presented elsewhere in the book.
- **Try This!** A quick procedure you can work through to test what you've learned. Of course, *Faster Smarter Home Networking* is in many ways one long Try This!, but I've thrown in a couple of these aids in spots where you can test my advice right away.

System Requirements

As home networking technologies continue to mature, you'll find that many new networking and multimedia capabilities are built right into your operating system. Where appropriate, I've listed the minimum requirements to run the three major operating systems I'm covering in this book (Windows XP, Microsoft Windows Millennium Edition [Me] and Microsoft Windows 98 Second Edition [SE]) and noted where some additional capabilities I mention in the book require a more powerful computer than what is needed to run the operating system itself.

Note You can create a home network using computers running Windows 98 Second Edition, which means that you can use pretty much any computer you have lying around the house to create a home network!

Here's What You Need to Run Windows XP

Windows XP, the newest operating system for the home and business, will often be installed on any computer you buy. But, just for the record, here's what you need to run Windows XP.

- PC with 300 megahertz (MHz) or higher processor clock speed recommended; 233-MHz minimum required; Intel Pentium/Celeron family, AMD K6/Athlon/Duron family, or compatible processor recommended.
- 128 megabytes (MB) of RAM or higher recommended (64 MB minimum supported; may limit performance and some features).
- 1.5 gigabyte (GB) of available hard disk space.
- Super VGA (800 × 600) or higher resolution video adapter and monitor.
- CD-ROM or DVD drive.
- Keyboard and Microsoft Mouse or compatible pointing device.

Using additional capabilities, such as Internet access or networking, does require additional equipment or services.

- For Internet access:
  - Some Internet functionality may require Internet access, a Microsoft .NET Passport account, and payment of a separate fee to a service provider; local and/or long-distance telephone toll charges may apply
  - 14.4 kilobits per second (Kbps) or higher-speed modem
- For networking:
  - Network adapter appropriate for the type of local-area, wide-area, wireless, or home network you wish to connect to, and access to an appropriate network infrastructure; access to third-party networks may require additional charges
- For instant messaging, voice and videoconferencing, and application sharing, both parties need:
  - Microsoft .NET Passport account and Internet access or Microsoft Exchange 2000 Server instant messaging account and network

access (some configurations may require download of additional components)

- For voice and videoconferencing, both parties also need:
  - 33.6-Kbps or higher modem, or a network connection
  - Microphone and sound card with speakers or headset
- For videoconferencing, both parties also need:
  - Video conferencing camera
  - Windows XP
- For application sharing, both parties also need:
  - 33.6-Kbps or higher modem, or a network connection
  - Windows XP
- For remote assistance:
  - Both parties must be running Windows XP and be connected by a network

Here's What You Need to Run Windows Me

The basic system requirements for Windows Me are:

- Pentium 150-MHz processor or better
- 32 MB of RAM or better
- Minimum 320 MB of free hard-disk space
- 28.8-Kbps modem or faster with current Internet connection
- CD-ROM drive
- Sound card
- Speakers or headphones
- Microsoft Mouse or compatible pointing device
- VGA or higher resolution monitor

If you want to use Windows Media Player 7, Microsoft recommends (apart from the requirements listed above):

- SVGA Monitor
- Pentium II 166-MHz processor or better
- 64 MB of RAM
- 1 GB of free hard-disk space

What You Need to Run Windows 98 SE

The following list describes the minimum hardware requirements for Windows 98 SE:

- A personal computer with a 486 DX 66-MHz or faster processor (Pentium central processing unit recommended).
- 16 MB of memory (24 MB recommended).
- A typical upgrade from Windows 95 requires approximately 195 MB of free hard disk space, but the hard disk space may range from between 120 MB and 295 MB, depending on your computer configuration and the options that you choose to install.
- A full install of Windows 98 requires 225 MB of free hard disk space, but may range from between 165 MB and 355 MB, depending on your computer configuration and that options that you choose to install.
- One 3.5-inch high-density floppy disk drive.
- VGA or higher resolution (16-bit or 24-bit color SVGA recommended).

Support

Every effort has been made to ensure the accuracy of this book. Microsoft Press provides corrections for books at the following address:

http://www.microsoft.com/mspress/support

If you have comments, questions, or ideas regarding this book, please send them to Microsoft Press via e-mail to:

mspinput@microsoft.com

or via postal mail to:

Microsoft Press
Attn: *Faster Smarter* Editor
One Microsoft Way
Redmond, WA 98052-6399

You can also contact the author directly at *cfrye@techsoc.com* with any comments or suggestions.

Please note that product support is not offered through the above addresses.

Chapter 1

An Overview of Home Networking

By itself, a computer is a powerful tool. You can use it to write reports, play games, surf the Web, or even create programs that do exactly what you want them to. Computers are so useful, in fact, that many households have more than one. For roommates who share a house or an apartment it makes sense for each to have his or her own computer, and in a family setting the kids can use their own computers and finish their homework at a reasonable hour, instead of waiting their turn and then getting to bed late. When you hook your home computers together, you'll find that the benefits of each individual computer increase dramatically.

If you and your coworkers use computers as part of your jobs, those computers are probably connected in a *network*. When computers are part of a network, you can choose to make some of your files available to your coworkers, print a hard copy of a report on the nice color printer on the other side of the building, or send e-mail to a lucky colleague who got to go to that week-long conference in Paris.

Lingo A network is a group of computers that are connected and able to exchange data.

Based on the fact that you're reading this book, I'm taking a guess you're interested in setting up a network in your home. Maybe you have a number of computers around the house and want everybody to be able to use the Internet at the same time, or maybe you want to let your kids print out interesting Web pages or their homework without buying them each their own printer or having them come traipsing into your home office at all hours. Or maybe you have friends who come over and play a role-playing or combat game into the wee hours of the morning.

But then you think about the size and complexity of the network in your office and how hard it must be to install. If you've never done any networking before, living with a home "sneakernet" (where you put on your sneakers and carry files from place to place on floppy disks) might not seem so bad after all.

Never fear! If you're worried that setting up a network is a tremendous undertaking that only the bravest, hardiest, and most technically savvy souls should attempt, you can set those concerns aside. If you can turn a screwdriver and rearrange your furniture, you have all the skills needed to connect your computers to a network. Yeah, you might need to add some software to your computers to make the network work, but it's not too much more difficult than putting in a game.

My job for the rest of this chapter is to introduce the hardware and software pieces you put together to build a home network. Once you can recognize the elements of a network, I'll give you an idea of how you can piece them together to make fun and useful things happen.

How to Recognize a Network When You See One

Because you've spent some time around computers, you know that there are usually a fair number of wires and cables running from the body of the computer to the bits that help it work, such as the monitor, keyboard, mouse, and *modem*. Of course, my editors know that I never make any errors when I type, so I don't really need the monitor for my work, but the keyboard and mouse come in handy all the time.

Lingo A modem is a device that lets you connect to other computers using a phone line or a cable Internet connection. Modem is short for "modulation/demodulation," which is what the device does to the signals it receives.

The monitor, keyboard, mouse, and modem cables all plug into jacks with hardware and software (usually included in the operating system, such as Microsoft Windows XP Professional) that can understand the signals being sent over the wire. When you press Enter on your keyboard, the keypress sends a specific signal over the wire, which your computer receives, interprets, and passes along to whatever application you're running.

Components of a Network

The principle that the hardware for a computer relies on physical connections (using the jacks) and software to interact with an application also applies to computer networks. You need to have the necessary hardware and software on each computer to send and receive signals, plus cables connecting the computers to the network. Here's a quick rundown of the hardware you need to build a network that includes Internet access, with full descriptions to follow:

- Computers, to give you something to network
- Modems, to connect you to the Internet
- Network interface cards, to let your computers plug into your network
- Hubs and routers, to serve as a focal point for your network
- Cat-5 cable, to connect your computers to your modem, hubs, and routers

> **Note** It is, of course, perfectly possible to set up a network without shared Internet access; I show you how to do that when I show you how to create a network with shared access.

Computers

You've probably already figured out that a computer network requires computers, but I thought I'd mention them anyway. The good news is that your computers don't have to be the newest models available. In fact, you can create the networks I describe in this book with any computer that runs Microsoft Windows 98 Second Edition (SE) or later. And your computers don't all need to be running the same operating system. Just as long as your computers are running Windows 98 SE or later, you can put them all together in a network. Of course, every new version of Windows has better networking capabilities than previous versions, so you should try to make the computer with the most recent operating system the focal point of your network. If you have an Internet connection, the computer with the most recent version of Windows should also be the computer with which you connect to the Internet.

Modems

If you want to share an Internet connection, the first thing you need is a modem. Almost every computer sold today comes with an analog modem, which lets you connect to the Internet at relatively slow speeds, but you need to either lease or purchase a broadband modem so you can connect to the Internet at speeds up to 100 times faster than is possible with an analog modem.

Network Interface Cards

Network interface cards (NICs), also known as network adapters or *Ethernet adapters*, connect your computer to a network, whether that network is the Internet or your home network. Many computers sold today come with an analog modem and a NIC, which is the most useful adapter for use in home networks. Some vendors might even offer computers with NICs for wireless network connections or other types of networks.

Lingo Ethernet is a standard for communicating data across a network. Older systems could transfer data at a rate of 10 Mbps (megabits per second), but practically all adapters sold today are capable of transferring data at a rate of 100 Mbps.

If your computer doesn't come with a NIC, you can install any one of a number of different types of adapters, depending on your needs and your computer. The most common type of adapter to buy is a card you plug into an *expansion slot* in your computer. The process for putting a card in an expansion slot is pretty straightforward, but you do need to make sure that the card you buy will fit into your expansion slot.

Lingo An expansion slot is an open socket on your computer's motherboard where you can plug in a device to enhance your computer's capabilities.

While there are many types of expansion slots in your computer, there are two types of expansion slots you can use to plug in NICs, Peripheral Component Interconnect (PCI) local bus and Industry Standard Architecture (ISA). You'll need to check your computer's documentation to figure out which kind of expansion slots you have.

See Also *For more information on nonstandard network types, see the section in Chapter 2 entitled "Networks Traversing Other Lines."*

If you don't have any available expansion slots (many discount computers come with only one or two free slots) or if you just don't feel like opening up your computer, you might want to buy an external NIC that connects to your computer through a universal serial bus (USB) port.

See Also *For more information on adding NICs to your computer, see the section in Chapter 3 entitled "Enabling Network Connections."*

Hubs and Routers

Once you have chosen the computer you want to serve as the focal point of your network, you need to buy a piece of equipment that lets you share the connection among other computers on the network. As always, you need to make some choices. The first is whether you want to have a simple Internet connection without a hardware barrier between your computer and other Internet users' computers, or whether you want to add security to your network and make those who would do you harm work a lot harder to get at you.

To set up a simple network, one without a hardware barrier between you and the Internet, you can buy a *hub*. These inexpensive boxes usually have from three to eight ports that share your Internet connection among the same number of computers. If you'd rather spend a bit more money to help keep your home network safe (not a bad idea, given what you'll learn in Chapter 5, "Making Your Network More Secure"), you can buy a *router*.

Lingo A hub is a piece of networking hardware that reads incoming network data and broadcasts it to every computer on your network. A router is a piece of networking hardware that reads the destination of incoming network traffic and routes it to the computer that requested the data.

Hardware That Does Too Much When you go into a computer store to buy your home networking hardware, you may see hardware that looks similar to a basic router or hub, but that is more expensive. These items are called *switches* and *switching hubs*, and you don't need them for a home network. A regular hub, which should cost under U.S.$100, broadcasts data it receives to every computer on your network. For a home network, that's fine–the computers can pick out the data they need, and you'll never notice the extra traffic. A *switching hub*, however, remembers the program or software process (such as a Web browser) that requested the data and sends it directly to that program, reducing the amount of network traffic. Switches and switching hubs are necessary for large corporate networks, but you don't need to spend the extra hundreds of dollars they cost to get what you need. They'll work, but it's like having your daily newspaper engraved on a silver platter.

Once you've figured out whether you want a hub or a router, or possibly both if you have a lot of computers, you need to decide what type of connections you want for your network. If you don't mind running cables around your abode, or if you live in a new house that came with Ethernet cable installed, you can go with a wired network. If you'd rather have more freedom of movement and don't mind spending more money on hubs, routers, and NICs, you can go with a wireless network.

Don't worry that I haven't gotten around to giving you all the information you need to make your decisions right now. I just want you to get a feel for what you'll need to think about when you look at the network scenarios in Chapter 2, "Envisioning Networks."

Cat-5 Cable

If you choose to put in a wired network, you'll become quite familiar with Cat-5 cable. Cat-5, which is short for "Category 5," a standard put forth by the Telecommunications Industry Association and the International Standards Organization, means that the cable is able to transmit data over your network at the highest speed your NICs can transmit it. (Your computer can process data much faster than you can ship it over a cable, so you don't need to worry about that.) You can buy cables in precut lengths, or you can make your own and, after an initial investment of a few bucks for tools, save money whenever you want to add a computer to your network or move a computer out of reach of an existing cable.

Network Topologies

Topology is a pretty fancy word, but in this context it simply means "layout" or "design." It's important to have an idea of what your network will look like before you start buying equipment to connect your computers. Although you can always return your purchases, the time you save running to and from the store (and any restocking fee the store may charge) is worth a little advance reading.

There are two basic topologies for computer networking, but there's really only one you need to worry about. I'll show you the first one, the *token ring* topology, as sort of a history lesson, and then describe the *star* topology, which is the basic jumping-off point for every type of home network you should consider when using personal computers. (This background piece involves a bit of hand waving and artistic license, so please forgive me if you know the technical details of token-ring networks.)

Back in the early days of computer networking, computers could be connected to share information, but the shape of the network was a circle. In other words, every computer was part of a ring, as shown in Figure 1-1.

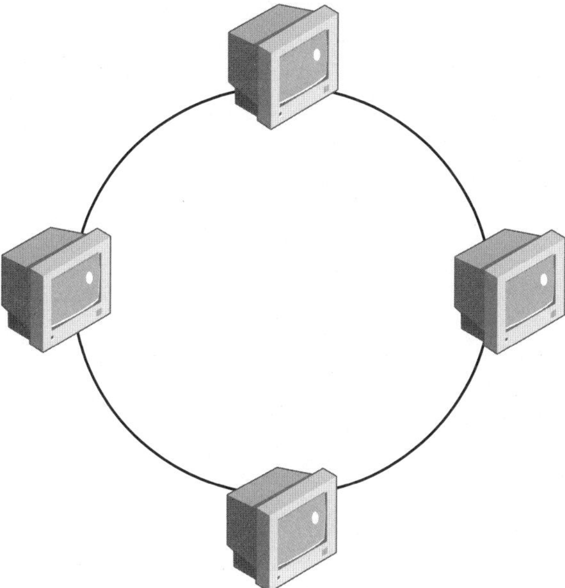

Figure 1-1 These computers are arranged in a token ring network, in which the computers connect in a chain.

In the four-computer network shown in Figure 1-1, if you wanted to get a file from the computer on the opposite side of the network, you would need to send the request through one of the computers next to the computer you were using. Your neighboring computer would pass the request along to the computer with the information you wanted, which would then forward the data along the circle until it reached you. The token ring topology was a great way to link computers together, but it suffered from one major flaw: a failure in any computer on the circle would break the chain, meaning any computer beyond the break was unreachable. It's kind of like those old strings of decorative lights where if one light burned out, the entire string wouldn't work. For companies with networks of more than three or four computers, the situation quickly became intolerable. Not knowing which machine to blame for the failure is unacceptable. After all, picking a random scapegoat might save your next performance review, but it won't get the network back up and running.

A better network topology is the star, in which a single computer serves as the focal point for the network. The star topology is shown in Figure 1-2.

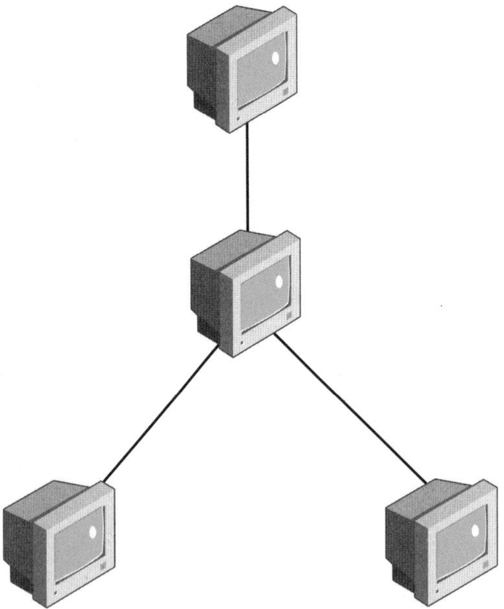

Figure 1-2 These computers are arranged in a star topology, in which only a failure in the hub or router will bring down the entire network.

The central computer is linked to the other computers in the network by a series of NICs attached to the network through a hub or router. In this configuration, if you can't get data from another computer on the network, you know that your computer isn't working, the target computer isn't working, or your hub isn't working. You can easily tell whether your computer is working, and you can try to get at files on other network computers to test your hub, so figuring out where the problem lies is usually pretty simple. After all, knowing what to blame is at least half the battle.

Note You can add all sorts of extensions to a star network, such as attaching another hub to include more computers in your network. The sample network shown in Figure 1-2 is a simple version of a star.

Put Your Network to Work...and Play

Part of what makes it worthwhile to have a home network is the convenience of being able to use the resources attached to any computer on the network from anywhere in your house. That statement is literally true if you have a wireless network and feel like taking your laptop computer out onto the deck so you can look at the sunset (or, in my case, the sunrise), and almost true if you have a wired network. And even then, you can still choose where in the house you want to work. The rest of this chapter introduces you to what you can do with a home network, while the following chapters show you how to make it happen.

Share Internet Access

My cable Internet access provider runs a commercial that sums up the appeal of home networks quite nicely. A dad is surfing the Internet, with the other three members of his family hovering over him impatiently. He says, "There are other computers in the house," to which his son replies, "Yeah, but this is the only one with a high-speed Internet connection." That's exactly the sort of aggravation that home networking can help you avoid. When I was a kid, the big fights were over the telephone and television, but the battle lines clearly have shifted to the computer.

By setting up a home network, you sidestep this problem completely. Every computer in your house can share your Internet connection. If you're lucky enough to have a broadband connection, another member of your household can be shopping online while you play bridge without having to wait impatiently for the screen to refresh after you overtrump. It'll be a bit slower going if you connect to the Internet using an analog modem, but the utility of the network and the simultaneous Internet connections more than make up for the lower speeds. If you can convince everyone, including yourself, to conserve bandwidth and avoid sites with a lot of large graphics, sound files, or animations, you can still use the Internet effectively. No, your setup won't be as nice as it is at work where you can download 1970s love songs all day without affecting the network's performance, but you will be able to get at the Web sites you just can't live without.

Share Files

Working out of your home office is a great way to eliminate your commute and spend more time with your family. Furthermore, if you're a sensible telecommuter or home-based worker, you probably don't have a television in your workspace. If, however, you need to get some work done on a document and there's a show on television you just can't miss, or if one of your kids has been especially good and has earned the right to watch television while doing his or her homework, you can make files on one computer available to other computers on your home network by sharing the folder containing the file.

Note Don't let your kids see this note, but I should tell you that I'm not a sensible home-based worker. I have a dual high-speed Internet and digital cable television outlet in my home office, but the arrangement works for me because I have a weaker will than many other folks and found that I lost a lot more time hanging out in the living room watching cable before I had a contractor install the second cable outlet in my home office. I tried sharing my files and working in the living room, but my couch is so comfy I never got anything done.

The main benefit of sharing a file across your network, as opposed to copying the file to a floppy disk and carrying it to another computer, is that you can reduce the risk that you'll save or copy the wrong version of the file and erase hours of work, the floppy could fail, or your file could be too big to fit on it. I had exactly that kind of nightmare during my senior year in college. I'd just finished a term paper for a class and somehow managed to overwrite the finished version of a 15-page paper with the 8-page partial draft I'd finished the night before. Needless to say, I went into panic mode and reconstructed the missing material in record time, but the paper wasn't nearly as good as it should have been. The only consequence for me was turning an "A" paper into a "B+," but if you're doing something important for work and get your versions mixed up, you could end up in your boss's doghouse for a while.

Tip When I work with multiple versions of the same file, such as a report I'm coauthoring with my colleagues, I always change the name of the document to reflect the date of the last change and who made it. For example, if I made the last change to part one of a report on home networking, I might name the file Hnpart1sep25CF.doc. The name indicates the file holds part one of the home networking report, revised on September 25 by Curtis Frye. Whatever naming system you come up with, be consistent.

Share Printers

Another advantage of home networks is that you can buy just one printer and make it available to anyone in your house. If you're tired of dragging files from computer to computer on the back of a floppy disk with Pack Mule on the label, you can add a printer to any computer on your network and print to it from any computer in your house.

Tip My acquisitions editor, Martin DelRe, had a great idea—don't put a shared printer in your home office. If your kids are doing their homework and need to print out their work, you don't want them traipsing in and out of your office while you're working.

Chat

Chat rooms, where computer users from all over the world can get together and converse about whatever topic is assigned to the area, have gotten a bit of a bad reputation from strangers preying on kids. For example, they may elicit information they need to commit robbery—or even worse crimes. Those things do happen, and you'll need to be on guard to protect yourself and your family, but chatting and instant messaging can also be a great way for you and your kids to meet other people with similar interests in a reasonably safe environment. You can also use chat tools over your home network to communicate with folks in other parts of your house after your resident early riser has gone to bed. Now, rather than having to walk to your roommate's room to see if she's on the computer or if she knows the answer to a question, you can open a chat window and ask her over the network. Using chat instead of yelling will help preserve your voice and the goodwill of that sleeping household member.

Secure Your Electronic House My parents didn't have eyes in the back of their heads, but they knew they could rely on the other parents in my hometown to keep track of my brother and me. Of course, I also grew up in a place where we kept our doors unlocked, and I had permission to walk into some of my friends' houses without knocking first. Some parts of the world are still like that, but you might live in an area where you feel more comfortable with a bit of physical security. Even if it simply means you lock your doors at night, that precaution helps you keep your mind on what you're doing when you're away from the front door.

If you want even more peace of mind, you can secure your home network against anyone who would try to break into your electronic "house." The simplest way to secure your network is to purchase a router that makes the computers on your network invisible to anyone on the Internet, but if you don't purchase a router you can use any one of a number of software firewalls to protect your computers from intruders.

If you're into getting the most out of chat programs, Web cameras let you set up video chats, where you send your voice and your image over your network to users elsewhere in your house or, if you have a fast Internet connection, to folks throughout the world. Of course, just as giving out information in a chat room can be dangerous, you should make sure you can trust the person on the other end of a video chat connection. My personal rule is that I need to know the person well and to have met him or her several times in person before I will suggest a videoconference.

Play Multiplayer Games

And now we get to the really fun part of having a home network, particularly one with a high-speed Internet connection: playing games. There are literally thousands of games you can play over the Internet, from role-playing games such as Asheron's Call to family classics such as Spades and Hearts to strategy games such as Age of Empires. If you're not a gamer, your shared Internet connection will still be useful. If you do play games, a shared Internet connection will seem like a breath of fresh air. And, with a home network, you can invite your friends over and play the game as part of a team. While you should be sure to keep the noise down, there's nothing quite like yelling "Help!" and having the other three people in the room yell "Where are you?" as they come to your aid, axes and swords swinging.

> **Note** By the time you read this, Microsoft will have launched a broadband network to which you can subscribe to play networked games on your Xbox game console. For more information, visit *http://www.xbox.com/LIVE/*.

Before I close this chapter, I'd like to warn you about a potential drawback to playing games on a network—it can become too much of a good thing. Think about how much time you want to spend sitting in a room by yourself playing games on a network and how much time you want to be, for example, sitting at the kitchen table with people playing with a deck of cards or a game board and a handful of die. There are differences between the two kinds of interaction, and both have advantages and drawbacks. Think about how you want to balance them. Pay attention to whether, and how, "virtual" interactions are affecting "real" ones.

Key Points

- Home networks aren't hard to put together; all you need is a screwdriver, some hardware, and an idea of what you're trying to accomplish.
- You can share an Internet connection among the computers in your house using a hub or a router. The hub is less expensive, but the router adds a lot of security to your network.

- Setting up your network in a star pattern, with a single computer as the focal point of the network, makes it easier to find problems should they occur.
- You can work on the same copy of a file from any computer on the network by sharing the file.
- Printing from the other side of the house is no problem once you connect your printer to the network.
- Consider how your home network can complement activities with family and friends, rather than take them over.

Chapter 2

Envisioning Networks

Whenever I begin work with something new, I always like to have a picture in my mind or, better yet, in my hands, of what I'm trying to accomplish. Creating a home network is no exception—it's a cliché to say that if you don't know where you're going, you won't know when you get there, but it's quite appropriate when you're hooking your computers together for the first time. This chapter clues you in on the "big picture" of putting in a home network; later chapters get down to specific steps.

Varieties of Home Networks

There are three basic kinds of networks:

- Networks that use wires to transmit data among computers
- Networks that use radio waves to transmit data among computers
- Networks that use both wires and radio waves to transmit data among computers

I know exchanging data using radio waves might sound like some exotic spy communication technology, but it's actually no more complicated than using a walkie-talkie. Well, maybe a little more, but you don't need to sweat the details.

Networks with Wires

When you think of a home network, you might think of a setup where your computers are hooked together by cables running from your connection point (a phone line for a DSL or analog modem connection, or a cable outlet for a cable modem connection) to a hub, which in turn manages the data traffic among all the computers on your network. One such layout is shown in Figure 2-1.

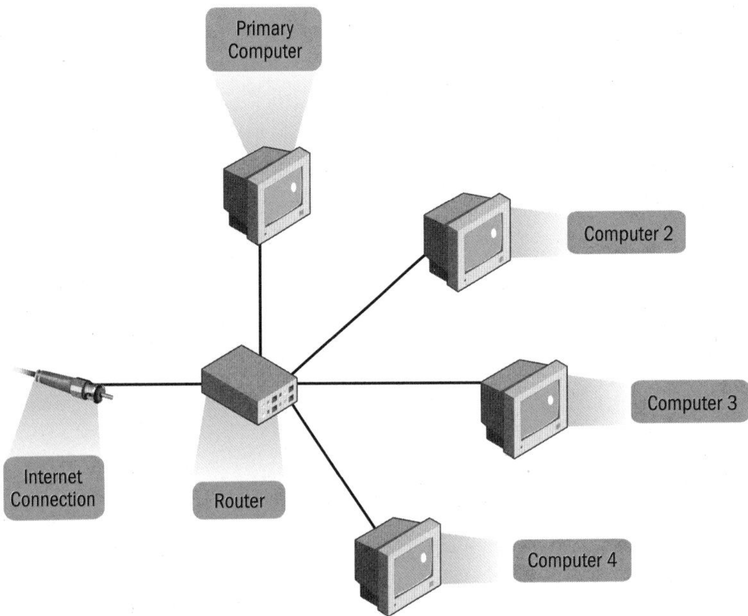

Figure 2-1 A typical home network sports an Internet connection, a router, computers distributed throughout a house, and cables connecting them all.

Pretty much every bit of wired networking hardware you find in stores today uses Cat-5 cable, though you might also see that variety of cable referred to as 10BaseT- or 100BaseTX-compatible. Those two seemingly cryptic designations refer to the speed at which your network will transfer data. 10BaseT networks transfer data at rates of up to 10 megabits per second (Mbps), while 100BaseTX networks transfer data at rates of up to 100 Mbps. The two new networking cards I bought when I started writing this book will handle either data rate. How do I know? The product names on their respective boxes are "Dual Speed 10/100 Ethernet Adapter" and "10/100 Mbps Fast Ethernet Card."

See Also *For helpful hints on managing cable in your home, see Chapter 4, "Making It Real—Putting In Your Home Network."*

As with all elements of computer networks, data transmission equipment and standards are getting better over time. The next entry in the Cat-5 family of standards is Cat-5e (the *e* stands for "enhanced"), which will transfer data at rates of up to 350 Mbps. Cat-5e cables are completely *backward compatible* with the Cat-5 standard, so if you buy Cat-5e cable instead of Cat-5 cable, you won't need to return it. And yes, there is a Cat-6 standard and a slew of other proposals under consideration by the Telecommunications Industry Association, so the manufacturers of networking equipment and cables will have the tools on hand to make everything work.

Lingo A piece of equipment is said to be backward compatible when it supports an earlier version of a standard.

Networks Without Wires

The main advantage of wired networking technology, especially in the area of home offices, is that the technologies have been around for a while and are well understood. Because the technologies are so established, it's possible for standards-making bodies to look at their existing equipment and determine where they can improve data transmission.

Of course, there's always a way to improve data transmission, and improving the speed at which data can be transferred over a wire isn't the only way to do it. In fact, wrangling yards and yards of cable can be a pain, so why not eliminate the wires entirely? The Romans communicated data over hundreds of miles by building a series of towers on hills and using reflected sunlight to signal messages. When the weather was good they could send data (okay, messages) from Rome to the hinterlands in a flash, so to speak. The alternative was a horse-and-rider relay that required weeks for the message and its reply to make the trip. That time frame was the best-case scenario, of course, and assumes no riders would get lost or waylaid, a horse wouldn't pull up lame, the weather would hold, and the message wouldn't be dropped on the road.

802.11b, the New Wireless Standard

The modern versions of the heliograph, at least as it applies to home networking, are wireless networking devices. These devices send signals from computer to computer using radio frequencies the U.S. government has made available for public use. There are a number of standards available (each standard covers a portion of the frequency *spectrum*), but the 802.11b, or WiFi, standard covers the part of the spectrum you'd most likely want to use around the house.

Lingo A spectrum is a range of things. For example, many wavelengths comprise the electromagnetic spectrum, which starts at radio waves and ends with gamma rays. The visible light spectrum within the electromagnetic spectrum—the only waves that we can see—consists of the colors of a rainbow.

Have you noticed that every major technology I've mentioned has its own industry association? Wireless networking is no exception—the equipment manufacturers and other stakeholders formed the Wireless Ethernet Compatibility Alliance (WECA). Some studies anticipate the entire wireless networking industry will generate as much as U.S.$1.6 billion in revenue in the year 2005, with lots of money being spent in the home networking market segment and for larger applications such as corporate networks and warehouses.

Note Many corporate networks actually use technologies based on a slightly different standard, 802.11a. That standard covers a different part of the radio frequency spectrum than the 802.11b standard and allows higher data transfer rates. At present, the two standards aren't compatible, meaning you can't connect to an 802.11a network with a computer with an 802.11b network interface card (NIC), but some vendors are designing NICs that can hook onto either type of network.

Wireless Infrastructure Networks

If you'd like to establish a wireless network, you can set it up so there are one or more *access points*, as shown in Figure 2-2, which are the equivalent of routers in a wired Ethernet network. Many access points also have Ethernet ports you can plug computers into, which can be quite handy when a computer doesn't have a wireless NIC and you don't feel like shelling out five times the cost of a wired Ethernet connection for all four computers in your house.

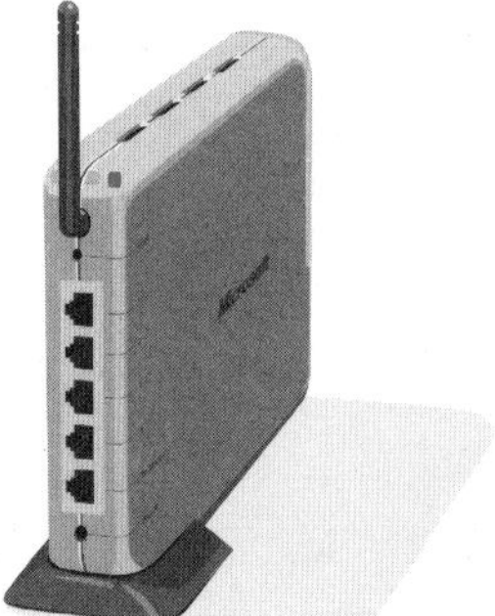

Figure 2-2 An access point is the heart of a wireless network.

Lingo An access point is a device that sends and receives radio signals and serves as the focal point of a wireless network.

If you travel a lot and have a laptop computer, you should strongly consider buying a wireless NIC. A growing number of airports around the United States and Europe have created wireless network infrastructures as a convenience for passengers. You can find out how to get on the network at any information kiosk and won't have to find a way to make a pay phone accept a modem connection. (Finally, good news about air travel!) And quite a few Starbucks coffee shops, particularly in the company's home city of Seattle, Washington, are part of that growing trend as well.

See Also *The easy accessibility of wireless networks can lead to security problems. For more information on securing a wireless network from prying eyes, see the section of Chapter 4 entitled "Encrypting a Wireless Network."*

You might also be interested in knowing that it's not only possible but also extremely feasible to set up a wireless access point in your house or apartment and share a broadband Internet connection with the neighbors. Why would you want to do that? Well, maybe your kids (read *you*) like to play games with your neighbors, or maybe you've found that your buddy next door spends so much time at your place "borrowing" your Internet connection that he has a regular spot at the dinner table. The signal from an access point can reach up to 150 feet indoors, even through walls, furniture, and pets, so you should have plenty of room to roam.

Caution Some Internet service providers (ISPs) specifically prohibit sharing a broadband Internet connection across more than one household. It's important that you read your terms of service agreement so you know what you can and can't do.

Peer-to-Peer (Ad Hoc) Wireless Networks

While most folks who set up wireless networks choose to go with the flexibility of a wireless router as an access point, you can choose to set up a network so a computer with a wireless NIC acts as the first link in a peer-to-peer network, which is also called a workgroup. In this model, computers directly communicate with each other and do not require a server to manage network resources. The main benefit of creating a peer-to-peer network is that you don't have to buy a relatively expensive (U.S.$150 or so) access point. However, you do pay a bit of a penalty in transmission range and data transfer rate, the latter because each computer on the network must maintain a link to every other computer on the network, and the overhead of sending bits back and forth between each pair of computers on a network increases quickly as the number of computers on the network grows. In general, a peer-to-peer network is most appropriate if you have fewer than 10 computers located in the same general area. Of course, if you have more than 10 computers in your house, you most likely can afford an access point and another five copies of this book.

Networks with Both

Remember that I mentioned that you buy wireless access points with ports where you can plug in devices using a wired Ethernet connection? You can take that concept one step further by plugging a wireless access point into your wired Ethernet hub or router and extending your network as shown in Figure 2-3.

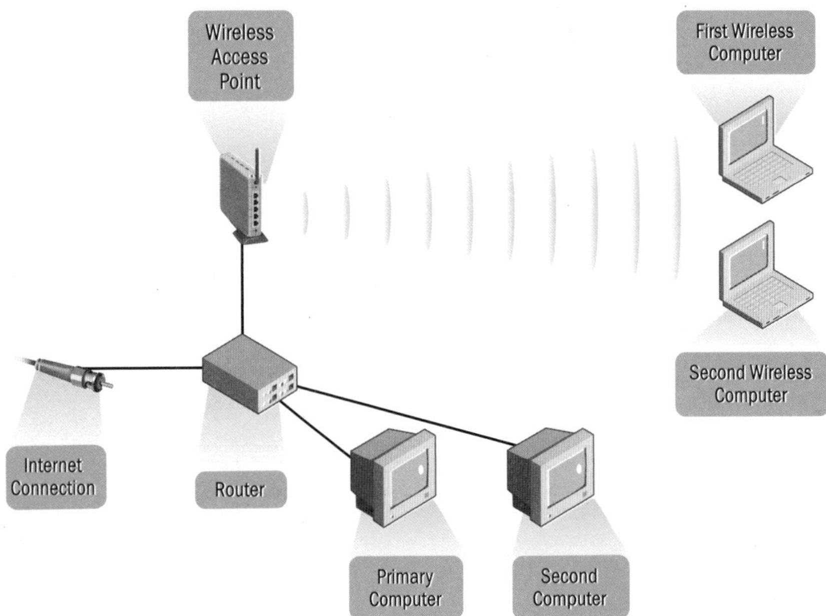

Figure 2-3 Attaching an access point to a hub or router lets computers with wireless NICs share in the bounty of your network.

You might wonder why you'd want to create a mixed wired and wireless network, but there are at least three times when it would be worthwhile to create a hybrid network:

- You want to add a computer to an existing wired network, but you believe running cable to a computer in an unwired room would entail more irritation than would buying and installing a wireless access point and a wireless NIC. You should always weigh the time it'll take to do something versus the cost.
- You want to bring a laptop computer home from work and need to connect to the Internet while you're working. Your employer probably would pick up the tab for the wireless NIC and might even go in for an access point.
- You don't want to shell out the money to buy a wireless NIC for every computer in your house, but you would like the freedom to move one or two of them around at will.

I'll go into more detail about what you need to do to make a mixed wired and wireless network happen in Chapter 4, "Making It Real—Putting In Your Home Network," but isn't it exciting to know you can do it if you want to?

Networks Traversing Other Lines

Whenever you add any new accoutrement to your place, whether it's a sofa or a bit of networking hardware, you need to make sure you have enough space for it. Of course, most of the time your networking hardware will fit into your computer or be set right next to it, so you might just need to slide the picture of your cat to the side to make room for your new universal serial bus (USB) connection. Running Ethernet cables from room to room can be a bit of a pain, but you can eliminate most of the cable wrangling by installing a wireless network.

There are, however, two other technologies in use that try to avoid the cable tangle by sending data over existing power or phone lines in your house. Although I don't really recommend either of the following network types for the average computer owner, both because of their expense and potential unreliability, I do want you to know they're available so you can make an informed choice.

Phone Cables

One method of connecting your computers using existing wires in your house is to transmit the data over already-installed phone lines. The Home Phoneline Networking Alliance established standards for phone line networking equipment a few years ago, though phone line networks run about 10 times more slowly than Ethernet or wireless networks. Once you've installed a phone line–compatible NIC in your computer, you can plug your computer into the network by running a cord from your phone jack to the card.

The first challenge the phone line technology developers overcame was to make sure there was no interference between your phone calls and data transmitted over the network, so you don't need to worry about your kids yakking with their friends for hours and making your network unusable. However, if you want to connect a phone and a computer to the same jack, you will need to buy a splitter, which is a plastic device that lets you plug two devices into the same jack. You can buy a splitter for fewer than U.S.$3 at your local hardware store, so the investment isn't too formidable.

Tip You should mark which hole on the splitter houses the line to the phone so you can disconnect your phone without disrupting your network connection.

There are a few things you should take into consideration before installing a phone line–based network in your home:

- You're still tethered to the wall. Just as you need to run a cable to your hub or router when you put in a wired Ethernet network, every computer does need to be connected to a phone jack.

- Your computer must be close to a phone jack, so you're limited to putting your computers in rooms with jacks.
- You might be using your phone jack for other things as well. For example, my digital cable boxes have internal batteries that are kept charged by a connection to a phone jack, so I already have a splitter in two of the jacks in my place. Also, my digital video recorder uses my phone lines to get programming information for its built-in scheduling software, so that's another jack gone.
- Your signal degrades as it travels over the phone lines in your house. If you're in a large house or have a lot of phone jacks installed, the amount of wire the signal must travel over, the number of telephone sets (including faxes) connected to the network, and the number of unterminated connections (that is, the number of jacks with nothing plugged into them) increase, negatively affecting network performance.
- Older houses might have substandard phone lines that will limit data transmission rates. Even though he has a 56K modem, one of my closest friends can't connect to the Internet at any speed faster than 28.8 because the phone lines in his house can't sustain higher data transfer rates.
- Power fluctuations can affect data transmitted over phone lines by adding electromagnetic noise to the system.
- All the computers on a phone line network must be connected to jacks that are wired for the same phone number.

Wired for Action? If you connect a computer to a phone jack but get no signal, and plugging a phone into the line and calling that number doesn't make the phone ring, you can tell whether the jack is wired for a given number by removing the faceplate from a jack with a phone number you know. You'll see a pair of wires leading to the back of the jack you plug the phone line into; note the colors of the wires (the usual pairs are red/green and black/yellow) and then replace the faceplate. Remove the faceplate from the jack you'd like to use for your network and see if the same pair of wires is attached to the jack. If not, switch the jack to the matching pair of wires and see if the jack works for that number. If it doesn't, the problem might be farther up the line, and you'll need to have a knowledgeable friend or a professional take a look at the line to locate the problem.

I visited the Home Phoneline Networking Alliance's Web site (*http://www.homepna.org/*) and followed their links to the sites of some of their members who sell phone line networking products. Their prices for routers, network adapters, and hubs are similar to those of wireless networking products available from Microsoft and other vendors, so if you're willing to spend the money and don't want to add new wires to your house, you should strongly consider going with a wireless network.

Power Line Systems

Another alternative to wired Ethernet or wireless networks is to send your computer traffic over the power lines in your home or apartment. Though it might sound hairy, it does actually work. There are a few caveats, however:

- Power line networks are a brand-new technology. In fact, the Home-Plug Powerline Alliance didn't finalize their initial standard until June 2001.
- A continuing bugaboo of power line networks is that they are susceptible to power fluctuations. While every piece of networking hardware has built-in error checking, if you have heavy appliances such as a refrigerator, an air conditioner, or a water heater, you might find there are more interruptions than you'd care for. Also, if you live in an area with a lot of rain, thunderstorms, or are just in an area with "dirty" (flickering or inconsistent) power, the errors can really add up.
- You're still tethered to the wall, though you probably have a lot more power outlets than you do phone jacks. If you plug in your monitor and computer to the same outlet, you will need to get a power strip so you have room to plug in everything. (You need to reserve one wall plug for your router; you can't run network traffic over a power strip.)
- Your computer network extends to other houses or apartments that draw power from your transformer. As with wireless networks, which extend to any computer with a wireless card within the broadcast range of your wireless router or access point, anyone with a power line router or an access point can hook the device into an outlet and gain access to your network. The power line routers I checked do have encryption options, so you can prevent unauthorized access by making some changes to your router's settings.

See Also *For more information about power line–based home networks, see the HomePlug Powerline Alliance Web site at* http://www.homeplug.com.

Summarizing Your Networking Options

I've given you a lot of information about your networking options. Hopefully you've memorized everything, but if you haven't, I've summarized the information in Table 2-1.

Table 2-1 Comparing Network Technologies

Name	Cost	Speed	Benefits	Drawbacks
Wireless	High	Medium (11 Mbps)	Easy installation; allows great freedom of movement	Expensive equipment; relatively low-speed connection
Wired Ethernet	Low to medium	Medium to high (10 Mbps or 100 Mbps)	Inexpensive equipment; high speeds; high reliability	Requires a cable run from your hub to each computer on the network
Phone line	Medium	Medium (up to 10 Mbps)	Uses existing wires; easy installation	Relatively slow connection; requires a phone jack by each computer; susceptible to power fluctuations
Power line	Medium	Medium (up to 14 Mbps)	Uses existing wires; easy installation	Relatively slow connection; susceptible to power fluctuations
Horse	Low up front, high maintenance	Low	Flexible transportation platform	Cleaning stables; saddle sores

What Your Network Might Look Like

In Chapter 4, I give you detailed instructions on how to build any one of several different types of home networks, but I want you to know what the ultimate goal I have in mind is when you read about setting up a shared Internet connection in the next chapter.

I've broken down the types of networks you might create into five scenarios:

- A wireless network with a hardware-based shared Internet connection
- A wired network with a hardware-based shared Internet connection
- A mixed wired and wireless network with a hardware-based shared Internet connection
- A wired network with a software-based shared Internet connection
- A wired network without an Internet connection

A Wireless Network with a Hardware-Based Shared Internet Connection

I put this scenario first because I expect it to be the most common method you will choose to create your home network. When wireless networking technology first came out, it had a few rough edges, not the least of which was that you usually couldn't use products from more than one vendor in the same network. The manufacturers didn't talk to each other, so their devices didn't either! But now that there's an industry association and everyone in the market seems to agree on the basics of how wireless home networking should work (or are at least keeping their differences to themselves), the freedom of working without wires, in my mind at least, is a powerful argument for going the wireless route.

Figure 2-4 shows one possible layout for a wireless home network used to share a broadband Internet connection and a printer.

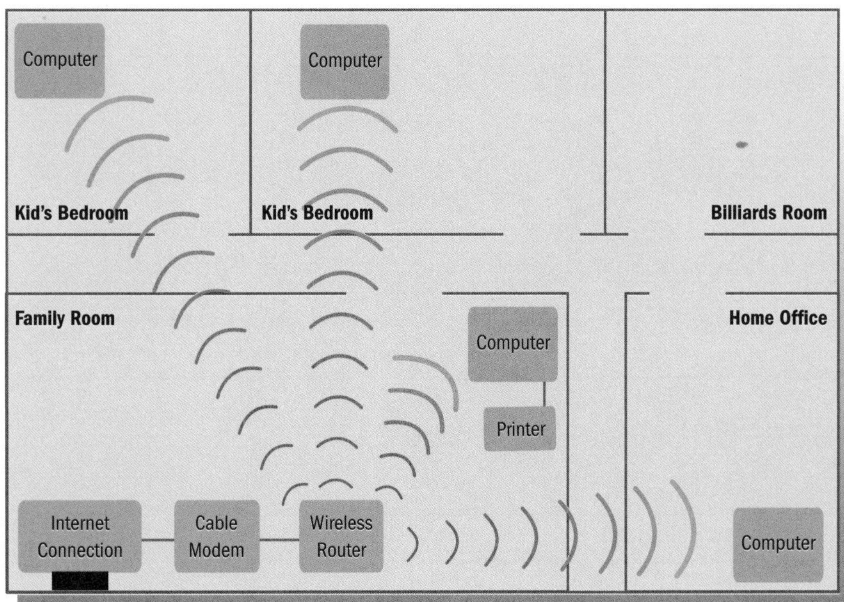

Figure 2-4 A layout for a house with a wireless network and a shared printer.

A Wired Network with a Hardware-Based Shared Internet Connection

If you don't want to spend the money to set up a wireless network (and, as partial to wireless networking as I am, I do understand there are plenty of other things you need to get you through the day), you can always count on your trusty friend Cat-5 cable. Not only is Cat-5 cable a commodity, but you can also buy NICs for U.S.$20 with a 6-foot run of cable included! That might not be enough cable to run from your office to your living room (I haven't seen your place), but it'll be cheap enough to buy or make the cable you need, even if you need to run around a wall to go through a doorway.

Figure 2-5 shows one possible layout for a wired home network set up for Internet and local gaming.

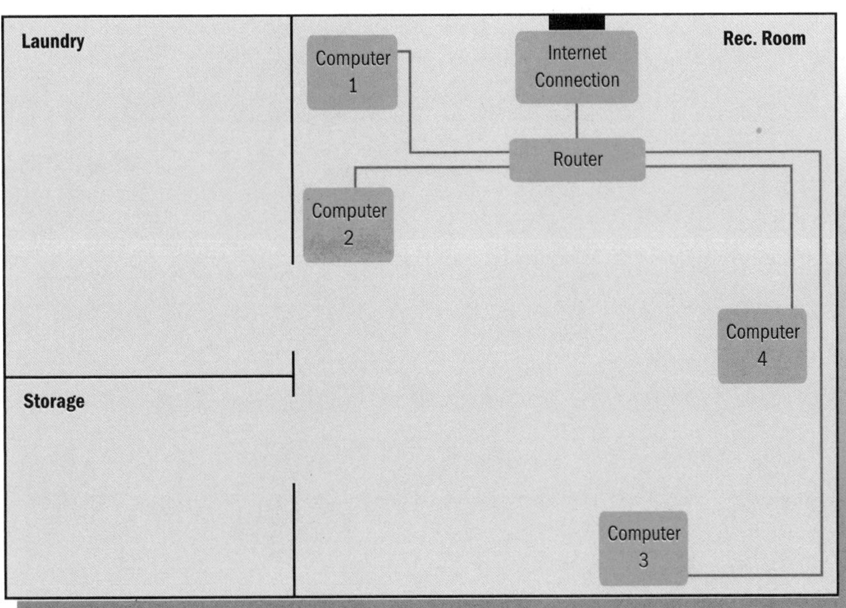

Figure 2-5 Serve it up! A home gaming network in the basement...how cool is that?

A Mixed Wired and Wireless Network with a Hardware-Based Shared Internet Connection

I'm glad the good folks at Microsoft Press decided against making this book a full-color spectacular, because I firmly believe the networking world comes in shades of gray. There are times when technologies are absolutely wrong or absolutely right for a situation, but there are also times when the compromise position is the best solution. For some homes, wired networks are great. For others, wireless is the best way to go. In my mom's house, the best solution was a mix of the two types of networks. My mom and her husband run a distribution business out of their home and have a little two-computer network hooked up to a high-speed Internet connection. Now, rather than sharing a single business computer, they can troll the Internet for competitive prices on the goods they sell, download online brochures, and so on.

Whenever I visited they'd let me use one of the computers, but they were always wary about me using a computer on which they had vital business and contact information, and they weren't keen at all on tripping over an Ethernet cable I'd drag behind me through the house. Fair enough. I bought a wireless access point, connected it to their router, and everybody was happy. I couldn't get at their files (they'd protected them, as I'll show you how to do in Chapter 7, "Getting Your Network to Work for You"), and I could surf the Internet from the living room, the guest bedroom, or wherever else I happened to be.

Figure 2-6 shows one possible layout for a wired home office with a wireless access point added for the convenience of laptop-toting visitors.

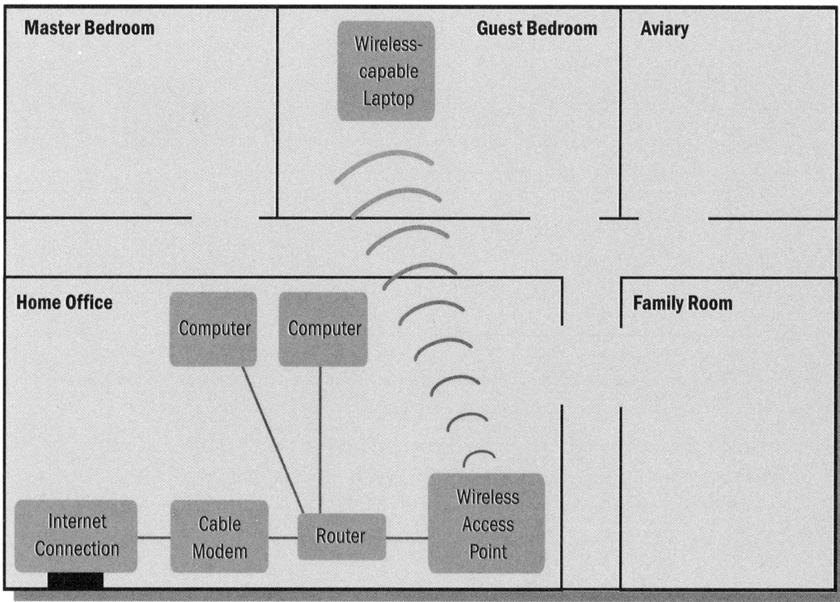

Figure 2-6 For her birthday, I bought my mom a wireless access point so I could check my mail and surf the Internet from the guest room before I went to bed. (Yes, I got her other stuff, too.)

A Wired Network with a Software-Based Shared Internet Connection

By far the safest way to connect to the Internet over a broadband connection is to put a router between your computer and the Internet. Most routers have built-in *firewalls* that act as a barrier between your computer and those on the Internet who would do it harm. If you can afford one, I highly recommend buying a router with a firewall. If you can't afford one, and they do cost around U.S.$150 as of this writing, you can buy a hub for U.S.$30 and use a firewall program to protect your computers.

Lingo A firewall is a bit of hardware, software, or both that prevents unauthorized data from getting at your computers.

Again, a router with a built-in firewall is your best bet, but if your budget just can't support buying a router right now, you do have options.

Note The firewall included with Windows XP Professional and Windows XP Home Edition, the Internet Connection Firewall, doesn't work for computers using Internet Connection Sharing.

Figure 2-7 shows one possible layout for a two-bedroom apartment where the roommates have separate computers hooked up to an Internet connection.

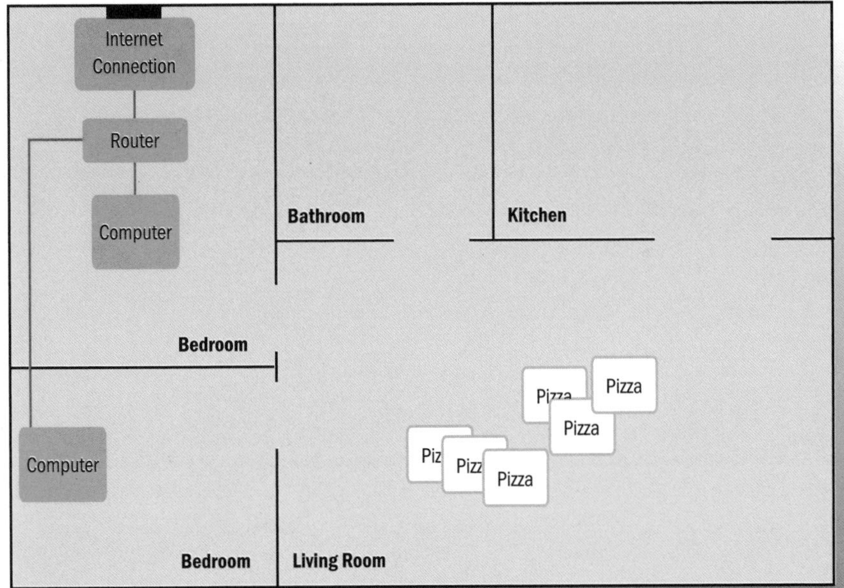

Figure 2-7 For many young people, high-speed Internet access is a bare necessity in their just-out-of-college apartments, even if it means skimping on networking hardware.

A Wired Network Without an Internet Connection

You might be wondering why anyone would want a network without an Internet connection of any kind. Believe me, most folks wouldn't choose this type of network, but they might have it imposed on them by circumstance. One instance in which a network without an Internet connection would work is if you run a research business out of a rented townhouse and want to have the ultimate security between the computers with your clients' information and the Internet. What type of security is that? An "airwall." A firewall tries to prevent people from getting at data on a computer with an Internet connection, but an airwall—meaning the computers with sensitive data aren't connected to *any* wires that extend outside your building—ensures that even the most daring and skilled hacker can't get at your stuff. You still need to worry about physical security, which is beyond the scope of this book, but locking your information away from the prying eyes of the Internet is a good start. If you use the Internet to do research, you can always have other computers in the office that are connected.

Figure 2-8 shows an office with a local network protected by an airwall and two other computers hooked up to an Internet connection.

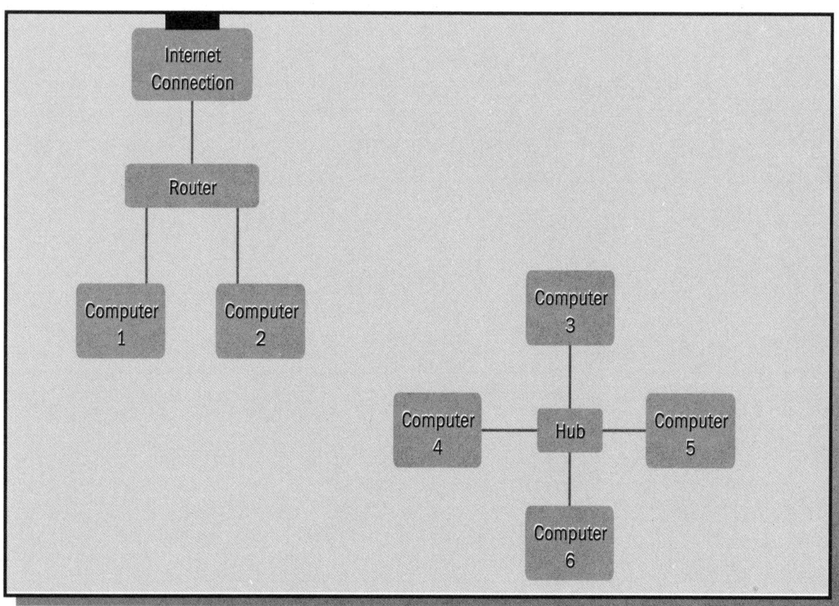

Figure 2-8 Not having Internet connectivity from your primary machine isn't much fun, but it might be a crucial element in protecting your information from snoopers.

Working from Home Using a Laptop

One of the joys of the electronic age is that it's now easier than ever to telecommute, or work from home. By working from home, you can avoid the mind-numbing drive to and from the office, run errands during the day without sneaking furtively out the side door, and maybe even avoid one or two meetings that would otherwise have taken away from an otherwise productive day. When you're working from home, though, it's important to realize that your network has become part of your company's security scheme. The operating system and software you use to connect to your work computers make all the difference in whether your connection is secure. Figure 2-9 shows a home office with a home network from which you connect to the network at your office.

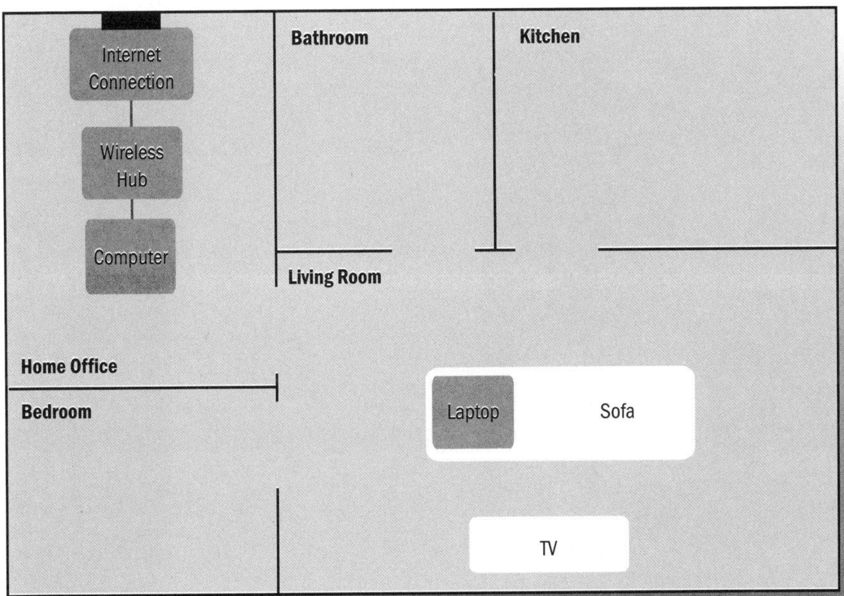

Figure 2-9 Working from home is great, but you need to be sure that the data you send to and from your company's computer is well protected.

Key Points

- Whatever your needs, living space, or budget, you can find a networking solution and get connected!
- Wireless networks give you the most flexibility in placing your computers, but they do so at an increased cost.
- Wired networks are less expensive than wireless networks, but you have to run cable throughout your house.

- Mixing wired and wireless networking hardware might be your best solution—if there's a computer in a hard-to-cable place or if you want to work on the deck with your laptop actually on your lap, you can reach it using a wireless device.
- There are alternatives to Ethernet-based technologies, but both power line and phone line networks have significant drawbacks.
- There's an industry association for *everything*.

Chapter 3

Preparing Your Computers for Action

As home networking increases in popularity, it's entirely likely that you can walk into a computer store and find machines that are set up and raring to go on a home network. No doubt the box or salesperson will proclaim the benefits of home networking, but make sure you aren't buying too much machine for your needs. Putting a computer on a home network doesn't mean you need to buy the newest equipment. If you're a gamer, you'll surely buy a computer that lets you run the latest and greatest strategy game or flight simulator, but that's way more power than you'll ever need for a home network.

Ready! You Need a NIC

The only things you need to add your computer to a home network are a modern operating system (Microsoft Windows 98 Second Edition [SE], Microsoft Windows Millenium Edition [Me], or Microsoft Windows XP) and a device to hook the computer to the network. Such a device is called a network interface card (NIC), also known as a network adapter. I'll be talking about NICs quite a bit throughout this chapter.

Set! Becoming Network-Capable

If your computer didn't come out of the box ready to hook up to a network, you can remedy that situation easily enough by purchasing a NIC. As with most other bits of computer hardware, you have a lot of choices.

- A device you put directly into your computer
- A device you plug into your computer through a universal serial bus (USB) port
- A device you plug into a laptop computer through a Personal Computer Memory Card International Association (PCMCIA) PC card port

You can buy any of these devices to serve as a connection for a wired or wireless Ethernet network. A wireless NIC, by necessity, will have an antenna, but that antenna might protrude from the NIC or be built into the body of the NIC.

Installing PC Bus NICs

The cheapest way to add a NIC to your computer is to buy one you plug directly into your computer's *data bus.*

Lingo A data bus is a set of wires used to transfer data from one part of the computer to another.

When you open up your computer, you might find one or two different bus types into which you can plug your network adapter *card.* The most common type of slot in newer computers is the Peripheral Component Interconnect (PCI) slot. A PCI slot is about 3.5 inches long and has two sections into which you can slide the gold "fingers" on the side of the card. One row of plugs is shorter than the other, so you can orient the card properly. Intel created the PCI standard in 1993, and it has been growing in popularity ever since.

Lingo A card is a device you plug into your computer. Many such devices were originally the size of small greeting cards, but now the size of some devices is closer to that of a playing card.

The second type of slot is the Industry Standard Architecture (ISA) slot, which is a much older standard than PCI. In fact, the last major change to the ISA standard was in 1984! Very few computers you'll buy these days have the 5.5-inch ISA slots in them, and finding new ISA-compatible NICs is nearly impossible, so if you have an older computer and need an ISA Ethernet card, you might need to shop at a store that sells secondhand computers. Note also that there appears to be no such thing as an ISA-compatible wireless NIC.

The third kind of slot is an Accelerated Graphics Port (AGP). This high-performance bus specification is designed for fast, high-quality display of 3-D and video images.

Figure 3-1 compares the of slots and shows you where they'll probably be located in your computer.

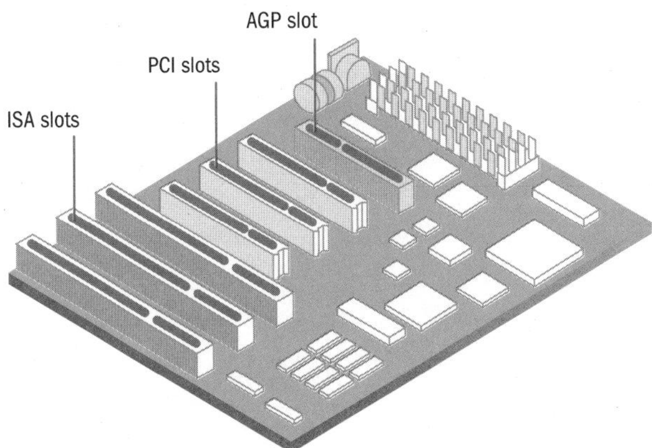

Figure 3-1 A look inside a typical computer: the ISA slots are at the bottom of the figure, with the shorter PCI slots just above them.

Note In computers with both ISA and PCI slots, the ISA slots usually are made from black plastic and the PCI slots from white plastic.

Not every computer cover comes off the same way. Some covers lift off of the chassis in one piece, while others are built so only one side slides off after you loosen a few screws. You can check your computer's documentation to see which screws you need to remove, or, if you can't lay your hands on the manual, look for screws that connect the cover to the edges of the chassis.

When you unscrew a screw, be sure you're using the right type of screwdriver (probably a Phillips) with a head that is very close in size to the grooves on the screw. Because the screws used in computers (especially inexpensive computers) are often made of softer metal than other machine screws, using a screwdriver with a head that is too big or too small runs the risk of stripping the head and making it extremely difficult to remove the screw. And don't use a screwdriver with a magnetic head! Magnets of any strength will damage computer hardware, meaning you could lose important files and possibly make your computer impossible to use.

Note When you open up your computer case, your biggest enemy isn't pressing too hard on a card or spilling a soda into the case. No, your biggest enemy is static electricity. Computer chips operate at relatively low power settings, both to reduce the demands on your machine's power supply and to keep the system from overheating. You might think static electricity shocks are annoying, but the amount of power behind a shock that makes you pull your finger back could very well ruin a chip. Please believe me when I tell you that you need to wear an antistatic wrist strap, which you can buy from any computer store. Or at the very least touch something metal before touching your computer. If you get a shock, you'll know you just saved the life of something expensive. And you'll also know you can safely reach into your computer case.

After you've added your NIC, plug your computer back in and restart it. Once you're sure the card passes the smoke test (that is, there's no smoke coming from anywhere), you can wait for Microsoft Windows to detect the adapter and either install software included in your version of Windows or ask you to provide a disk with a *driver* for the card. Your card should have come with installation instructions—be sure to follow them!

Lingo A driver, or device driver, is a software program that tells your operating system how to communicate with the device you just installed.

Many devices are built to the Universal Plug and Play (UPnP) standard, which is a specification Windows manufacturers can follow to ensure their devices work out of the box. When you add a UPnP device to your computer, it knows how to tell Windows what it does, how it transmits data, and how it expects data to be transmitted to it.

To add a PC bus NIC to your computer, follow these steps:

1. Put on your antistatic wrist strap, unplug your computer from the wall, and remove the cover from your computer.
2. Unscrew and remove the faceplate protecting the expansion slot, and put the faceplate someplace where you won't forget it, such as in a utility drawer or with your other computer gear, in case you ever need to remove the NIC and want to seal up the hole to prevent dust and other debris from getting into your computer. Do hold on to the screw, though; you'll need it to secure the NIC.

3 If there is a metal plate, as shown below, sealing off the expansion slot from the outside world, use a flat-head screwdriver to pry it up enough so you can twist the plate until it breaks free.

4 Remove the NIC from its packaging and then orient it so the side with the pins lines up with the expansion slot. Then, exerting equal pressure with both thumbs, push the card into the slot. You might need to use a bit of force to get the card to go in securely, but it's a "pushing" force, not a "hitting" or "leaning on it until something snaps" force.

Note If you're having trouble getting the card to go in, pull the card out and make sure there are no stray wires or protrusions from other devices blocking your way. You should also make sure the card's pins are lined up exactly with the slot; if you're shifting even a little bit to either side, you won't be able to put the card into the slot.

---

5 Using the screw you saved after removing the expansion slot's faceplate, secure the bracket of your NIC to the frame and then replace the computer's cover.

6 Turn on your computer. Windows should recognize the NIC you just added. If it doesn't have the drivers for the NIC included in its operating system, Windows will prompt you to use the manufacturer's software, which should be in the same box as the NIC. If the installation instructions included with the NIC recommend a specific procedure, by all means follow that procedure.

Note Manufacturers often release improved versions of their device drivers as performance issues are discovered and resolved, so you should visit the manufacturer's Web site every so often to see if there are any new drivers for your network adapter.

Why UPnP Is Vital for Effective Home Networking I gave you a quick overview of why UPnP is important for your home networks, but I want to go into a bit more detail so you can have a more complete understanding of UPnP and how it solves a very sticky problem. This discussion is a little bit technical in places, but if you read through it, you'll get a feel for how the computers on your home network interact with the world.

The first thing you need to know is how computers identify themselves on the Internet. The quick answer is that every computer on the Internet is assigned an Internet Protocol (IP) address. For example, if you have a computer connected to the Internet over a cable modem or DSL hookup, that computer is assigned an address made up of four numbers separated by periods.

The IP address of the main Microsoft computer, for example, is 207.46.230.218. Any data sent over the Internet that's bound for microsoft.com is routed to the machine at IP address 207.46.230.218. (The engineers who designed the Internet realized that humans would have a hard time remembering numbers with no pattern, so they made it possible to assign a name to the computer at an IP address.)

What the individual groups of numbers stand for isn't really important, but it's interesting to note that the numbers in each group can go up to 255 (with zero reserved for administrative purposes), meaning that there are a total of 255 x 255 x 255 x 255 IP addresses available for machines connected to the Internet. You should note that I say "machines" and not "computers." That's because wireless phones, game systems, and personal digital assistants are all on the cusp of full Internet access.

The total number of IP addresses may seem close to infinite, but the influx of Internet devices of all stripes has made IP addresses a precious commodity. One of the Internet oversight bodies recognized that there might be a shortage, so it did two things to help ease the pain. First, it decreed that only the computer directly connected to the Internet had to a have a unique IP address. Second, it set aside a group of IP addresses (192.168.xxx.xxx) so folks could create private networks and still use Internet protocol to send data to and from the computers on their network.

As an example, consider Figure 2-1 in the preceding chapter. In that figure, a computer is connected to the Internet through a high-speed modem, and a bunch of computers share the connection through a router. The computer connected to the high-speed modem has an IP address assigned by the Internet service provider (ISP), the router is treated as a computer and is given its own IP address, and every computer on the network is assigned an IP address for the local network. In this example, the router is 192.168.0.1, and the other computers have addresses ranging from 192.168.0.2 to 192.168.0.5.

You're probably wondering how UPnP relates to your computers' addresses. The trick is that when a computer on your network tries to establish a direct connection with another computer on the Internet, such as when you're playing a multiplayer game or trying to get help using the new Windows XP Remote Assistance feature, the program needs to be able to translate a local IP address, such as 192.168.0.2, into an address the computer on the other network can use.

For example, imagine the person you're trying to contact also has a home network. If your computer represents its IP address as being in the 192.168.xxx.xxx range, the computer on the other end of the connection will think the connection request is coming from a computer on its own local network.

How does the UPnP standard solve this problem? Through the Network Address Translation (NAT) protocol. By using NAT, a UPnP-compatible device can translate a local IP address (that is, an address in the 192.168.xxx.xxx range) into an IP address that other computers on the Internet can use to communicate directly with your computer.

The bottom line: when you buy home networking hardware, be sure it's UPnP-compatible.

Installing USB Adapters

Adding a NIC to your computer isn't that difficult, but there are a few reasons you might not want to add an internal NIC. One reason that I can identify with very easily is that you might not want to open up your computer and mess around with its insides. For years I lived in mortal fear of doing something wrong and breaking an important part. After I replaced a few video cards so my games looked better and added a new hard disk or two, I began to feel more comfortable poking around inside a computer case.

I still have a healthy respect for my components and understand that pushing a little too hard can cause something to snap, but it's no longer my dominant thought when I crack open the case. And remember, if you unplug the computer from the wall before you start working, you won't get shocked!

Another reason you might not want to add an internal NIC is that your computer might have come with a warranty that explicitly prohibits anyone who isn't a certified technician from modifying the physical makeup of the computer. I sympathize with this—while I don't care for limits on what I can do with a machine I paid perfectly good money for—and I'd probably choose to play by the rules and not add a card. And, last but not least, you might not be able to add an internal NIC to your computer because you might have added so many devices to your computer that you just don't have any slots left. All that gaming hardware adds up, after all.

So, whatever your reason, if you don't want to add an internal NIC, you can buy an Ethernet adapter that connects to your computer through a USB port. Figure 3-2 shows you what a USB port and connector look like.

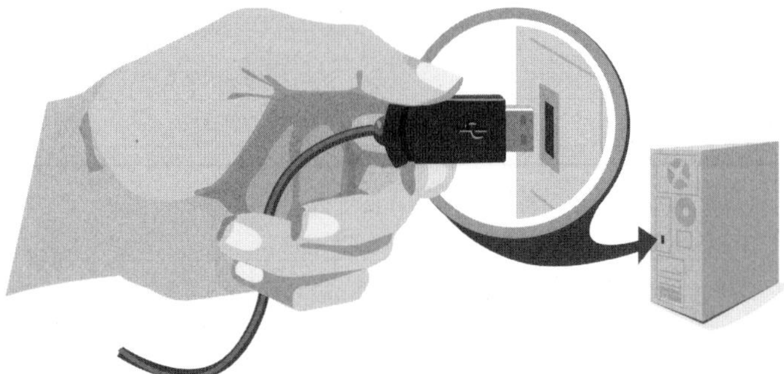

Figure 3-2 You can add devices to your computer using the ultra-convenient and fairly speedy USB connection.

I kind of gave away the benefit of using USB devices in the figure's caption; USB ports live up to the *Universal* in the standard's name by letting you plug any kind of device into your computer. For example, as I write this I have an extra hard disk, a CD-ROM burner, and a laser printer plugged into the USB ports of my main computer at home. At other times I've attached a digital camera, scanner, and personal digital assistant (PDA) to my computer. How do you attach a USB device to your computer? You push the adapter into the port, Windows recognizes it, and, if necessary, you run the manufacturer's installation software included with the device. And that's all there is to it.

Note Yes, there is an industry association for USB technology: the USB Implementers' Forum. You can visit the USB-IF's Web site at *http://www.usb.org*.

Most of the time when you want to move your USB device to another computer, all you have to do is unplug the device from its home and move it to the other computer. For some devices, however, you need to tell your operating system you want to unplug it so Windows can prepare for the shock of losing one of its friends. If you see the Unplug Or Eject Hardware icon on the taskbar, click it to display a list of devices you must identify to Windows before you unplug them. If you don't see the Unplug Or Eject Hardware icon on the taskbar, you can unplug your USB device with a clear conscience.

If the Unplug Or Eject Hardware icon appears on the taskbar, follow these steps to unplug a USB device:

1 Click the Unplug Or Eject Hardware icon on the taskbar. From the list of devices that appears, click the device you want to unplug.

2 Click OK and then unplug the device from your computer.

Most computers built these days come with two or four USB ports, but if you have a USB-connected printer, CD burner, hard disk, scanner, keyboard, and game controller, you might find that you've run out of slots. And, while it's great that you can unplug a device you're not using, if your system only has two USB ports, you might not want to unplug your keyboard or your printer.

As it turns out, you can buy USB hubs that let you increase the number of devices you can plug into a single USB port. USB hubs are very much like power strips you plug into electrical outlets; the hub plugs into a single USB port but has (usually) four ports of its own, meaning that on a computer with two built-in ports you can use two hubs to add as many as eight devices to your system. And, should you need to add even more devices, you can plug another hub into one of your hub's ports and add another four devices!

Note You can connect as many as 127 USB devices to your computer at a time. If you do end up attaching that many disk drives, cameras, and speakers to your system, you might need to take out a loan to pay your electricity bill.

Figure 3-3 A USB hub can be used to connect yet another USB hub.

Caution You should plug a NIC only into a USB hub that is connected to your computer's data bus. Some keyboards and monitors have built-in USB ports, but those ports are meant for low-power equipment such as your mouse and other input devices, not a NIC.

USB is a great technology, but there is one potential problem that you need to watch out for. It used to be that any USB device would plug into any USB port and run right out of the box, but that's no longer the case. In 2001, the USB-IF introduced an updated version of the USB communications standard. High-speed USB 2.0 devices can transmit data at rates up to 50 times faster than could similar devices using USB 1.0. As any good standard should be, USB 2.0 is backward-compatible with USB 1.0, so you'll be able to run your existing USB hard disks and CD burners on systems with USB 2.0 ports, but you might not be able to run USB 2.0 devices on USB 1.0 ports. Some products can detect the type of port they're connected to and run at either speed, but a fair number of products have been built specifically for USB 2.0 connections.

Note Most computers built in 2002 and later have USB 2.0 ports, but you'll need to check your machine's documentation to be sure. If you do want to add USB 2.0 devices to your system but it didn't come with a compatible port, you can always buy an upgrade kit and install your own USB 2.0 ports. Of course, that means you'll need to crack open your computer, so if you went the USB route to avoid fiddling with the inside of your system, you'll just need to bite the bullet and add the card. You can do it—really!

Installing Laptop NICs

If you travel a lot for your job, you understand how important it is to have a laptop computer. Laptops are also handy because you can take them home when you need to make a few changes to that report you didn't quite finish before you took off for your kids' soccer games. One thing laptop manufacturers, not to mention employers, don't take kindly to is your taking apart a laptop computer and adding components on your own. With laptops getting smaller and smaller, you really do need special training to get in there and make changes effectively.

Note Laptop computers are often called notebook computers, reflecting the small size and light weight of modern portable computers.

So how do you add your laptop to your home network if the little guy doesn't have a built-in Ethernet card? Fortunately, computer manufacturers have made it possible for you to add components to your laptops without much fuss at all. Practically every laptop computer made these days comes with USB ports, so you can plug a USB-based wireless or wired Ethernet NIC directly into your computer. Your laptop probably also comes with a PCMCIA slot, also known as a PC Card slot.

PCMCIA is short for the Personal Computer Memory Card International Association, which is yet another industry association. Founded in 1989, the PCMCIA is a focal point for companies that make peripherals for laptop computers, digital cameras, and other electronic devices that let you transfer data from one device to another. For example, you can use a PCMCIA-based memory card to record photos you take with a digital camera, and then transfer the files from the camera to your laptop by inserting the memory card into a reader you attach to your laptop.

Figure 3-4 Here's an enlargement of a PC card as well as how it looks when inserted into a laptop.

Ready, Set, Go (Online)! Making the Internet Connection

Now that you've selected the network adapter that's best for you (if your computer didn't come with one), you are ready to experience one of the greatest advantages of a home network—every computer can share a single Internet connection. That means you don't have to drag all your work to the family room, beg your grandparents visiting from Florida to turn down the volume on the television, and do your research while the cat jumps on your lap. Instead, you can use Internet Explorer in the comfort of your home office with your own music playing at a reasonable volume.

Modem Connections

Even though high-speed Internet connections are becoming increasingly popular, the vast majority of home computer users around the world still connect to the Internet over a phone line with an analog modem. And now that the developers of popular Web sites have gotten wind of the fact that the majority of their audience aren't willing to wait fifteen minutes for a cool but unnecessarily hip home page to finish loading, logging on using a modem isn't so bad. Sure, the speed of a cable or Digital Subscriber Line (DSL) connection is great, but I get along just fine when I visit my cousin, who lives in such a remote area that she's lucky to have phone service at all.

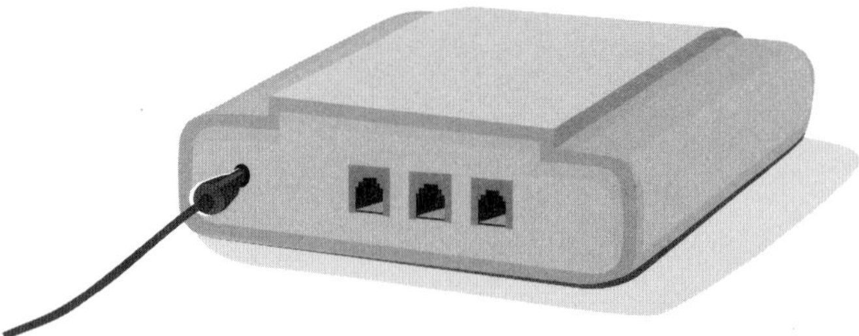

When modems first became popular for the average user in the 1980s, there were a lot of variations in the settings you used to connect to your access provider (maybe an Internet company, but in the early days it was more probably a bulletin board system). Now, however, you don't need to worry about much beyond the phone number you dial to connect to your ISP. Windows makes it easy for you to set up an Internet connection using the Network Connection Wizard. The wizard is a bit different in each operating system, so I'll show you how to create a modem connection in Windows 98 SE, Windows Me, and Windows XP.

To create a new Internet connection in Windows XP, follow these steps:

1. Click Start, and then choose Control Panel.
2. Click Network And Internet Connections dialog box (or if you're using Classic view, click Network Connection) and then click Set Up Or Change Your Internet Connection. In the Internet Properties dialog box, click the Connections tab.

Note Throughout this book, we assume that readers will use the default view, which is Category View, rather than Classic View.

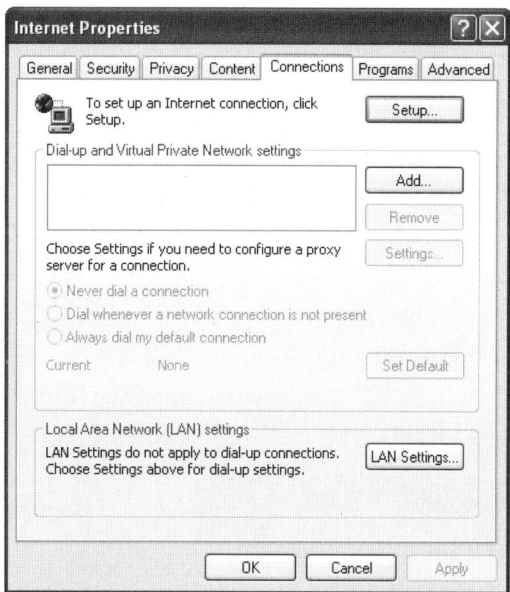

3 Click Setup to open the New Connection Wizard. Click Next.

4 Click Connect To The Internet and then click Next.

Note If you are setting up an Internet connection for the first time, you may be asked to supply your area code and dialing rules, such as whether or not you need to dial the area code for local calls.

---

5 Click Set Up My Connection Manually and then click Next.

6 Click Connect Using A Dial-Up Modem and then click Next.

7 Type the name of your ISP in the ISP Name box and click Next.

8 Type the phone number of the service you're calling in the Phone Number box and click Next.

9 Type your user name in the User Name box, type your password in the Password box, and then type your password again in the Confirm Password box. Select Use This Account Name And Password When Anyone Connects To The Internet From This Computer, Make This The Default Internet Connection, and Turn On Internet Connection Firewall For This Connection. Click Next.

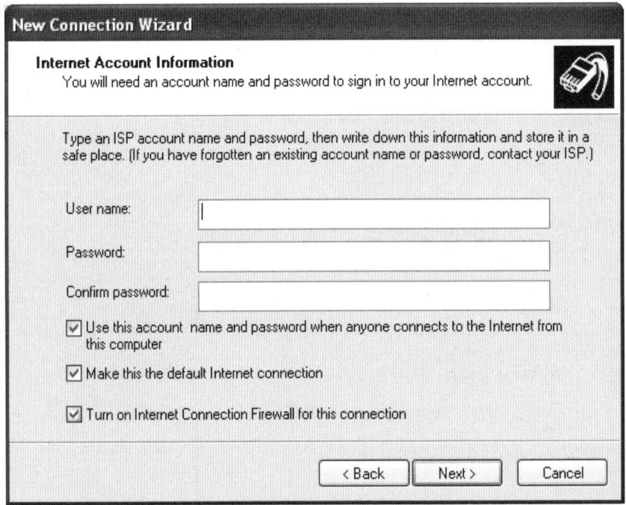

Note If you type different passwords in the Password and Confirm Password boxes, Windows shows an alert box indicating that you made an error and lets you try again. Of course, if you make the same mistake in both boxes, you might not be able to use this connection. The good news is that all you'd need to do to fix the problem is create a new connection.

10 If you'd like to add a shortcut for this connection to your desktop, select Add A Shortcut To This Connection To Your Desktop. Click Next and then click Finish.

See Also *For more information on the Internet Connection Firewall, see the section in Chapter 5 entitled "Add a Firewall."*

To create a new Internet connection in Windows Me (or Windows 98 SE), follow these steps:

1 To run the Make New Connection Wizard, follow either of these steps:

- In Windows Me, click Start, choose Settings, and then choose Dial-Up Networking.
- In Windows 98 SE, double-click My Computer, and double-click Dial-Up Networking.

2 Double-click Make A New Connection.

3 In the Make New Connection Wizard, type a name for your connection in the Type A Name For The Computer You Are Dialing box.

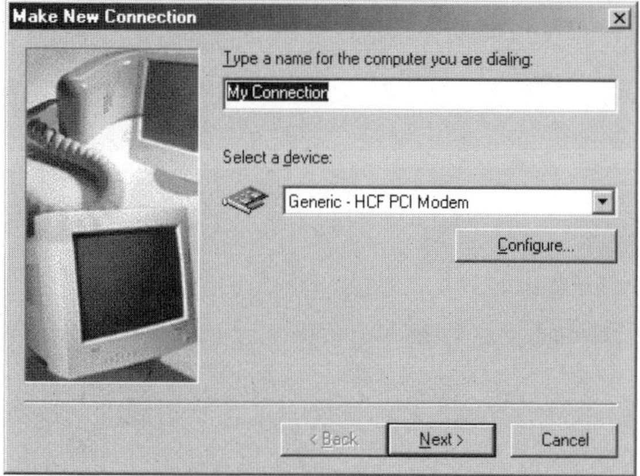

4 If necessary, click the Select A Device down arrow and select the modem you want to use to connect to the Internet. Click Next.

5 If your area has 10-digit dialing or if you need to dial an area code to reach your service, type the area code in the Area Code box. Type your ISP's phone number in the Telephone Number box and then, if necessary, click the Country Or Region Code down arrow and select your locality. Click Next.

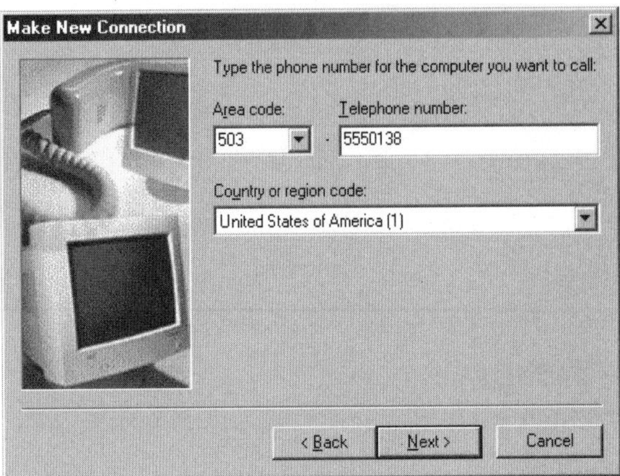

6 The name of your connection appears in the box at the top of the wizard page. Click Finish.

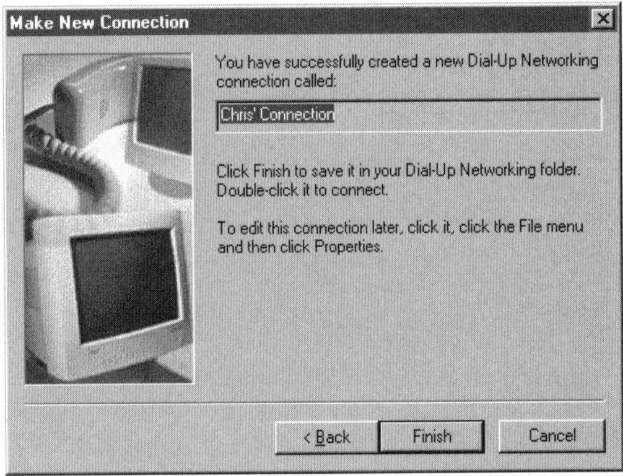

Note You can't actually edit the name of your connection here, but you can step back through the wizard and rename it if you like. You could also rename the connection as you would any other file on your computer.

Now that you've created your dial-up connection, you can log on to your ISP by double-clicking the icon representing your connection. A dialog box will appear, asking you for your password and giving you the opportunity to change any of your information. If your dialing information does change, you can modify your connection to change your dialing properties, user name, or other options.

To modify a modem connection, right-click the icon representing your modem connection, choose Properties, and then follow any of these steps:

- On the General tab, you can type a new area code for your connection in the Area Code box or type a new phone number in the Telephone Number box. If you'd like to add codes, such as a comma to wait for a solid dial tone or *70 to turn off call waiting for the current call, you can put those codes in front of the number.
- In Windows Me, on the Dialing tab, use the controls in the Redialing Options section of the dialog box to change the number of times the modem attempts to connect, the amount of time it waits between attempts, how long it should wait to hang up if there's no activity, and whether it should redial automatically if your connection gets dropped.

Troubleshooting: What to Do When Your Modem Connection Isn't Working

Q. What do I do if I don't get a dial tone when I try to connect to the Internet?

A. After you verify that your phone line is plugged into the wall and into your modem, make sure the phone line is plugged into the proper RJ-11 jack on your modem. Most modems have two jacks, one labeled "Wall" and the other labeled "Phone." The phone line should come from the phone jack on the wall and be plugged into the modem jack labeled "Wall." The modem also acts as a pass-through device, so you can plug your phone into the jack labeled "Phone" and use it without switching cords.

Q. I hear a dial tone, but there's a "stutter" indicating I have a voice mail message waiting. How do I dial out without clearing my messages?

A. You can tell your modem to wait for a solid dial tone by putting a comma in front of the phone number. For example, if your access number were 4255550138, you should type **, 4255550138**.

Q. I connect just fine, but my calls get dropped a lot. What might be happening?

A. What might be happening is that you're getting a call waiting tone on your line, which is often sufficient to break a modem connection. You can turn off call waiting for the current call by putting *70 in front of the number you dial.

DSL and Cable Modem Connections

The next step up from a standard modem connection to the Internet is a *broadband* connection using either a DSL or cable modem. DSL connections let you connect to the Internet over an existing phone line at rates of up to 50 times faster than a standard 56KBps modem connection, while with cable modems you hook up to a digital cable outlet and can usually transmit data even more quickly than that.

Lingo The term *broadband* refers to a high-speed connection that uses multiple frequencies to transmit and receive data. Just as more water flows through a large pipe, more data will flow through a "broader" connection.

You will need to have a few things on hand to set up a high-speed Internet connection:

- **A cable or DSL provider in your area** Cable Internet and DSL connections aren't something you can just turn on, unfortunately. For DSL, your residence must be close enough to a phone company switching station so that the signal doesn't degrade to the point of uselessness, while for cable your provider must have upgraded its services to offer access.
- **A phone jack or cable tap within a few feet of your computer** My cable Internet provider recommends that the modem be within 5 feet of a cable tap to limit the distance over which the signal travels before it gets to the modem. The modem acts as an amplifier (for an analog system) or a repeater (for a digital system), ensuring that a high-quality signal reaches your computers.
- **A DSL or cable modem** After the usual industry shakeout in which some modems didn't work with some providers, you can now buy modems at your local computer store and, for the most part, not worry whether a particular modem will work with your provider. If you don't know if a particular modem will work with a given system, check both the modem manufacturer's and the service provider's Web sites for information.
- **The Media Access Control (MAC) address for your modem** This unique 12-digit code, which is permanently assigned to your modem, identifies it both to your network and to your provider's network.

Caution Under no circumstances should you enter another device's MAC address for your modem! If your provider's network detects two devices with the same MAC address, one or both of you will be dropped from the network and you'll have to answer some questions before the provider will let you back on. Why is it such a big deal? Network integrity. If your computer has the same MAC as another computer on the network and you request a Web page, the network is just as likely to pass that Web page to the other computer as to your own. So, not only would you be messing up your own data, but you'd be hurting someone else's as well.

- **Your provider's installation software** In many cases, installing a cable or DSL modem is a relatively straightforward process, but you can often get custom installation free as part of a promotional offer or pay a small fee to have the technician who enables your connection install everything. The great thing about getting the technician to install the connection is that he or she can't leave until you sign the papers acknowledging everything is in working order, so make sure you're satisfied everything is fine before you let him or her go. You have the power, but use it wisely.

Microsoft Hardware and a Broadband Connection

Microsoft recently introduced a line of wireless broadband networking products that let you share a broadband connection with every computer in your home. The centerpiece of the Microsoft Broadband Networking Wireless Kit is the router, which can support up to 200 wireless devices at a time! There are also four wired Ethernet ports on the back of the router, so, if you like, you can make full use of the speed advantage wired Ethernet connections currently have over wireless connections. And, just as you can do with USB ports, you can extend the capacity of the wired Ethernet connections by plugging an Ethernet hub into an open port, as shown below.

The Broadband Networking Wireless Kits come in two flavors: one with a USB-based network adapter for desktop computers, and one with a PCMCIA card adapter for laptop computers. You'll see a lot more of these products in Chapter 4, "Making It Real—Putting In Your Home Network," in which I show you how to get to work and build a network.

Key Points

- Static electricity is your enemy! Wear an antistatic wrist strap or touch something metal before you handle any computer equipment.
- Always undo the screws at the edge of the computer case to get the cover off. The screws in the middle might be holding up something vital, such as the power supply.
- When you add a card to a Peripheral Component Interconnect (PCI) slot in your computer, press firmly with both thumbs. You will need to use some force, but don't go overboard.
- There are two versions of the universal serial bus (USB) standard: 1.0 and 2.0. While every USB 1.0 device will work with a USB 2.0 hub, it's not true in the other direction. If you buy a USB 2.0 device, you'll need to verify it'll work with a USB 1.0 port.
- If you see the Unplug Or Eject Hardware icon on your taskbar, click it to see if you need to stop your USB device before you remove it from your system.
- PCMCIA is a standard for cards used in laptops and other portable devices; it is not a new U.S. government intelligence bureau.
- In the United States, dialing *70 in front of the ISP phone number you identify in your modem's Properties dialog box will turn off call waiting and help prevent dropped modem connections.
- When you set up a broadband Internet connection, make sure you enter the correct Media Access Control (MAC) address for your modem.

Chapter 4

Making It Real—Putting In Your Home Network

Whenever you decide to make any changes around the house, you have two options: to hire someone to do it or to do it yourself. Hiring someone to put in a home network for you might seem like to easy way to go, but I'm sure that's not why you bought this book. The good news about putting in a home network is that you've got a lot of components you can install easily—such as Peripheral Component Interconnect (PCI) bus cards—or mindlessly easily—such as universal serial bus (USB) network adapters. After you've decided which type of network you want to install, you can make it happen quickly. In this chapter, my job is to go through the five scenarios I originally outlined in Chapter 2, "Envisioning Networks," and to give you step-by-step instructions for setting everything up.

Note It's always easy to spend other people's money, but I do ask you to seriously consider upgrading from Microsoft Windows 98 Second Edition (SE) to Microsoft Windows XP if you want to install a home network. Windows XP handles everything much more cleanly, and Windows 98 SE came out just as home networking was starting to become popular. You can do home networking in Windows 98 SE, but it's a lot easier if you have Windows XP.

Positioning Cables

There are a few technical things you need to know to install any network, but if you're putting in a wired Ethernet network, the real trick is to find an elegant way to run the wires in your home. The easiest way to send cable through your home is to run it along the walls, at the bottom of the baseboards. If you have several computers in the same room, such as the basement gaming extravaganza I described in Chapter 2, "Envisioning Networks," all you need to do is put the router right next to the computer with the high-speed Internet connection and run the cable along the walls to each of your computers.

I agree, running a cable all the way around a room when you could save 20 feet by running it across the middle of the floor might seem like a waste, but believe me when I tell you that the small amount of money you spend on a longer cable is more than worth reducing the likelihood that you'll trip on the cable and sprain a wrist trying to catch yourself as you fall.

Note If you're adamant about running cable across the middle of a room, be sure to at least put some carpet over the cable and *tape the carpet down*! The carpet strip, which theater technicians call a runner, does no good if it can slip and slide around. You can also spend a bit more money and buy cable covers, which are plastic strips rounded just enough to cover the cable (fancy that) while having a slope that's gradual enough that you'll be unlikely to trip over them. The better models, which are slightly more pricey, run the cable through a tunnel in the cover, while the less expensive (but perfectly serviceable) covers look like someone heated up flat sheets of plastic and bent them a little in the middle (which, I think, is exactly how they are made).

If you have computers in two adjacent rooms, such as those of the roommates just out of college that you saw in Figure 2-7 in Chapter 2, "Envisioning Networks," you can drill a hole in the wall, tie some cable to a straightened coat hanger, and feed it through to the other side. Plug one end into the router or hub, the other into the computer in the other room, and you're golden! If you want to run cable to one or more rooms that are on a different floor from the computer with your Internet connection, you need to decide whether you want to run cable from your router to every computer, meaning you need to run multiple cables between floors, or whether you want to run a single cable from a router on one floor to a hub in a central location on the other floor and run cables from that hub to the other computers. You can use an extra hub to extend your network, but there are some things you need to keep in mind when you add an extra hub. The first consideration is that you might need to connect your router and the hub with a *crossover cable*; the only way to know for sure whether you need a crossover cable is to check the documentation for both your router and the hub. The good news, however, is that you can buy crossover cables wherever you buy regular cables, or you can make them yourself.

Lingo A crossover cable is a cable that lets you hook an additional hub to a router, which in turn lets you extend your network by as many more computers as there are ports on the hub.

The second thing you need to do is to ensure your hub has an *uplink port*, which is usually located at one end of the hub and has the word *uplink* above it. That's the port you plug the crossover cable from your router into.

Lingo An uplink port is a specially designated port on a hub that you must use to extend your network to computers connected to the hub.

Things get a little trickier if you want to run cables between rooms that are on the same floor but aren't that close together, which is often the case with the family room and a bedroom, or to rooms separated both horizontally and vertically. "Measure once, cut twice" is a cliché of the first order, but the aphorism got promoted to cliché for a very good reason: it's true. If you don't have a good idea of where you're going, you won't know what to do to get there. (Sorry, that second cliché kind of snuck up on me and wormed its way into the paragraph.)

Suggestions for Wheel Inventors

My technical editor, Chris, has spent a lot of time wiring houses (he just finished wiring his new home, which is the second house he's set up for home and entertainment networking), so he came up with some great practical advice for anyone who is wiring his or her house for the first time.

First, don't be afraid to cut or drill through a wall to run your cables where you want them to go. Obviously you need to ensure you don't cut through electrical wires or pipes, but there are some rules of thumb you can use to avoid water pipes and electricity. The first is that you need to remember that anyone who works for a living finds the best way to do everything, and in a world where you pay for every foot of wire, contractors run wires in straight lines. So, by using your light switches and power outlets as guides, you can figure out where the wires are. The second is that you generally don't want to go through the wall blind. To be safe, a better method of putting a hole in a wall is to score the wall with a utility knife and bang the interior of the cut piece with a hammer. If you don't see any wires when you look through the hole, you found the right spot!

Note When you score wallboard (also known as drywall), you don't cut all the way through it. Instead, you cut about halfway through the board. Wallboard is typically less than an inch thick, so you don't need to cut that far into it to weaken it enough so that you can make a reasonably neat hole with a hammer. If you have a keyhole saw around, you can use it to smooth out the edges of the hole you made. On the off chance you cut in the wrong spot, you can either put in a blank face plate to cover the hole, or fill in the gap with another piece of drywall and a lot of spackle.

Second, take the time to see how the rooms and walls in your house line up vertically. One of the visual tricks I play on myself is that I imagine the rooms in a house always align vertically, but that is rarely the case. You might have the downstairs recreation room below a smaller guest bedroom, a bathroom, and a closet, for example. If you have the plans for your house, by all means refer to them, but you can give yourself a more accurate guide about how your house is laid out by putting the layout onto presentation transparencies (or tracing paper) and laying them one over the other. If you don't have the plans for your house handy, you can still map your house onto transparencies by measuring your house and rendering it in a drawing program or just tracing it onto transparencies with a marking pen.

Third, find the best way to run your cables behind walls, or in areas such as unfinished basements or garages where no one will care if there's some wiring showing. Closets are great, but (if your local building codes allow it) you can also use runs of 2-inch or 4-inch diameter PVC pipe as channels for your cables, depending on how many you run. Chris went a little crazy and ran four Cat-5 cables and two coaxial cables to every room, ending up with over 3000 feet of cable in his house! He says he knows it's a little extreme, but he's happy because everything is in place for whatever he wants to do.

And finally, drilling through the ceiling probably won't enhance your decor, but you can make it a lot less painful to look at by drilling only in closets. Unless you're some sort of closet fanatic, you won't need to do anything to dress up the hole except to vacuum up the dust. You can then run the cable from the closet to your computer. If there's room under the closet door, the cable can come out that way, or you can drill through the jamb and hook it out onto the wall.

Note Make sure you drill on the right side of the door! A friend of mine (not Chris) has an extra hole in his wall because he forgot he wanted to drill on the right side as he was coming out of the closet, not as he was looking in. You should also be sure the hole is a bit larger than the cable so the cable can run without scraping too much or crimping. And, as sort of a dessert for the cable-running meal, you might also consider spraying the exposed wood in the hole with a dry lubricant so the cable won't catch at all.

Your Home Networking Toolkit

When you get ready to start installing your home network, you should assemble a number of tools to make your life easier. Here are the basics.

- **A motorized drill** Battery-powered drills tend to be more expensive than corded drills, but they are also more convenient. Whether you choose to buy a corded or a cordless drill, be sure to verify with a salesperson that the motor is strong enough to drill effectively, without draining your battery or straining the motor.
- **Paddle bits for your drill** Unlike standard drill bits, which are round and have a spiral cut to move the bit through the wood, a paddle bit has a flat extension on the end of a standard bit, which lets you bore a wider hole. And remember that you're not drilling a hole for a single cable—in most cases you'll want to run more than one cable through a hole, whether it's to wire several computers or to run a spare cable or two. The best widths for paddle bits are ¼ inch, ½ inch, and ¾ inch. As you might imagine, running a wide, relatively square paddle bit through wood demands a lot more of your drill's motor than does a round bit, so be sure your drill is up to it!

Tip It's always a good idea to run a spare cable or two so you don't have to go through the process of running a fresh cable if something should go wrong.

- **An installer bit** This drill bit takes a cable along with it as it drills through wood. You may be able to do without this tool if you're using your paddle bits to drill wide holes, but if you need to run just a single cable through a wall, you can use an installer bit to make the job simple. Installer bits are also quite tough—you can use them to cut through nails and such.
- **A keyhole saw** Keyhole saws have a small, semi-circular handle and a thin blade. They are perfect for cutting through drywall or soft wood.

If you need to widen a hole or cut out a square for a patch panel (which I'll describe later), you can use a keyhole saw with much more precision than a larger saw.

- **An electrician's fish tape** No, this isn't a roll of tape you use to fix a trout; it's a roll of flexible steel wire to which you can attach a cable. You can then feed the wire into a hole in your wall, or into a bit of conduit or duct work, and then "fish" the tape out of the hole on the other end of the run. Because the tape is steel, you can use a magnet to find the tape and pull it through the hole. The only down side to using an electrician's fish tape is that it can be expensive. If you plan to install only a few short runs of cable and don't need to do too much work behind your walls, you don't need a fish tape. If, on the other hand, you're going to be running several 100-foot or longer cables through several walls, or if you're building or remodeling a home and want to do some work on your own, a 150-foot fish tape might be a very good investment.

> **Note** If you don't want to buy a fish tape, you can tie a fishing sinker and a cable to the end of a string and drop the sinker through any holes you drill. Because the sinker is made of metal you can use a magnet to bring the cable from the depths of your crawlspace so it can see the light of day in your office.

- **And more** You'll also need a utility knife, blades, a hammer, a screwdriver, and other common tools you use for tasks around the house.

Sprucing Things Up

Finally, after you've run your cable, you can make the visible cable more attractive (that is, less obtrusive) and more secure by trying the following approaches.

- Use a patch panel to have all your cables come out of a single point on your wall. A patch panel, which has connections for four or more Ethernet cables and often one or more coaxial cables, is a plate you screw into your wall. Patch panels make your cabling much neater to look at and easier to deal with. Be sure to label which outlet is connected to which computer!
- Paint your cable to match your baseboards or carpet. If you can't buy cables of the color you want—and there are quite a few different colors available—buy some paint and get to work. I suggest latex-based paint, because I'm leery of putting oil-based paint on plastic.

- Ensure the cable run stays straight or follows a gentle curve, which means you might need to cheat the corners of a room a little if you're running it around the baseboards. Nail the cable to your baseboard or floor using U-shaped nails. Again, make sure the nails fit around the cable and don't pinch the outside of the cable at all. One benefit of this approach is that the nails form a track for the cable, which should still run freely after the nails are in place.

Buying Cables or Making Your Own

If you're going to put a wired network in your home, you'll need to figure out the best way to run your cables. Once that's done, you'll go to the store to buy the cables so you can do the deed and hook everything together. If you need to buy only a few cables, you can safely open your wallet and buy premade ones. If, on the other hand, you need to run several hundred feet of cable, you might balk at the price, not be able to find any cables that are long enough for your project, or decide you just don't want to buy a 150-foot cable for a 101-foot run. In any case, you can always buy a 500-foot spool of Cat-5 (or Cat-5e) cable and make the cables yourself. There are two major advantages to making your own cables:

- They're always exactly the right length. You don't need to fool around with loops of Cat-5 hanging around behind your computer or rearrange your furniture because the cable you bought doesn't quite reach. With that in mind, you should always add several feet of slack to any long cables you make, just in case you want to move your computers around. You don't want to have to cut again, this time a 102-foot cable so you can move your desk over a foot.
- You save money on long cable runs. I checked prices for a 500-foot spool of Cat-5e and found out that it cost only a few dollars more than a premade 75-foot cable. That's right! You can get over six times as much cable for the same price.

Note Cat-5 cables come with two different coatings: PVC and Plenum. Plenum is generally more expensive, and you don't really need it for home use.

In addition to the cable, you do need to buy a few other things to make the raw cable ready for prime time. And what are those things? They are few in number, their stories quickly told:

- **RJ-45 connectors** These connectors look like larger versions of the connector you see on the end of a phone line (an RJ-11 connector). If you pay more than approximately U.S.$10 for a bag of twenty RJ-45 connectors, they'd better come with a free meal.
- **A wire stripper** Make sure you choose a wire stripper that's meant for use with Cat-5 cable. A wire stripper removes the cover from a cable without damaging the wires underneath. Most wire strippers have holes for use with a variety of cables, so you just need to be sure the one you buy has a hole for Cat-5 cable. Odds are that if you buy your wire stripper in a computer store, it'll have the hole you need, though I firmly believe in the adage "trust, but verify." Wire strippers of acceptable quality, which double as cable cutters, can be had for as little as U.S.$2.
- **A crimper** You use this to seat the wires firmly in the RJ-45 connectors at either end of the cable. Be sure your crimper has an RJ-45 setting. Crimpers cost less than U.S.$20, and you might even be able to find a tool that is a combination wire stripper and crimper for a few more bucks.
- **A cable tester** These testers cost around U.S.$100, but they're very useful if you're putting in a lot of cable. The good ones will even tell you which wires have failed, so you can try to fix the problem.

Caution Make sure you save your crimper's packaging. It most likely has instructions on how to use it to seat the wires in a connector.

An important part of creating a Cat-5 cable from scratch is to put the eight wires within the cable in proper order in each connector. There are two standards you can follow, the Telecommunications Industry Association's 568A or 568B. Both standards specify an order for the wires in a cable, and both will work when you make a patch cable as long as you don't mix them in the same cable. Mixing the standards results in a crossover cable, so the cable you make won't be completely useless. Figure 4-1 shows the order of wires in the 568A and 568B standards, counting from left to right.

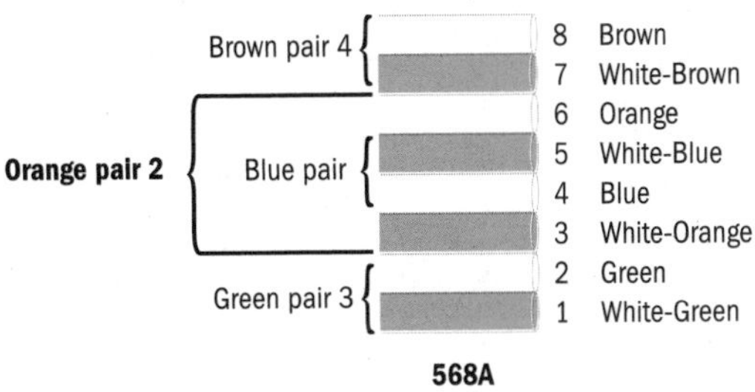

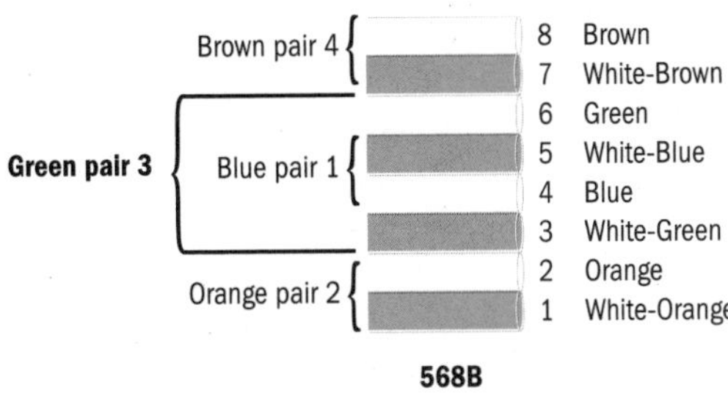

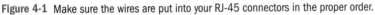

Figure 4-1 Make sure the wires are put into your RJ-45 connectors in the proper order.

Note Note that the wires in a Cat-5 cable come in pairs: one wire in the pair is of a solid color (white, green, blue, or brown), and the other is of the same color with white mixed in.

Building Your Own Cables

Once you've assembled the fixin's to make your own Ethernet cables, follow these steps:

1. Cut the cable to the desired length, taking into account that you might need to run the cable to your computer through an indirect route and that you might want to move your computer from its original location. In any event, too long is much better than too short.
2. Use the wire stripper to remove about one-half inch (or so) of the outer coating from one end of the cable. In this case, you should err on the short side until you see how much exposed cable you need to feed into the RJ-45 connectors.
3. Slide the four sets of wires into the holes in the RJ-45 connector.
4. Position the crimper so it covers the point where the wires enter the connector, and squeeze firmly so the contacts in the connector are snug against the wires. Your crimper should come with instructions and tips on how to complete this step.

5 Look at the other end of the cable and ask yourself, "Do I see an RJ-45 connector?" If you don't, repeat steps 1 through 4 on that end.

Tip You can also use Cat-5 cables instead of phone lines. A phone line usually has two pairs of wires: a red-green pair for your first line, and a black-yellow pair for your second line. On a Cat-5 cable, the blue–blue/white pair works for your first line, while the orange–orange/white pair works for your second line.

Troubleshooting Cables

In general, there are two times when you should test a Cat-5 cable: when you make it, and just after you've run it through your wall. Problems are easiest to fix when you have the entire cable sitting in front of you, and when you're new to making cables it's entirely possible you'll put some wires in the wrong order or not seat the wires securely in a connector, but the problems are generally easy to fix at that point. After you've run your cables, though, there is still the danger that an installer could put a nail or screw through a cable, or that a wire could break as it's being run around a sharp corner.

Note Because accidents can happen, you should test every cable you install, whether it's store-bought or homemade.

To troubleshoot a Cat-5 cable that has failed, follow these steps:

1 Use a cable-testing unit to determine which wires aren't functioning properly. The unit will have a series of lights on the base (and possibly the other end as well) to indicate problem areas.

2 Check the body of the cable for any breaks, such as sharp bends or incisions from nails or screws. If there is a break, you may need to scrap the cable.

Note If a cable has failed, don't despair! You may be able to use it after all. If you don't mind running a bit more slowly, and two pairs of wires are working, you can attach one pair of wires to pins 1 and 2, and another to pins 3 and 6, and send data over the cable at 10-BaseT rates.

---

3 Check the ends of the cable to ensure the wires are arranged properly in the connector. If you suspect there's a problem at the end of your cable, cut off the RJ-45 connector and reattach it.

It's Almost Show Time

And now it's time for the rubber to meet the road. Before you decide what you want to do, take a look back at the scenario summaries in the section in Chapter 2 entitled "What Your Network Might Look Like." Read through this chapter's descriptions for setting up each of the topologies. If you have friends who have installed home networks, find out what worked or didn't work for them. Once you have all that information in hand, you'll be in a position to make the best possible choice for your home network. The rest of this chapter describes your options in some detail.

Scenario 1: Setting Up a Wired Network with a Hardware-Based Shared Internet Connection

Of all the types of home networks you can set up, this one is the simplest. You buy a router, plug your cable or Digital Subscriber Line (DSL) modem into the designated modem port, and then run Cat-5 cables from the router to every computer you want to connect to your network. If your router has a built-in firewall (which you should insist on before you buy your router), the router serves as a barrier between your computer and the rest of the Internet, you don't have to worry about setting up any wireless equipment (not that it's that hard), and your data is transmitted at speeds that make networked gaming a joy. Even though this particular topology is pretty straightforward, you do need to think about where you want to put your router.

Note For simplicity's sake, I'm assuming you link every computer on your network directly to your router, but everything would work the same if you use one or more hubs to extend your network.

When you plan a home network that uses a router to share an Internet connection, you will appreciate very early on that the router is the star of the show. Do you remember the star network topology I mentioned in the section in Chapter 1 entitled "Network Topologies"? The router is the leading lady with her name above the title on the marquee.

Note Your leading lady needs to get along well with the rest of the cast (in this case, the Windows operating system), so you should visit *http://www.microsoft.com/hardware/broadbandnetworking/default.aspx* for more information on wired Microsoft Broadband Networking solutions.

Because everything revolves around the router, you need to choose its position carefully. One common mistake many first-time home network installers make (and I can say so because I did it) is to assume that you need to put the router right by the computer with which you connect to the Internet. Not so. You connect the computer with the cable or DSL modem the same way you connect every other computer to the router, so if you can position your router at a convenient middle point of your home and save 100 feet or more of cable, it'll probably be well worth it to do so.

Note Like all computer equipment, routers are very sensitive to heat, dust, electrical surges, and magnets. You should avoid putting your router on top of stereo speakers or behind a computer. Speakers use magnets to produce their sound and computer power supplies generate strong electromagnetic fields, so either one of them can erase a disk or knock the delicate internal workings of a router out of kilter. If you have a closet that's centrally located and stays relatively cool, you could put your router there.

To create a wired network with a hardware-based shared Internet connection, follow these steps:

1. If you're using Windows XP, make sure you're logged on as an administrator. If your router or base station came with a Setup program, you should run it now and follow the directions in that program. If not, follow the instructions in the printed manual. If you don't have a printed manual, follow the steps I've outlined.
2. Unplug the cable running from your cable or DSL modem to your computer's network interface card (NIC). Leave the cable plugged into the modem.
3. Plug the free end of the Ethernet cable coming from the modem into the modem port on the router. The modem port might be on the back of the router or at either end of the row of connections on the front of the router.

Note The "modem" port might be labeled *modem* (as it is on my router), *WAN* (short for Wide Area Network), or something else, depending on the router's manufacturer. Consult your documentation to see into which router port you should plug the Ethernet cable from the modem.

---

4. Plug a Cat-5 cable into the first open port on the router and then plug the other end into the NIC of the computer through which you originally connected to the Internet.
5. If your router has a power adapter, connect it to the router and then put the plug into an electrical outlet. The power indicator on the router will light up.

6 Configure your router using the method described in the router's documentation. You might need to run a Setup program on the router's installation disk, access the router itself using a Web browser such as Microsoft Internet Explorer, or perform a combination of those tasks.

7 When you are done setting up your router, turn your entire computer system off, including the router and all peripherals, such as printers and scanners, wait 30 seconds, and then turn everything back on.

8 Plug Cat-5 patch cables into the NICs of the remaining computers you want to share your Internet connection and plug them into open ports on the router. Because all the routers I checked were Plug and Play–compatible, the computers will detect the connection and configure themselves to work on the network without your needing to lift a finger.

Scenario 2: Setting Up a Wireless Network with a Hardware-Based Shared Internet Connection

I'm a big fan of doing things as inexpensively as possible, but I also value my time. When a friend of mind inquired about installing a home network, I checked the prices of all the available technologies. At the time he had three computers, so my math ran something like this: he could buy a wired router, Ethernet cable, and NICs for his computers, or buy a wireless router for the same price as the wired router, buy one Ethernet cable to run to the computer close to the wireless router, buy one wired adapter, and buy one wireless NIC for four times as much as the wired NIC. You will need to do some math to see whether a wired or wireless network would be better for you, but don't forget to consider intangibles such as installation time and aggravation!

Many wireless routers have a series of Ethernet connections as well, which you can use to connect computers that are in the same room as the router. The Microsoft Broadband Networking Wireless Base Station, for example, has four Ethernet ports on its back for connecting to nearby computers.

I'm not a guy who avoids hard work—I can sit and watch it for hours—but I wasn't too keen on wrangling Cat-5 cable through an attic crawlspace to the other end of my friend's house. In the end, he went for the wireless option, which I think was a great choice for him.

To set up a wireless network with a hardware-based shared Internet connection, follow these steps:

1. If you're using Windows XP, make sure you're logged on as an administrator. You also need to turn off any firewall or Internet Connection Sharing software you're running, such as the Microsoft Windows Internet Connection Sharing protocol. If your wireless router came with a Setup program or printed instructions, follow them now. If not, follow these instructions.
2. Unplug the cable running from your cable or DSL modem to your computer's NIC. Leave the cable plugged into the modem.
3. Plug the free end of the modem cable into the modem port on the router. The modem port might be on the back of the router or at either end of the row of connections on the front of the router.

Note The "modem" port might be labeled *modem* (as it is on my router), *WAN* (short for Wide Area Network), or something else, depending on the router's manufacturer. Consult your documentation to see into which router port you should plug the Ethernet cable from the modem.

---

4. Plug a Cat-5 cable into the first open port on the router, and then plug the other end into the NIC of the computer that was originally connected to the Internet.
5. If your router has a power adapter, connect it to the router and then put the plug into an electrical outlet. The power indicator on the router will light up.
6. Configure your router using the method described in the router's documentation. You might need to run a Setup program on the router's installation disk, access the router itself using a Web browser such as Internet Explorer, or perform a combination of those tasks.
7. When you are done setting up your router, turn your entire computer system off, including the router and all peripherals such as printers and scanners, wait 30 seconds, and then turn everything back on.

Once you've configured your router, you need to create a network for your computers to connect to.

Note The instructions in this section are meant as an example only–you should follow the instructions that came with your router.

To define a wireless network, follow these steps:

1. Access the router's configuration utility using the instructions that came with the router. For one brand of routers, you type the Internet Protocol (IP) address for the router in the Address bar of your Web browser. You can find the specific IP address in your manual, though most routers use either 192.168.0.1 or 192.168.1.1.

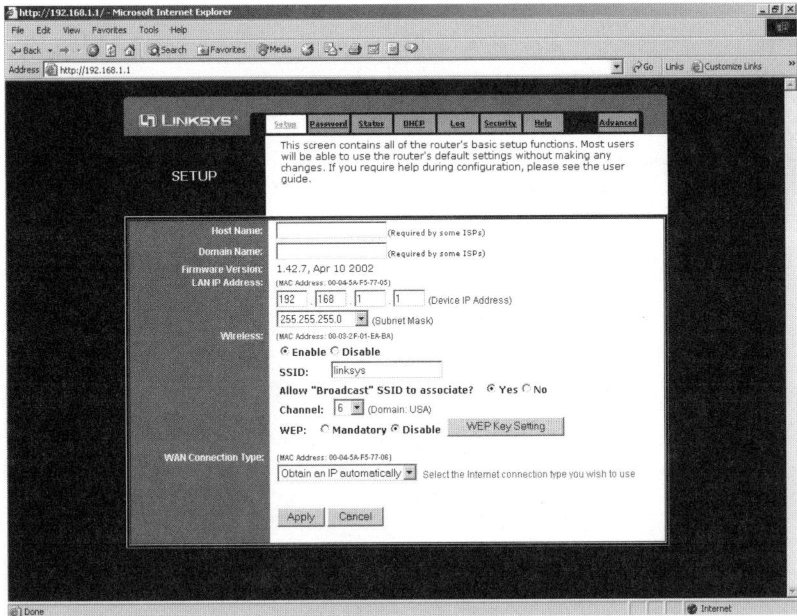

2. Type a name for your network in the SSID box. You should always change the name of the network from the default choice because that choice is too easy to guess and might leave your network open to unauthorized use.
3. Click Apply.

You might need to perform some additional setup tasks, such as choosing whether you want to encrypt the connection among your router and the computers on the network. Where those steps appear in the configuration process will depend on the wireless router you purchased. If you aren't given the opportunity to encrypt your network during the initial setup process, you should definitely do so afterwards.

See Also *For more information on encrypting a wireless network, see the section later in this chapter entitled "Encrypting a Wireless Network."*

Positioning Your Receivers

As with most other computer devices, you need to be sure your computers are away from any sources of electromagnetic interference, such as large stereo speakers or major appliances. It might be tempting to put your computer desk right next to the refrigerator so you don't have to get up to get a drink, but the likelihood that you could lose your work or network connection because of the fan or motor makes leaving your machine in the den much more practical. Beyond those considerations, you can put your wireless receivers pretty much anywhere you like. That's the beauty of wireless connections.

Encrypting a Wireless Network

One of the nice things about setting up a wired home network is that pretty much the only way someone can find out what's going on in your network is to connect to it. If you set up a wireless network, on the other hand, there's no telling who can connect to your network. All someone who wants free Internet access or to see what's on your network needs to do is guess the name of your home network and they get the run of the place. That, as I like to say, is a suboptimal occurrence. You can hide your network traffic behind a wall by turning on the *Wired Equivalent Privacy (WEP)* protocol.

Lingo The Wired Equivalent Privacy (WEP) protocol is a method of making data unreadable to any computer you don't want on your network.

What WEP does is scramble the data that traverses your network so that it can be read only if you know the method used to scramble it and the phrase you provide when you set up encryption. The mathematics of the type of encryption used is understood by a select few mathematicians and engineers, but essentially what happens is that you enter a password that the system uses as a base for the scrambler. For example, if you wanted to scramble the word *wireless* with the password *phantasm*, you could "add" the letters together to generate a new letter of the alphabet. Figure 4-2 shows you what would happen in that case.

```
wireless
phantasm
mqssfflg
```

Figure 4-2 If you "add" the words *phantasm* and *wireless*, you get a jumble. Of course, if you know one word, the result, and the method, you can find the other word.

You might think that it would take someone pretty strange to latch onto your network, and you'd be right, but there are plenty of folks out there who might not mind getting a little free Internet access from a neighbor who didn't protect himself or herself. Or you could be the target of a "drive-by," where folks cruise around with their wireless-enabled laptops on, looking for networks they can glom onto for nothing. You'd be surprised how many networks are left completely unprotected, without so much as a network name or password to protect them. I read an article recently about a security consultant who drove around downtown Washington, D.C. (my old stamping grounds), trolling for open connections. On some blocks he could have chosen from several corporate networks!

See Also *For more information on security threats and how to deal with them, see Chapter 5, "Making Your Network More Secure."*

The specific method you'll need to follow to enable WEP encryption on your wireless connection will vary depending on the equipment you buy, but you will do something akin to the follow steps:

1. Access your router's Setup program using the method described in the owner's manual. If you password-protected your router's configuration settings, which you should have done, you will be prompted for the password. Type it in, and then press Enter.
2. Click Encryption.
3. In the encryption setup dialog box, click the Encryption (WEP) down arrow (which has 64 Bit selected in the example shown here) and select the highest number available in the list of values. The higher the number, the longer the "password" the router uses to encrypt your network traffic and the harder it is for someone to guess it.

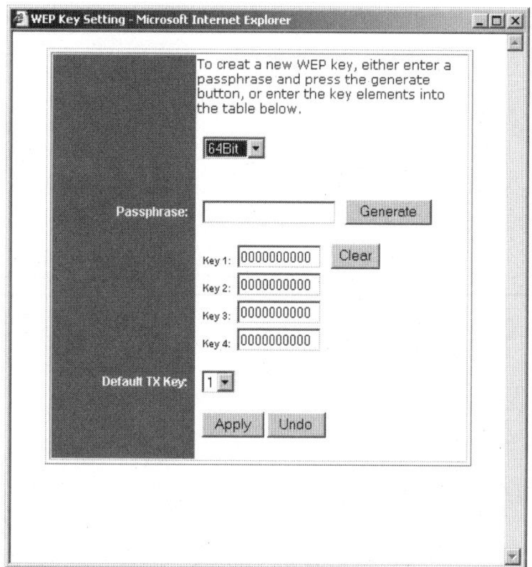

4 Type a password for your network in the password box.

See Also *For more information on creating secure passwords, see the section in Chapter 6 entitled "Making a Password Strong."*

---

5 Click Apply (or OK, depending on your router) to save your settings. You can then either close the program or quit your Web browser to end your session.

Building a Network with Microsoft Products

Home networking is taking off in popularity, in no small part because wireless networking technologies make it easy to put in a home network. With that thought in mind, Microsoft kicked off the Microsoft Broadband Networking Initiative. The Initiative culminated in the production of several pieces of wireless networking hardware that work hand in hand with the Microsoft Windows operating system to let you create home networks with a minimum of fuss. Those products are

- The Microsoft Broadband Networking Wireless Base Station
- The Microsoft Broadband Networking Wireless USB Adapter
- The Microsoft Broadband Networking Wireless Notebook Adapter

You can also buy kits with a router and either a USB or notebook (Personal Computer Memory Card International Association [PCMCIA]) adapter.

To install a network using Microsoft Broadband Networking equipment, follow these steps:

1. To install the software, insert the Setup CD-ROM into the CD-ROM drive of the computer attached to your broadband modem. If the Setup Wizard does not start automatically after a few seconds, open My Computer, double-click the CD-ROM icon, and then double-click Setup or Setup.exe.
2. Follow the steps in the Setup Wizard to install the software and set up your base station. When the wizard asks which device you are setting up, select Base Station. Continue following the instructions in the Setup Wizard. When the wizard asks you to connect the base station, position the base station close to your modem and computer and near the center of your intended network area. If you want to position the base station vertically, attach the optional stand.
3. Unplug the modem Ethernet cable from the back of your computer and plug it into the port labeled To Modem on the back of the base station. The base station is now connected to your modem.
4. Plug one end of the blue Ethernet cable that came with your base station into the Ethernet port labeled 1 on the back of the base station and plug the other end into the Ethernet port on the back of your computer.
5. Plug one end of the power supply that came with your base station into the Power port on the back of the base station, and plug the other end into an electrical outlet.

> **Tip** When prompted by the wizard, use the blank floppy disk included in the box to save your network settings.

6. When you reach the end of the wizard, click Finish. Remove the Setup CD-ROM and the floppy disk that contains your network settings from your computer. Keep both items handy for setting up additional computers on your network.

Scenario 3: Setting Up a Hybrid Network with a Hardware-Based Shared Internet Connection

If you're not quite ready to go all out and buy a wireless router and an 802.11b NIC for each of your computers, you do have an in-between option. If you like, you can connect the computers close to your wired router with Cat-5 cable and connect to the computers in the remote reaches of your home by plugging a wireless *access point* into your router.

Lingo An access point is a wireless networking device that acts like a hub on a wired network; you can plug it into a port on your wired router and extend the network's reach.

You should consider using this scenario as the basis for your home network if you have a number of computers very close together and one or two computers far enough away from your router that it would be an absolute pain to string cable through your house to get to them. If you have an existing home network and want to add wireless capabilities to it, you should take a look at buying a wireless access point. Wireless access points don't cost much more than a wired router, so they are a good investment in your network.

Positioning Your Router

When you create a hybrid network, one with both wired and wireless components, you can put your wired Ethernet router much closer to the computer with your Internet connection and use an access point to extend your network to the hard-to-reach portions of your home. As always, remember to keep your router away from sources of electromagnetic interference, and don't let it get too hot.

Note Your wired router is the touchstone for this system and should work with your operating system flawlessly. You can get more information on Microsoft's wired networking products by visiting *http://www.microsoft.com/hardware/broadbandnetworking/default.aspx*.

Adding a Wireless Access Point

When you pull a wireless access point out of its box, you realize that it looks a lot like a wireless router. In fact, the only difference, aside from the price, is that the access point has no wired Ethernet connections. So when, you might wonder, would it be worthwhile to buy a wireless access point instead of a wireless router? The most obvious time would be if you want to enable wireless connections within your home but don't want to spend the money for a wireless card for every computer you own. You might also have an established wired network but want to be able to use your laptop anywhere in your house without worrying whether there's an Ethernet cable in that room you can unplug from another computer. If you're going to do that, you might as well run cable to every room and hang a loop from the ceiling!

To create a hybrid network with both wired and wireless components, follow these steps:

1. Set up the wired portion of your network as shown in the earlier section entitled "Scenario 1: Setting Up a Wired Network with a Hardware-Based Shared Internet Connection."
2. Plug a Cat-5 cable into the Ethernet port on the access point, and then plug the other end of the cable into an open port on your wired router.
3. Install the software that came with the access point, most likely on a floppy disk or a CD-ROM.
4. Run the software you just installed and follow the directions in your owner's manual to set up the wireless portion of your network. You'll probably find that the access point setup is very much like setting up a wireless network through a router.

See Also *For more information on setting up a wireless network using a router, see the earlier section entitled "Scenario 2: Setting Up a Wireless Network with a Hardware-Based Shared Internet Connection."*

Scenario 4: Setting Up a Wired Network with Software-Based Internet Connection Sharing

Setting up a shared Internet connection with a router is a great option for folks who want the very best security and connectivity for their network, but I know for a fact that it's not for everybody. In fact, a lot of folks I know start looking at the amount of money they stand to spend for a wireless network and figure, "Hey, I'm not getting paid to write about this stuff—where can I cut costs and still get a decent connection?" The answer is here—you don't need expensive hardware to create a network. In fact, you just need to buy a second NIC for the computer with which you connect to the Internet, a hub to serve as the backbone of the network, and enough cable to connect everything together. And, as I explained earlier, you can make your own cables on the cheap. The only software you need to share your Internet connection is part of the Windows operating system that most likely came with your computer.

Of course, a drawback of connecting directly to the Internet with one of your computers is that you don't have the added security of a router standing between the bad guys and your computer. Also, if that computer goes down, none of the computers on your home network will be able to reach the Internet.

See Also *For more information on securing your computer against attack, see Chapter 5, "Making Your Network More Secure."*

Positioning Your Hub

Setting up a wired network using Internet Connection Sharing is, at least on its face, very similar to setting up an Internet connection you share through a router. You still need to use a hub to distribute the Internet connection to the other computers in the network, though, so you should pay close attention to where you put the hub. As with positioning a router, you should remember that the hub doesn't need to be right next to the computer with the Internet connection. In fact, if your Internet connection is in one room and there are two other computers in another room, it would make sense to place your hub in the other room and just run a single cable from your connected computer to the other two.

In addition to considerations of where you should place your hub, there are two very important points you should keep in mind when you set up a wired network that uses Internet Connection Sharing:

- The computer you use to connect to the Internet must have two NICs—one for the cable coming from your modem and the other to connect to the hub you use as the hardware backbone of your network. If you use a dial-up modem to connect to the Internet at 56 kilobits per second (Kbps), that device counts as the first NIC, but the second adapter must be a 10/100 megabits per second (Mbps) Ethernet adapter of some variety.
- You should always use the computer with the most recent version of the Windows operating system to connect to the Internet. The reason you want to use the newest version of Windows as your base of operations is that part of the setup for sharing an Internet connection is to create a floppy disk with files that can be used on computers with the same operating system or a previous version. The logic is that programmers can write a script to start Internet Connection Sharing on a computer with an earlier version of Windows, but as a rule you can't expect them to write a script to invoke Internet Connection Sharing on a version of the operating system that hasn't been created yet. It's this consideration that puts the *backward* in *backward compatible.*

Configuring Internet Connection Sharing in Windows XP

As you might imagine, there's a lot going on under the hood when you add an Internet connection for a computer. Sharing that single Internet connection among a number of computers, some of which might not even be running the same version of Windows as the connected computer, makes it even more challenging. Fortunately, Windows XP comes with a wizard you can use to share your Internet connection with other computers on your network. You don't have to fiddle with the internal workings of Windows to make everything happen correctly, and you don't need to do anything more complicated than answer a few questions about your computer.

To configure Internet Connection Sharing in Windows XP, follow these steps:

1. Connect the computers on your network to the hub, and make sure your Windows XP computer is connected to the Internet.
2. Log on to Windows XP using an administrator account.
3. Click Start, and then choose Control Panel. Click Network And Internet Connections.

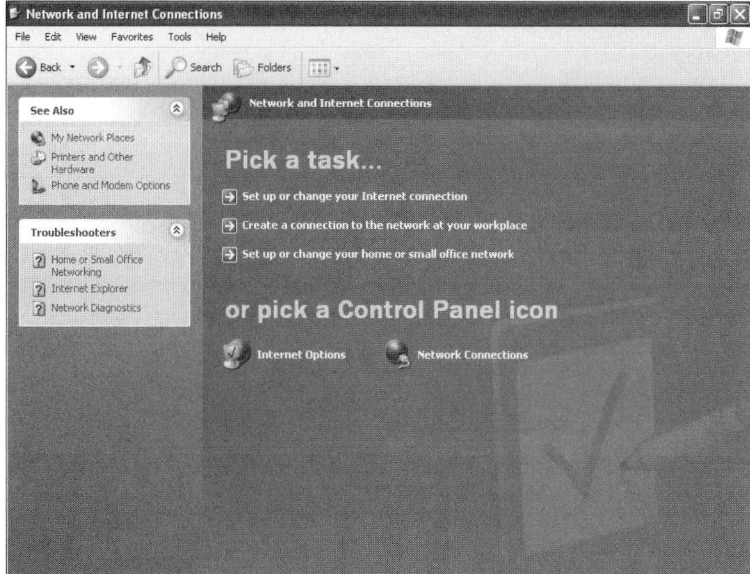

4. In the Network And Internet Connections dialog box, click Set Up Or Change Your Home Or Small Office Network. In the Network Setup Wizard, click Next twice.
5. If a wizard page appears indicating you have a disconnected NIC, plug in the cable for that adapter, and then click Next. (If you make the same mistakes I did when I first tried setting up a home network, you probably forgot to plug your second NIC into your hub!)

6 Select This Computer Connects Directly To The Internet, and click Next.

7 Select the connection by which your computer connects to the Internet, and click Next.

8 Type a description and name for your computer in the Computer Description and Computer Name boxes. Click Next.

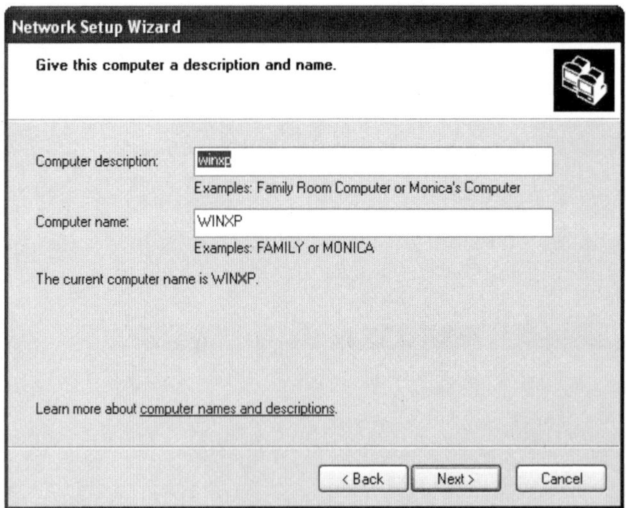

9 Type the name of your network in the Workgroup Name box, and click Next.

10 Verify your settings are correct, and click Next to implement them. This is the last chance you'll have to change any of the settings you chose during this run of the wizard.

Note If you do want to change any aspect of your home network, all you need to do is run the Network Setup Wizard again.

---

11 Select Create A Network Setup Disk, and click Next. Put a disk in your computer's floppy disk drive and click Next to copy the files to the floppy disk. If the disk needs to be formatted to accept data, click Format Disk.

Note If you have your Windows XP installation CD-ROM handy, you can select Use My Windows XP Installation Disk and then use your Windows XP installation CD-ROM instead of a network setup disk.

---

12 Click Next, and then click Finish.

To add Internet Connection Sharing capabilities to other computers on your home network, insert the network setup disk you created into the floppy drive of a computer you want to add to the network, display the disk's contents in My Computer or Windows Explorer, and double-click Netsetup.exe. Follow the instructions in the Netsetup program, and your computers will be ready for your network.

Configuring Internet Connection Sharing in Windows Me

As in Windows XP, you use a wizard to configure Internet Connection Sharing on a computer running Microsoft Windows Me. The wizard takes you through the process step by step, making it easy for you to let everyone on your network take advantage of a single Internet connection.

To set up Internet Connection Sharing in Windows Me, follow these steps:

1 Click Start, choose Programs, choose Accessories, and then choose Communications. Choose Home Networking Wizard, and click Next to move past the introductory wizard screen.

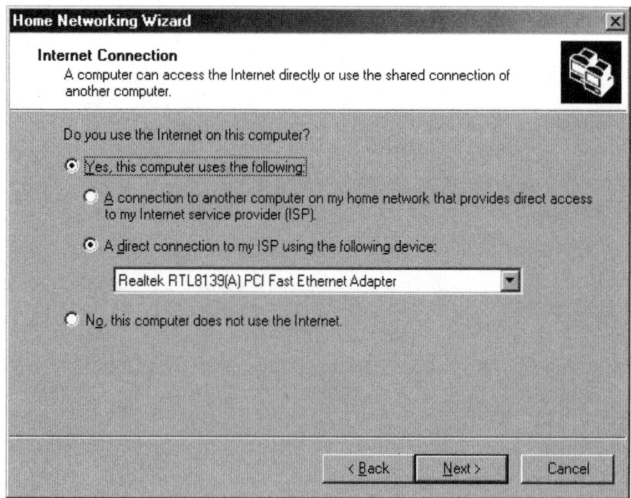

2 Select A Direct Connection To My ISP Using The Following Device and then, if necessary, click the down arrow and select the NIC you use to connect to the Internet. Click Next.

3 If desired, type a new name for your computer in the Computer Name box. Then either click Next to accept the default workgroup name of

MSHOME or select Use This Workgroup Name, type a new workgroup name in the box, and then click Next.

Note If you do type in a new workgroup name, be sure to verify that all other computers on your network have the same workgroup name.

---

4. Select the My Documents Folder And All Folders In It check box to share the contents of your My Documents folder with other users on your network. Likewise, you can make any printers attached to your computer available to other folks on your network by selecting the check box next to the name of printers you want to share. You can remove printers from the sharing by clearing the check box next to their name. Click Next.
5. Select Yes, Create A Home Networking Setup Disk and click Next. Put a disk in your computer's floppy disk drive, and click Next to copy the files to the floppy.
6. Click Finish.

To add Internet Connection Sharing capabilities to other computers on your home network, insert the home networking setup disk you created into the floppy drive of a computer you want to add to the network, display the disk's contents in My Computer or Windows Explorer, and double-click Setup.exe. Follow the instructions in the Setup program, and your computers will be ready for your network.

Configuring Internet Connection Sharing in Windows 98 SE

Unlike Windows XP and Windows Me, Internet Connection Sharing isn't included in the recommended Windows 98 SE installation. To add the Internet Connection Sharing software to your system, you'll need to find your Windows 98 SE installation CD-ROM and be ready to put it in your CD-ROM drive part of the way through the process of adding Internet Connection Sharing to your computer.

To configure Internet Connection Sharing in Windows 98 SE, follow these steps:

1. Click Start, choose Settings, and then choose Control Panel. Double-click Add/Remove Programs.

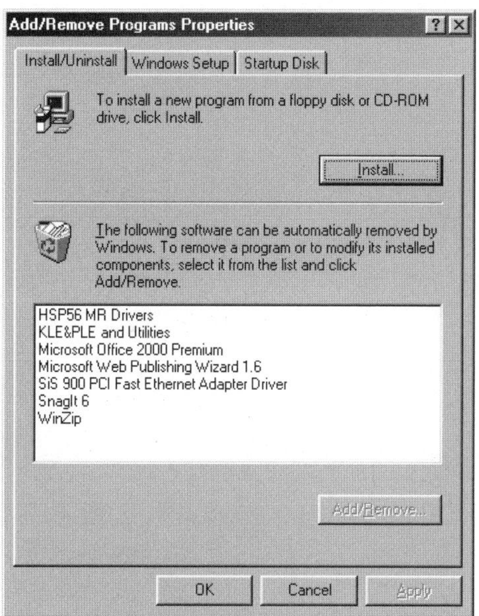

2 In the Add/Remove Programs Properties dialog box, click the Windows Setup tab. In the Components pane of the dialog box, select Internet Tools and click Details.

3 Select the Internet Connection Sharing check box, and click OK. A message box will appear, instructing you to put your Windows 98 SE CD-ROM into your computer's CD-ROM drive. After doing that, click OK.

4 Click Next. Select the option button representing the type of Internet connection you have from this computer, and click Next.

5 Select the NIC you use to connect to the Internet, and click Next.

6 Click Next to begin creating a Windows 98 SE Internet Connection Sharing client disk. This disk will contain a Setup program you will run on other computers on your network.

7 Insert a disk into your computer's floppy disk drive, and click OK. When the disk is ready, remove the disk and click Finish.

8 If you're prompted to restart your computer, close any other programs you have open and click OK.

You can configure other computers on your network to take advantage of Internet Connection Sharing by inserting the client disk you created into the computer's floppy disk drive, displaying the disk's contents in My Computer or

Windows Explorer, double-clicking Icsclset.exe, and following the instructions in the Client Setup program.

To turn off Internet Connection Sharing in Windows 98 SE, follow these steps.

1. Click Start, choose Settings, and then choose Control Panel. Double-click Internet Options.
2. In the Internet Properties dialog box, click the Connections tab and then click Sharing.
3. In the Internet Connection Sharing dialog box, clear the Enable Internet Connection Sharing check box. Click OK twice.
4. If you're asked to restart your computer, click Yes.

If Internet Connection Sharing is installed on your system but isn't enabled, follow these steps to enable it:

1. Click Start, choose Settings, and then choose Control Panel. Double-click Internet Options.
2. In the Internet Properties dialog box, click the Connections tab and then click Sharing.
3. In the Internet Connection Sharing dialog box, select the Enable Internet Connection Sharing check box and click OK twice.
4. If you're asked to restart your computer, click Yes.

Scenario 5: Setting Up a Wired Network Without an Internet Connection

If you're in a neighborhood without reliable Internet connectivity, you just don't care to have an Internet connection, or you want to set up your basement so you and your friends can play games over a LAN, you can set up a wired network without an Internet connection. Windows XP and Windows Me are both set up to handle that task quite nicely, letting you choose a connection-less network early on in the wizards you use to create your network. You can also create a wired connection in Windows 98 SE, but you need to do it manually.

Note One thing I've found that helps when you're creating a home network is to create a dial-up connection from your computer's modem, even if you will never use it. Many of the wizards in Windows expect to see an Internet connection of some sort, and creating a "dummy" entry might save you some headaches.

Configuring Networking in Windows XP

As you might expect from the latest version of Windows, Windows XP has the most complete and effective wizard for creating home networks, with or without an Internet connection attached.

To configure networking in Windows XP, follow these steps:

1. Click Start, choose Settings, and then choose Control Panel. Click Network And Internet Connections.
2. In the Network And Internet Connections dialog box, click Set Up Or Change Your Home Or Small Office Network.
3. In the Network Setup Wizard, click Next, ensure you have performed all the tasks mentioned on the wizard page except for establishing an Internet connection, and then click Next.
4. If a wizard page indicates that Windows found disconnected network hardware, verify your computer is connected to the network. If your computer is connected and the disconnected hardware is for a second NIC, select the Ignore Disconnected Network Hardware check box and click Next.

> ***See Also*** *For more information on when you might put more than one NIC in a single computer, see "Encouraging Unity: Bridging Networks in Windows XP," later in this chapter.*

5. Select Other to bypass the Internet connection options offered, and click Next.

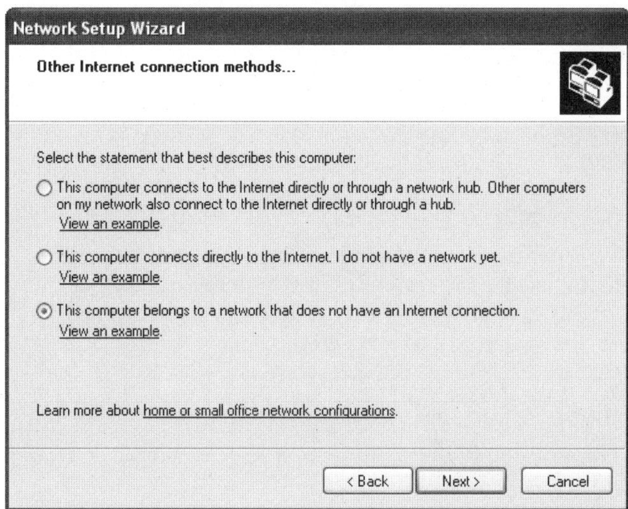

6 Select This Computer Belongs To A Network That Does Not Have An Internet Connection, and click Next.

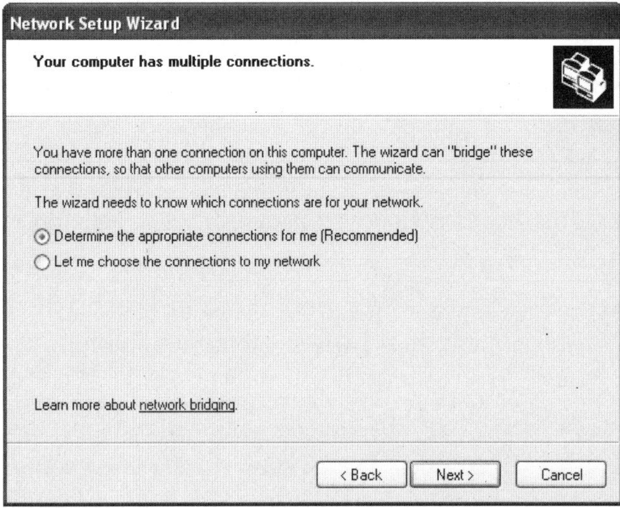

7 If your computer has more than one NIC, a wizard page will appear asking if you want to bridge the connections. Select Determine The Appropriate Connections For Me (Recommended), and click Next.

8 The description and name you provided for your computer when you first set up Windows XP appear. Change the computer's description by typing a new description in the Computer Description box, and change the computer's name by typing a new name in the Computer Name box. Click Next.

9 If you want to change your workgroup's name, type a new value in the Workgroup Name box. Click Next.

10 Click Next to accept the listed changes, click Back to retrace your steps and make any changes, or click Cancel to halt the wizard. After you click Next, Windows XP will take a few minutes to apply your settings.

> **Note** This is the last wizard step where you can use the Cancel button to undo your changes, and the Back button won't let you move to this screen. If you want to change your network settings, you will need to run the wizard again.

11 Select Create A Network Setup Disk, and click Next. The network setup disk you create will have all of the files you need to add other Windows computers to your network.

12 Insert a 3.5-inch floppy disk into your drive and click Next. Windows will copy the required networking files to your floppy disk.

13 Read the instructions on using the network setup disk. Click Next, and then click Finish.

Configuring Networking in Windows Me

Just as in Windows XP, Windows Me has a wizard you can follow to create your home network. In fact, if you're creating a home network, the name makes a bit more sense: the Home Networking Wizard. The best part of the Home Networking Wizard, at least as far as this scenario is concerned, is that you can choose to set up a home network without a shared Internet connection.

To configure networking in Windows Me, follow these steps:

1 Click Start, choose Programs, choose Accessories, and then choose Communications. Click Home Networking Wizard, and then click Next.

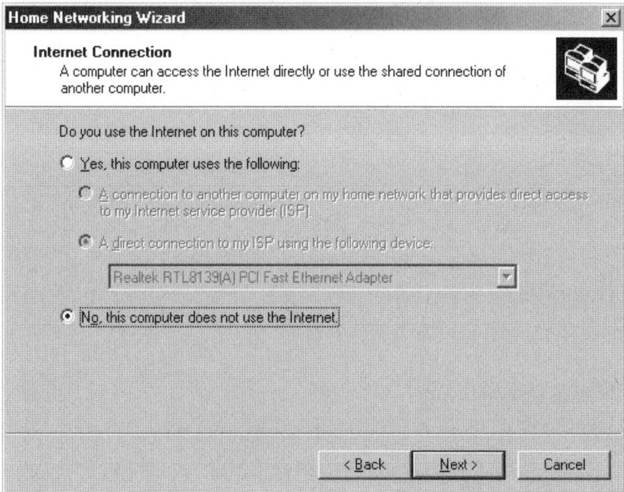

2 Select No, This Computer Does Not Use The Internet and click Next.

3 If you like, you can change the name of your computer by typing a new name for it in the Computer Name box.

4 Click Next to accept the default workgroup name, which is MSHOME.

5 If you want to share the contents of your My Documents folder, select the My Documents Folder And All Folders In It check box. To share any printers listed in the box at the bottom of the wizard screen, select the check box next to the name of the printer you want to share. Click Next.

6. Select Yes, Create A Home Networking Setup Disk, and click Next.
7. Insert a floppy disk into your computer's floppy disk drive, and then click Next to have the wizard create a setup disk.
8. Click Finish to save your settings or click Cancel to exit the wizard without setting up home networking on your computer. If you're asked if you want to restart your computer so the changes can take effect, click Yes.

Configuring Networking in Windows 98 SE

Configuring networking, as opposed to creating a shared Internet connection, is a bit different in Windows 98 SE than it is in later versions of Windows. Rather than using a wizard that steps you through the process, you need to let Windows know you want to make the files and folders (and maybe printers) on your Windows 98 SE machine available to other folks on your network. In other words, if you didn't know the effect of networking your computers, you wouldn't know where to look (unless you read this book, of course)!

See Also *For more information on sharing files, folders, and printers in Windows 98 SE, see the section in Chapter 7 entitled "Making Your Files and Folders Available to Others."*

To configure networking in Windows 98 SE, follow these steps:

1. Click Start, choose Settings, and then choose Control Panel. Double-click Network. In the Network dialog box, click the Configuration tab and click File And Print Sharing.

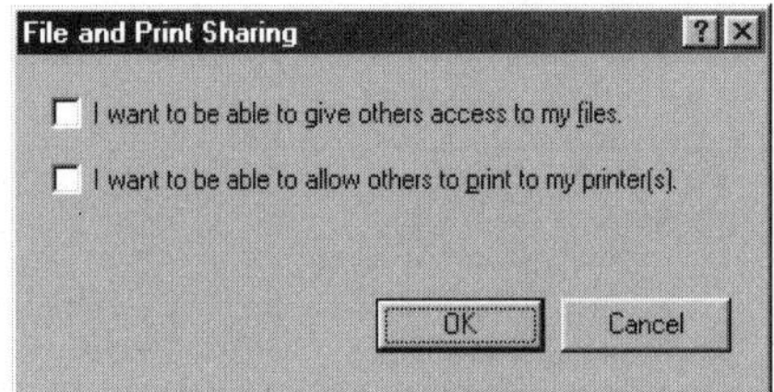

2. In the File And Print Sharing dialog box, select the I Want To Be Able To Give Others Access To My Files check box and click OK twice. Click Yes to restart your computer for the changes to take effect.

Encouraging Unity: Bridging Networks in Windows XP

When you build a home network, you should design it so it fits in with your living space. The most basic sort of home network, as exemplified by the basement computer gaming utopia depicted in Figure 2-5, is made up of computers with one NIC apiece that are all connected to the same hub. Now, imagine two computers in an upstairs office that share a high-speed Internet connection. Because the groups of computers don't have a common connection, they can't talk to each other. If you were to connect the two groups of computers, presumably so the computers in the basement could take advantage of your Internet connection, each separate network would become a *segment* of a single network.

Lingo A network segment is a self-contained group of computers that have a common connection. For example, you might have four computers in your home, all of which are connected to the same router.

For example, in my home I have a single computer connected to a high-speed Internet connection in my office, and I have a network of computers in my rec room. It's not quite geek Nirvana, but it's close. The backbone of the operation is a wireless router in my home office, into which I have plugged my office computer. I also installed two NICs (one wired, one wireless) into one of my three Windows XP Professional computers in the rec room (the other two computers have a single wired NIC). The wireless adapter exchanges signals with the wireless router, and the wired Ethernet adapter has a Cat-5 cable running from it to a hub. The other two computers in my rec room are also connected to the hub, completing the chain and letting all three computers in the rec room use my Internet connection.

Confused? Figure 4-3 should help you visualize what I just tried to explain.

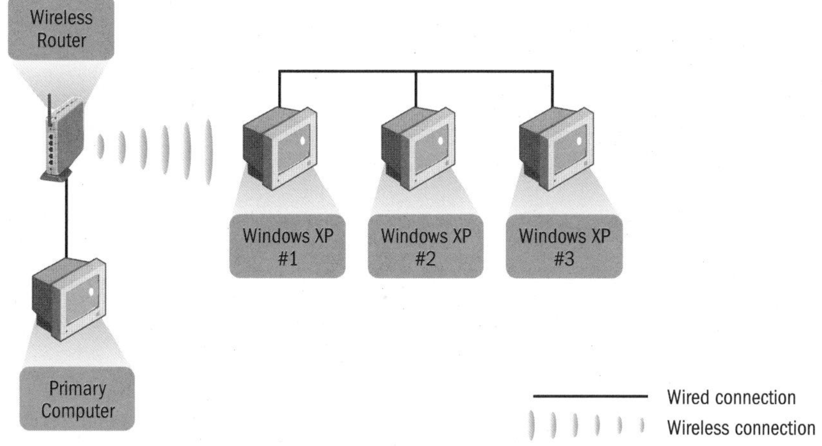

Figure 4-3 My network has two segments, connected by a bridge in my Windows XP computer.

When you run the Network Setup Wizard, Windows XP will likely detect that you have two NICs in your computer and will offer to create a bridge between the two adapters. Yep, the operating system is set up to recognize what you're trying to do! If you added a second NIC after you ran the wizard the first time, or if for some reason the bridge isn't there, you can always create a bridge on your own.

To form a bridge between network segments, follow these steps:

1. Click Start, choose Settings, and then choose Control Panel. Click Network And Internet Connections.
2. In the Network And Internet Connections dialog box, click Network Connections.

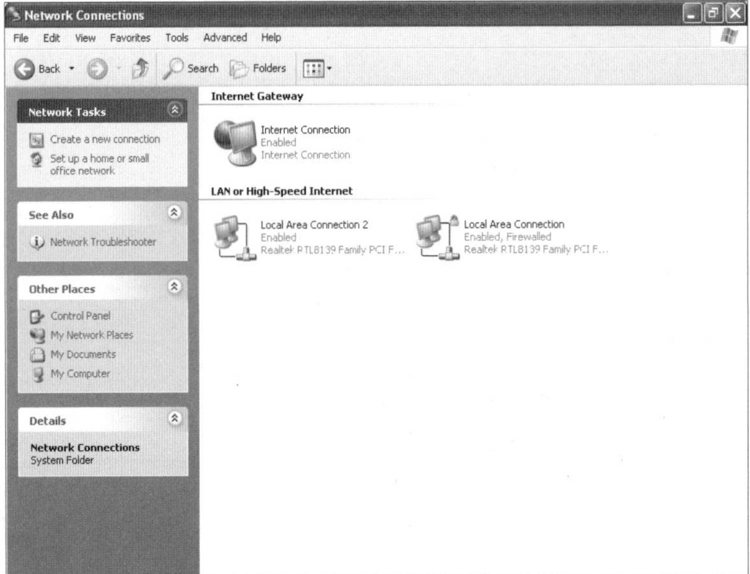

3. In the LAN or High-Speed Internet section of the dialog box, select each of the private network connections that you want to be part of the bridge.
4. Right-click one of the highlighted private network connections, and then click Bridge Connections.

Note You're not limited to two network segments. If you need to set up another few computers in another part of your house, you can copy the rec room segment in other areas of the house.

Adding a Macintosh to Your Network

If you own a mix of Macintosh and Windows computers, you probably turned to this section first to see if there is any easy way to add a Macintosh computer to a mostly Windows network. You'll be happy to know you can add a Macintosh to your network and surf the Web or download files over the Internet with no difficulty, but up until August 2002 there was no easy way to exchange files between a Macintosh and a Windows computer.

Time. Some things time just can't do ...

With the introduction of Mac OS v. X 10.2, code-named "Jaguar," you can have your Macintosh masquerade as a Windows computer, enabling you to share files and printers on a Windows-based home network.

To add a Macintosh computer running Jaguar to your Windows-based home network, follow these steps:

1. Click the Apple, and choose System Preferences.
2. Click System.
3. On the Services tab, select the Windows File Sharing check box.
4. On the System Preferences menu, choose Quit System Preferences.

If you're not running Jaguar on your Macintosh, you can still connect your Macintosh to your network with a standard Ethernet cable and surf the Web. Of course, using the Web is one thing, but sharing files and printers on a mixed network is quite a bit trickier. Fortunately, there are two programs available that take a lot of the guesswork out of sharing files between Macintosh and Windows computers. If you want to add a Macintosh to a mostly Windows network, you should look into Thursby Software's DAVE. If you want to add a Windows computer to a mostly Macintosh network and share PC files with your Macintosh computers, you can buy PCMACLAN, a program created by Miramar Systems.

Note You can visit Thursby Software's Web site at *http://www.thursby.com/* and Miramar's Web site at *http://www.miramar.com/*.

Troubleshooting

Q. What do I do when I can't access the Internet from a guest computer on my network?

A. If you're having trouble accessing the Internet from a guest computer, first make sure the computer is plugged into your network, whether into a hub or router. Then power cycle the computer to reset the system and look at the NIC you installed in that computer. Most adapters have a small green light by the RJ-45 jack to indicate whether they are active. If the green light is off, there might be a problem with the adapter; try reinstalling it. If the adapter is okay, you might need to run the Internet Connection Sharing software again. Get the disk you created when you first ran the networking wizard on your computer and run the Setup program on the machine you're having trouble with.

Q. What do I do when I'm having trouble seeing a Windows 98 SE machine on a network with a Windows XP Professional machine?

A. If you are having trouble seeing a Windows 98 SE machine, make sure both computers have the same workgroup name in their networking settings. If they are the same, you should also check to be sure you have an account with the same name on both computers. You can get more information on establishing user accounts in Chapter 6, "Creating User Accounts."

Q. What do I do when my computer tries to establish a modem connection whenever I try to connect to another computer on the Internet, even when I'm already connected to the Internet?

A. Click Start, choose Settings, and then choose Control Panel. Click Network And Internet Connections, click Internet Connections, and in the Internet Properties dialog box, click the Connections tab. Select Never Dial A Connection, and then click OK twice to save your changes.

Key Points

- When establishing a home network that shares an Internet connection, you should always connect to the Internet with the computer that has the most recent version of Windows.
- You don't always need to put a router right next to the computer with your Internet connection.
- You can make your own cables to save a lot of money and paint them to match your decor (saving your eyes).
- A wireless network will cost a bit more than a wired network, but you'll save installation time up front and won't need to work as hard to add computers to your system.
- You should always encrypt a wireless network, whether it's through a wireless router or access point.
- You might be able to take advantage of bridges to create the optimal mix of wired and wireless connections on your network.
- Never, ever lose the setup instructions for your router.

Chapter 5

Making Your Network More Secure

The Internet has often been compared to the Wild West, where gunslingers ply their trade and the common folk scamper about doing their business and trying to avoid trouble as best they can. That was once the case, but the law has started to catch up to the electronic frontier, and the homesteaders aren't as helpless as they're made out to be. In fact, you've got quite a few tools at your disposal to make sure you can go about your business all peaceable like and not have to worry about the bad things that can happen. Of course, you get to avoid worrying only if you've done some work up front to protect yourself, but that's part and parcel of life on the range.

My job in this chapter is to describe the seamier side of life on the Internet and to tell you how to protect your computers from exploitation. You'll learn how to protect yourself from viruses, worms, Trojan horses, and intruders of all kinds. You'll also learn what sorts of information folks can often find on a computer and what steps you can take to ensure your personal information stays safe at home.

Know Your Enemies

I don't know why, but some people are just intent on ruining everyone else's good time. Whether it's cutting you off in traffic or arguing with a waiter over nothing, these folks exhibit a trait known as *schadenfreude*: taking an unhealthy delight in the misfortune of others. When these folks gets their hands on a programming tool that lets them write files that can do serious damage to others' computers, there's little doubt in their minds that they've found their calling. Thank goodness these rogues are relatively few in number, but the damage they can do is significant—especially when it happens to you.

Viruses

I'm sure you've heard reporters and your computer-using friends say the word *virus* as if it were a curse. And they're right—it is a curse. If you've ever had a bad cold, you know all you need to know about viruses: they're nasty, hard to get rid of, and best dealt with by avoiding them in the first place.

Lingo A virus is a program that attaches itself to a "host" program and can cause damage to hardware, software, and files.

What kind of damage can a virus do? If you're using an administrator account on your computer, or if you can add or run any program you want, you're wide open to abuse. The virus is, after all, a computer program. The whole point of writing a virus is to ensure the infection spreads to other computers, whether the virus does damage or not. Some folks do create benign viruses for the sheer challenge of seeing whether they can write a program that makes the virus protection industry scramble for a while. But there are also the folks who delight in doing damage, in punishing people for not being smart, wily, or attentive enough to fend off attacks from all angles. As if you didn't have better things to do with your time.

See Also *For more information on the different types of accounts and how they can affect your computer's security, see Chapter 6, "Creating User Accounts."*

So how does a computer virus infiltrate your computer? There are a number of ways the little beasties can sneak past your defenses:

- As an e-mail attachment.
- As e-mail sent to a Web-based service, such as Hotmail.

- Through files you share by disk or over a network. (I can tell you from firsthand experience that college computer labs are rife with virus-infested files.)
- From a Web site that tricks you into downloading malicious code.

One type of virus that is particularly insidious is the *macro virus*. One of the benefits of Microsoft Office products is that you can automate repetitive tasks by recording a macro. For example, if you have to copy a number of tables from a Web site into a Microsoft Word report you're preparing, reformatting the table as you go, you can record the steps you go through the first time and then run the macro whenever you need to bring in another table. The macro scripting language, Microsoft Visual Basic for Applications (VBA), is powerful and flexible—powerful enough, in fact, to make it possible for individuals to manipulate your computer and its contents in unsavory ways.

Lingo A macro virus is a program attached to a document that uses the macro scripting language to do harm to your computer.

Every virus-scanning program worth its salt can detect all sorts of viruses. If one does happen to slip by your scanner, however, you still have a chance to prevent it from wreaking havoc on your computer by choosing not to enable it when you open the document.

Each Office program, with the exception of Microsoft Access (the database program, which doesn't use VBA as its macro scripting language), lets you determine if and when Office macros will be run on your computer. There are three different settings:

- High, which rejects any macros from a source you don't trust
- Medium, which lets you choose on a case-by-case basis whether to run a macro
- Low, which runs all macros

To set the macro security on your computer in any Office program except Access, follow these steps:

1. From the Tools menu, choose Macro, and then choose Security.

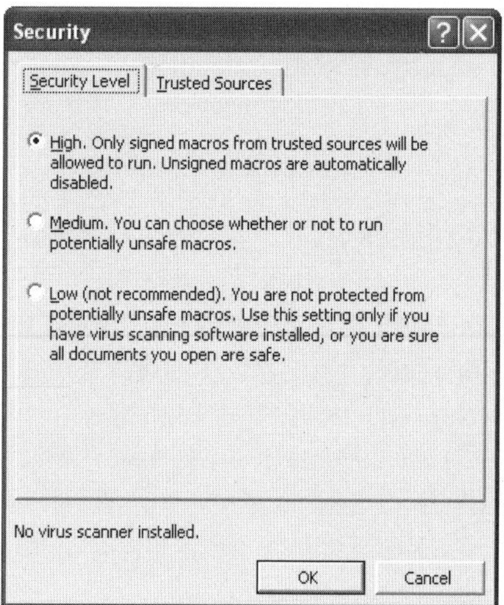

2 In the Security dialog box, click the Security Level tab and select the option button representing the macro security level for your computer. There are three levels to choose from, but under no circumstances should you set your security level to Low! Letting any old code that wanders into your neighborhood take over your computer is foolhardy at best.

3 Click OK.

If you set your macro security level to Medium, a dialog box appears whenever you try to open a file that contains macros. The dialog box has three buttons that let you enable macros, disable macros, or view the Help files for virus safety and security. If you know the file's sender, expected to receive the file, and the file passes through your virus checker with no problems, you can *probably* run it without worrying about whether it contains a macro virus. There's always that flicker of doubt in the back of my mind, but I've driven in Washington, D.C., during rush hour and understand that there is no life without risk.

Worms

Another type of malicious program you might come across is the *worm*, which spreads from computer to computer, using increasing amounts of your computer's resources until the system can't cope and shuts down. The term *worm* was first used in John Brunner's 1975 science fiction novel *The Shockwave Rider* to describe programs individuals used to tunnel through computer networks, much as worms tunnel through dirt. And that's how worms operate; they exploit a flaw in your computer's programming to spread across the Internet, taking up valuable processing power and transmission capacity and generally bringing things to a crashing halt.

Lingo A worm is a stand-alone, self-replicating program that invades computers and consumes memory, thus causing a computer to crash.

On a Personal Note The first well-publicized worm to hit the Internet (then known as the ARPAnet, named after the U.S. Defense Department's Advanced Projects Research Agency, which funded the Internet in its early days) was released in 1988 by a Cornell University graduate student whose father, ironically enough, was a senior computer security expert for a government agency. How do I know? I was pursuing my undergraduate studies about an hour north, at Syracuse University, and working as a student consultant for Academic Computing Services. As the most mediagenic person in the department (pickings were indeed slim), I was interviewed by two local television stations about the worm. The federal investigators visiting the area saw the interview and asked around briefly if it were possible that I knew anything else about the worm, but I had the perfect alibi: I was a political science major!

These days worms don't travel alone. Instead, the most recent worms carry with them a program that either tries to help spread the worm by mailing itself to everyone in the computer's e-mail address book or by leaving behind a program that the person who sent the worm could use to attack another computer on the Internet. Here's how it works. The person who created the worm puts the address of the computer to be attacked in a program carried along by the worm. Then, at a time also written into the worm, every infected computer begins sending hundreds of requests for Web pages from the victim's computer every second. This type of attack is called a *distributed denial of service* attack, and it's really, really nasty. Fortunately, most virus-scanning programs also look for worms, so you don't need to buy any extra software to protect yourself.

Trojan Horses

The last type of harmful software I'll cover here is the *Trojan horse*. According to myth, the Greeks left a great wooden horse outside the gates of Troy after ten years of unsuccessful siege. As the Greek fleet appeared to sail away, the Trojans pulled the horse inside the city's walls. Of course, there were a number of Greek soldiers in the belly of the horse, including the great hero Achilles, and they crawled out in the dead of night, dispatched the guards, and flung open Troy's gates to the returning army. And, just as the Greeks had their way with Troy, a Trojan horse that you unsuspectingly run can devastate your computer.

Lingo A Trojan horse is a computer program that appears to be useful but conceals an unexpected function that is typically damaging.

Trojan horse programs are *executable* files, meaning they can be run on their own without the aid of another program, as is required with a macro virus. They'll usually have a file extension such as .exe or .com, the latter of which is the most dangerous for practical purposes. Both types of files will run without another program, but a .com, or "command," file can be dressed up to look like the address of a Web site. Another type of file that can be used as Trojan horse is the screen saver (.scr).

Most virus-scanning programs also know how to look for Trojan horses, so you have your bases covered.

A Few Commonsense Rules for Dealing with Strange Files

I'd love to tell you how to stay perfectly safe, but there's no surefire way to protect your computer or files from infection. The best strategy is to do a few simple things and keep your eyes open. The following measures are the most important steps you can take to protect your computer from viruses:

- Install antivirus software and keep it current. (There is more information on keeping your virus checker up-to-date in Chapter 11, "Maintaining Your Home Network.")
- Use Microsoft Windows Update to scan and update your Windows operating system with the latest free software patches, including those for Microsoft Internet Explorer and Outlook Express. For more information on updating Windows, visit *http://www.microsoft.com/security/articles/update.asp.*
- Use Microsoft Office Products Update to keep Outlook and other Office programs up-to-date to help guard against virus intrusions. For more information on updating Office, visit *http://office.microsoft.com/productupdates/.*
- Install a firewall, especially if you use a high-speed Internet connection. (I'll show you how to set up a firewall later in this chapter.)

Here are two more good practices to follow:

- Be cautious about visiting unknown or untrusted Web sites. Untrusted or disreputable Web sites can transmit a virus directly into your computer. Staying on the main routes of the information highway will help keep you safe.

- Don't open e-mail attachments from anyone you don't know—and be wary of ones from people you do. Some viruses spread by mailing themselves to contacts in an infected computer's address book. If you have any doubts about the safety of an attachment, check with the source before opening it.

By using discretion, keeping your antivirus software up-to-date, and erring on the side of caution, you can help correct and protect the health of your computer system. Prevention is the best medicine.

Scanning Software

What's the backbone of a solid and effective computer security plan, relatively inexpensive, and could very well save you from days spent rebuilding your computer and weeks spent rebuilding your sanity? It's virus-scanning software, and it's your best friend.

As the name implies, virus-scanning software inspects files before they are written to your computer's hard disk, or afterward if you have the program inspect your files while you grab some shut-eye. And believe me, if you have a lot of files on a large hard disk, it will take your computer an hour or more to work through them all. There are a lot of good virus-scanning programs, and all of them allow you to do the following:

- You can update the files the programs use to search for viruses, often on a weekly basis.
- You can have the programs scan your incoming e-mail messages for attachments that contain viruses.
- You can set up regular system scans to ensure your hard disks are free from infection.
- You can choose to have the program fix infected files, delete infected files, or move infected files to a quarantine area so you can try to fix them later.

Any virus scanner you consider purchasing should also give you the option of creating a set of emergency rescue disks you can use to diagnose and, with luck, fix your computer if you suspect it has been taken over by a virus, worm, or Trojan horse. If you do nothing else I recommend in this book, make that set of disks. They could save your data—and your sanity. If you've ever had to reformat your hard disk, reinstall your operating system and programs, and re-create an entire directory full of files that were destroyed by a virus, you understand what I mean when I tell you to make the disks.

Tip Make those disks.

It's absolutely vital that you keep in mind that virus-scanning programs can detect only the viruses that software manufacturers know about. To that end, you should always keep an eye on your computer to see if something just doesn't look right. For example, if your hard disk is working overtime for more than a few minutes at a time when you're not optimizing your disk or backing up your files, your computer might have been taken over by some remote code and is being used as a zombie, mindlessly following the will of its controller, who might well be halfway around the world. You should still be able to use your computer in other ways, because if you weren't you'd just pull the plug and stop it from whatever it was doing. However, if your hard disk's light flashes consistently while you're not using the computer and your network traffic is high, you might have a problem.

See Also *For information on updating your virus-checking software, see the section in Chapter 11 entitled "Updating Virus Signature Files."*

If you think a virus, worm, or Trojan horse might have infected your computer, follow these steps:

1. Turn off your computer and unplug it from your network. At the very least, you want to minimize the damage the infection will cause.
2. Insert the emergency boot disk that came with your program, or that the program prompted you to make when you installed it, and reboot your computer.
3. Follow the instructions on the screen or in your antivirus program's manual to scan your computer for malicious code.

Virus Checking and Microsoft Windows XP

Microsoft Windows XP marked a significant leap forward in terms of operating system security, but you still need to have virus software to do the dirty work of scanning the files on your system to make sure nothing untoward happens to you and your data. I've put together a list of virus scanners that work well with Windows XP. I don't doubt there are other programs available, but this list is a good place to start.

Table 5-1 Virus Scanners That Work Well with Windows XP

Manufacturer	Product	Status
Central Command Software	AVX Professional 5.9.1	Windows XP Compatible
Computer Associates	eTrust Antivirus	Designed for Windows XP
Computer Associates	eTrust InoculateIT	Designed for Windows XP
Computer Associates	InocuLAN Anti-Virus NT 4	Windows XP Compatible
Computer Associates	InoculateIT Workgroup Edition for NT 4.53	Windows XP Compatible
Data Fellows Ltd.	F-Secure AntiVirus 5.2	Windows XP Compatible
Data Fellows Ltd.	F-Secure AntiVirus 5.21	Windows XP Compatible
HAURI	ViRobot Expert	Designed for Windows XP
McAfee.com	VirusScan Online for Windows XP	Designed for Windows XP
Network Associates	McAfee Internet Security	Designed for Windows XP
Network Associates	Active Virus Defense Suite 4.5	Windows XP Compatible
Network Associates	McAfee VirusScan Professional	Designed for Windows XP
Symantec Corporation	Norton AntiVirus 2002	Designed for Windows XP
Symantec Corporation	Norton AntiVirus 2000 6	Windows XP Compatible
Symantec Corporation	Norton AntiVirus 2001	Windows XP Compatible
Symantec Corporation	Norton AntiVirus Corporate Edition 7.5	Windows XP Compatible
Symantec Corporation	Norton AntiVirus Corporate Edition 7.51	Windows XP Compatible
Trend Micro	Pc-cillin 2002	Designed for Windows XP
Trend Micro	Virus Buster 2002	Designed for Windows XP

How Do I Know You're a Real Virus Alert? The Internet, as wild and rough as it can sometimes be, is populated by people who want to make things easy for newcomers. It's also true that folks, for one reason or another, will write fake virus alerts. They're sort of the urban legends of the Internet and are often kind of humorous in how they try to play on our fallibilities. There are a number of online resources you can visit to see if the virus warning you just received for the fifth time this morning is real or a gag:

- Microsoft Security at *http://www.microsoft.com/security/*
- Vmyths.com at *http://www.vmyths.com/*
- Virus Bulletin at *http://www.virusbtn.com/hoax*
- Carnegie Mellon Software Engineering Institute (CERT) at *http://www.cert.org/*
- TruSecure at *http://www.trusecure.com/*
- Your virus software vendor

Finally, if someone e-mails you a file that purports to provide protection against a virus, don't install it. The file probably contains the virus it claims to protect against!

Social Engineering, or "Hacking by Talking"

Social engineering might sound like what you study in school if you want to build attractive and usable public parks, but it's actually the somewhat disingenuous term used to describe techniques used to get information out of people. Some of the best hackers in the world aren't all that skilled with computers. Instead, they know how to get people to talk about themselves. By seeming interested in someone's personal goings-on, especially if that someone has been cooped up in a windowless office for a few weeks finishing up a project, unscrupulous individuals can glean all sorts of information from the unwary.

Here are some of the verbal and nonverbal techniques social engineers use to get useful information out of their marks:

- Pretending to be a technical support representative who needs your password to add functionality to your account. Don't you believe it! A real technical support person won't need your password because he or she will be able to access your account and other personal information without using your password. Never, ever give out your password over the phone.
- Hanging around while you type your password, also known as "shoulder surfing." With a little practice, these social engineers can track your fingers as you type your password. Even if they don't get it right the first time, there are only so many combinations they'll need to try. My solution is to stare fixedly at anyone who tries to watch my hands—I won't start typing until they avert their eyes.
- Going through your garbage, also known as "trashing." Some hackers have been known to get jobs at companies as janitors just so they'd have access to offices when no one was around to supervise them. Have you ever thrown away a credit card statement? A note card with a password on it? A travel itinerary that might let someone know you'll be out of town? The best way to keep that sort of information from getting into the wrong hands is to buy a crosscut shredder, one that doesn't just cut your paper into strips, but cuts it into strips and then cuts the strips as if the shredder were dicing a carrot.

Protect Your Privacy

I take privacy seriously, both yours and mine. I'm tired of all the junk mail, telephone solicitations, and unsolicited commercial e-mail I get day in and day out. But I've fought back. I subscribe to a phone company service that has reduced the number of telemarketers calling me to practically nil, I toss most junk mail unopened, and I have the fastest Delete key this side of the Mississippi River. If you're on the Internet, privacy is as much a technical problem as it is a social or legal problem. Fortunately, you've got the means to secure your information against the bad guys. But what, you might ask, are the bad guys looking for? A good question, and one I will answer right now.

What Interesting Information Do You Have on Your Computer?

If I were someone intent on getting at your computer so I could get your personal information and use your good name to my advantage, there are *lots* of things I'd search for on your computer:

- Passwords from services you signed up for. Lots of services mail your passwords back to you so you know what they are, which is completely silly. You must know what it is—you just typed it in! And because a lot of folks reuse passwords, that password might let someone else in to other services to which you subscribe.
- Credit card numbers.
- Social Security or Social Insurance numbers.
- Bank account numbers.
- Vacation plans. Not home? Maybe I'll drop by.
- Your address book. Who do you know?
- Proprietary information from work. Knowledge your company uses to make money is knowledge I can sell to make money.

Remember, if I know enough about you, I can mimic you well enough to convince a mutual stranger, such as a credit card issuer, that I *am* you.

Protecting Your Information

The real key to protecting your personal information is to be certain that anything that might be useful to someone trying to create a false identity isn't on your computer. So where does that leave you with regard to any online banking or money management you do with programs such as Microsoft Money? There are a few things you can do to make your information more secure:

- Set passwords for your programs, especially if they contain financial information.

See Also *For more information on creating secure passwords, see the section in Chapter 6 entitled "Making a Password Strong."*

- Never send e-mail messages, or any other kind of message, containing any credit card or account information, discourage others from sending sensitive information by e-mail, and immediately delete any messages that do contain sensitive information.
- Don't add the computer with your sensitive information to your network. It's a pain, but an "airwall" between your data and a network connection is a computer's ultimate defense, short of unplugging it.

Identifying a Secure Connection

These days lots of Web sites require you to register before gaining access to their sites or placing an order. While I guard my credit cards viciously, I do buy a fair number of things online. While there's been a lot of hubbub about how dangerous it is to send your credit card number to parts unknown, it's also dangerous to hand over your card to a waiter who hasn't been tipped in days and who carries a pen and paper around as part of the job. Of course, just as I told you that you shouldn't send your credit card numbers zooming around the Internet in e-mail messages that sit around on servers or your computer unprotected, you need to make sure the computer you're sending your purchasing information to is doing its part to safeguard your transaction.

When I want to make a purchase or fill out a form with sensitive personal information, I always look to make sure the connection is encrypted. In Internet Explorer, there are two ways to tell if the connection is secure:

- The Web page address begins with *https*, which indicates that the connection uses the Secure Sockets Layer (SSL) encryption standard.
- There is a locked padlock icon on the Internet Explorer status bar, at the bottom of the program window.

See Also *For more information on the benefits of encryption, albeit in a slightly different context, see the section in Chapter 4 entitled "Encrypting a Wireless Network."*

The SSL standard provides a standard toolkit for Web servers to create secure connections with their customers. Before SSL came along, the warning not to use a credit card on the Internet was absolutely correct. Now that all the obvious bugs have been worked out of the system, I think it's fine to send personal information over a secured connection. I do it all the time. But if a site asks me for anything other than my e-mail address, which is more or less public knowledge, it had better secure that information on the way to and from its computers.

Your Browser History

Another category of files that you or someone else might find "interesting" is your browser's history file and temporary file cache. What are those things? Simply put, your history file is a list of every Web page you've visited within the last 20 days or so. (The default number of days a page is kept in your history is 20.) The main benefit of keeping a list of the pages you've visited is that your browser retains a copy of the site and all of its files, including images, so it can save you time the next time you visit the site.

How does that work? If you ask to see a site, your browser sends a request to the hosting computer to see if the page has changed since the last time you viewed it. If it hasn't, your browser just loads in the page it has in memory and you're on your way without hesitation. If some items on the page have changed, such as when the site owner puts in a new title graphic, your browser downloads the new files and reads the rest from its cache. Another benefit of having your browser retain a history of your Web activity is that you can find a site you've been in contact with, even if you've forgotten the site's name and address.

To view your browser's history file, follow these steps:

1. In Internet Explorer, click the History button on the Standard Buttons toolbar.
2. In the History pane, click the time period representing the set of links you'd like to view.
3. Click any of the links to visit the Web page it represents.

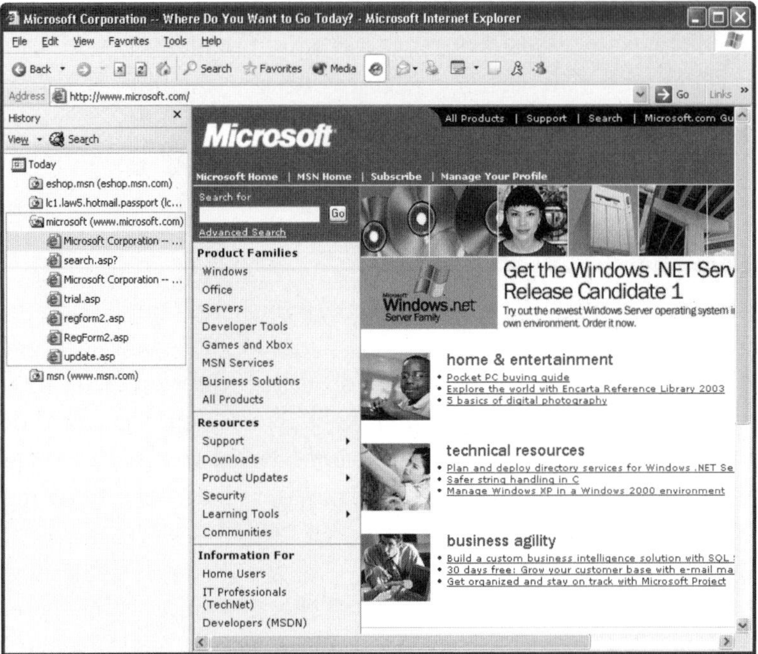

Note You can change the order in which your history file is displayed by clicking the View button in the History pane and choosing a new order, or you can search your links by clicking the Search button in the History pane and typing the word you want to search for in the box.

4 Click the Close button on the History pane to hide your history.

Deleting Your Browser History and Temporary Internet Files

Of course, if anyone visiting your place were interested in which Web pages you've seen, all they'd need to do is pull up your history file and read through it. It's probably not a big deal, but if you share your computer and want to keep some things private, you might want to delete your history file while your guests stay over.

To delete your browser history or your temporary Internet files, follow these steps:

1 In Internet Explorer, choose Internet Options from the Tools menu.

2 On the General tab, which should appear by default, either:

- Click Delete Files to delete your temporary Internet files
- Click Clear History to delete your browser history

Note If you're running out of disk space, deleting your temporary Internet files is a great way to free up a few megabytes.

Cookies and Your Web Experience

If you used the Web in the early days, way back in 1993 and 1994, you remember when there weren't even any pictures; it wasn't until a year or so into the Web that you could visit the Smithsonian site to see approximately five images of dinosaurs. Also, there was no way to record where you had been on a Web site. Oh sure, every Web server software suite kept log files that the Web site owner could process to see where visitors came from and what they did, but there was no way for the server to "remember" visitors from one visit to the next. That all changed with the advent of cookies.

What Are Cookies?

A *cookie* is a small file that a Web server writes onto your computer and subsequently reads whenever you return to the site that wrote the cookie. Yes, this functionality is built into your Web browser—it's not as if the Web site programmers are finding a way to bypass your security settings. The reason Web browsers are set to allow sites to write cookies to your computer is that individual cookies are extremely limited in size and can contain only text, not executable program code. Also, only computers from the same organization that set a cookie can read that cookie. For example, only computers from microsoft.com can read cookies set by computers in the microsoft.com domain.

Lingo The name cookie, or magic cookie, is a term programmers have used for years to describe any text file or other token that is written onto another computer.

Cookies can come from a variety of sources, however. The server software powering a site you visit might set a cookie on your computer, but it's also possible for so-called third parties to set a cookie on your computer. As an example, consider the advertisements you see on the Web. Most of those ads are actually stored on ad agency computers elsewhere on the Web. Just as you can set up a link to another Web page on your personal site, commercial sites create links to advertisements stored on other servers. The trick is that, unless you forbid it, the servers providing the ads can also write cookies onto your computer. Why is it important that other computers can write these innocuous-seeming cookie files onto your personal computer? Remember, for sites that provide Web advertisements, it's all about tracking where you've been.

Note I don't want to harp on the negative side of cookies too much. In and of themselves, cookies aren't bad things. For example, if you purchase a subscription to a Web site, the site might write your logon information to your computer using a cookie. Then, whenever you return to the site, your information would be there. Cookies are also useful for corporate sites, where the computer to which you're trying to connect can check the validity of your user name, password, and a cookie on your computer.

What Kind of Data Is Stored in Cookies?

There are a lot of myths surrounding cookies, most of them centering around the supposed capabilities of cookies to root around on your hard disk and find your personal information. I'm here to tell you it just ain't so. There are only two types of data that can be written to a cookie:

- Something the owner of the site already knows, such as a unique code the server assigned you the first time you visited the site or the Web pages you've visited on the site
- Information you type into a form

Most of the time a server will write a cookie to your computer that simply assigns you an identification code. Then, whenever you return to the site, the server can read your code and associate your activity on the site with your previous visits. If you've ever made a purchase on a site such as Amazon.com, you've probably noticed that the site greets you with a personalized message (and even a store named in your honor) whenever you return. That information, of course, comes from the form you filled out when you made your purchase.

Here's the tricky part. Suppose an advertising company provides ads for more than one site you frequent. Because the ad company can read cookies it has set, it can tell which other sites you've been to. For example, if Tailspin Toys were to provide ads for every page on every site you've ever visited, the company would be able to record your movements in a database. What's more, if you ever filled out a form with your name, address, and phone number, Tailspin Toys could correlate that data with your personal information and reach into the consumer marketing data pool used by direct mail companies and telephone solicitors to market to you more effectively. Whether you see that as a blessing or a curse is up to you, but if you want to take action, you can do so.

Viewing and Deleting Cookies

Because cookies are stored as text files on your computer, you can open those files and read your cookies any time you like. In Microsoft Windows 98 Second Edition (SE) and Microsoft Windows Millennium Edition (Me), your cookies are stored in the C:\Windows\Cookies directory, while in Windows XP your cookies are stored in the folder assigned to your user account. If your name were Jenny, for example, your cookies would be stored in the C:\Documents and Settings\Jenny\Cookies directory.

Each cookie is stored as a separate text file, so it's a pain to open each file individually. Plus, a lot of the data runs together and you can't tell what's what. There is, however, a tool you can use to view all your cookies at once in a neat, clean window. That tool is Karen Kenworthy's Cookie Viewer, and it's available at that most magical of prices: free. Figure 5-1 shows you what your cookies look like when seen in the Cookie Viewer.

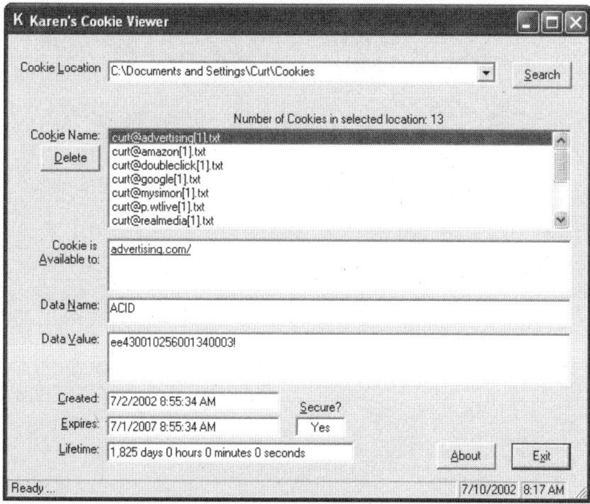

Figure 5-1 You can use the Cookie Viewer to look at and manage your cookies through a single, compact interface.

Note You can find Karen Kenworthy's Cookie Viewer on her site, *http://www.karenware.com/*. There are plenty of other free programs there that you might find useful as well.

You can delete cookies individually in the Cookie Viewer by clicking the cookie you want to get rid of and then clicking Delete, but you can delete every cookie on your system and start fresh from within Internet Explorer.

To delete all cookies on your computer, follow these steps:

1. In Internet Explorer, choose Internet Options from the Tools menu.
2. In the Internet Options dialog box, click the General tab and then click Delete Cookies.
3. Click OK twice.

Choosing Which Cookies to Let Through

Even though I make cookies sound like something you should avoid, they perform some vital functions that make the Web a nicer place to be. For example, would you like to get along without online shopping carts, which track items you want to buy so you don't have to write down everything and enter product identification numbers and prices into a form by hand? Cookies make using shopping carts possible. Do you like it when some Web sites remember you were there and pull up items that might be of interest to you and sometimes do a good job at it? Cookies again.

Internet Explorer 6.0 has a number of built-in cookie management tools you can use to control which cookies are placed on your site. In fact, you have a wide variety of security levels to choose from. (These security levels are cumulative, so the Medium security setting incorporates all protections mentioned for the Low security setting.) You can choose

- Accept All Cookies, which lets anyone set a cookie on your computer
- Low, which rejects cookies from third parties (such as advertising companies) that either use your personal information without your consent or don't have an identifiable privacy policy
- Medium, which restricts first-party cookies from sites that use your personal information without your consent
- Medium High, which blocks first-party cookies from sites that use your personal information without your consent
- High, which blocks all cookies whose sites do not have a privacy policy or that use your personal information without your consent
- Block All Cookies, which blocks all cookies

You might be wondering what Internet Explorer 6.0 considers a "privacy policy." After all, it's not as though Microsoft programmers have the time to check out the privacy policies of every site on the Web. The answer is that the World Wide Web Consortium (W3C), the body that sets the standards for the Web, sponsored the Platform for Privacy Preferences Project (P3P). The standard, which was officially recommended for use in April 2002, lets site owners put their policies for personal information distribution and use into a machine-readable form. Now rather than forcing you the human to dig through a site in search of a written privacy policy, your browser can detect the site owner's privacy practices and determine whether to allow that site to set cookies on your computer. I should note that a site without an online policy is treated as having no privacy policy at all.

See Also *For more information on the W3C and P3P, visit http://www.w3.org/P3P.*

To change Internet Explorer's cookie settings, follow these steps:

1 Choose Internet Options from the Tools menu.

2 In the Internet Options dialog box, click the Privacy tab.

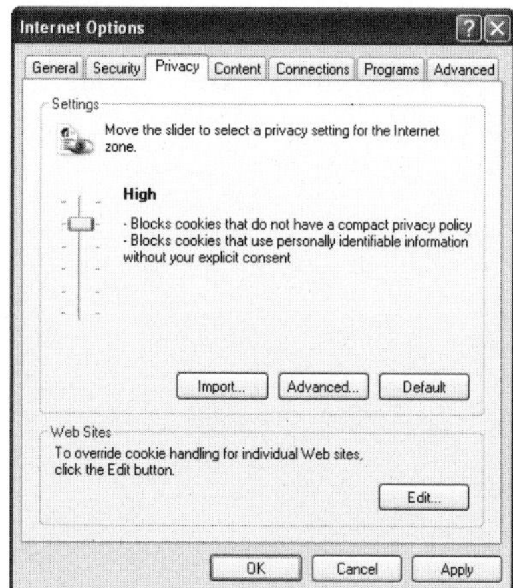

3 Drag the vertical slider so that it reflects the cookie management policy you want to set for your computer, and then click OK.

Note I have my cookie management policy set to High, which keeps out cookies from sites that don't bother to let me know what they're going to do with my personal information or that have policies I disagree with.

Allowing or Rejecting Cookies from Individual Sites

Another way that Internet Explorer 6.0 lets you deal with the Internet on your own terms is to let you allow or reject cookies from specific Web sites. All you need to do is identify the site you want to manage and then choose whether to accept or reject cookies from that site, which are identified by their domain name and machine name. For example, the Web address *http://www.microsoft.com* refers to the Web host for Microsoft Corporation, but *http://mspress.microsoft.com* refers to the computer that hosts the Web site for Microsoft Press. Both computers are part of the microsoft.com domain, but the computers are two separate entities within that domain.

Note You can only accept or reject cookies from an entire domain, not a subset of that domain. For example, you couldn't block cookies from microsoft.com while still allowing cookies from mspress.microsoft.com.

To allow or reject cookies from a specific site, follow these steps:

1. In Internet Explorer, choose Internet Options from the Tools menu.
2. In the Internet Options dialog box, click the Privacy tab and then use the slider to choose a privacy setting other than Allow All Cookies.
3. Click Edit.

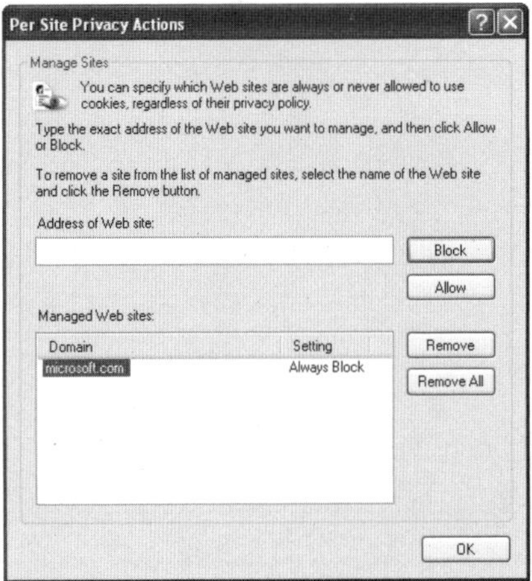

4. In the Per Site Privacy Actions dialog box, type the address of the site you want to manage in the Address Of Web Site box and then either:
   - Click Block to block all cookies from that site
   - Click Allow to allow all cookies from that site
5. Click OK twice.

To change or remove per site privacy settings, follow these steps:

1. In Internet Explorer, choose Internet Options from the Tools menu.
2. In the Internet Options dialog box, click the Privacy tab and then use the slider to choose a privacy setting other than Allow All Cookies.
3. Click Edit.
4. In the Per Site Privacy Actions dialog box, click the domain in the Managed Web Sites pane whose settings you want to change and then do one of the following:

- Click Block to block all cookies from that site
- Click Allow to allow all cookies from that site
- Click Remove to remove restrictions for that site

Note You can remove all per site restrictions by clicking Remove All in the Per Site Privacy Actions dialog box.

Add a Firewall

What's a firewall? My car has one, as do almost all cars. My car's firewall sits between the motor and the forward wall of the passenger compartment, ready to fend off any external combustion emanating from my internal combustion engine. In electronic terms, a *firewall* does the same thing—it stands between your computer and potential sources of harm. Firewalls are so important that most routers come with one installed, and Windows XP has one built right into the operating system.

Lingo A firewall is a hardware device or computer program that protects unauthorized data from getting onto your computer.

Routers with Firewalls

As I described in Chapter 4, "Making It Real—Putting In Your Home Network," routers designed for home networks serve a vital security function. If you think of the Internet as a party, which is a metaphor I find particularly compelling, a home networking router is like someone who sits at the edge of the room, arms folded, avoiding eye contact, and moving only to walk to and from the punch bowl. You know they're there, but there's no good way to interact with them. At a party it means someone is having a vile time of it, but on the Internet it means that your router is stonewalling those who would breech your defenses and do much worse than ask "What's your sign?"

Note Every router I checked when I researched Chapter 4, "Making It Real—Putting In Your Home Network," claimed to have a firewall built in, but you should still read the box or online product description to be sure one is included in any router you buy.

Windows XP Internet Connection Firewall

Just as there are hardware firewalls, there are software firewalls that protect your computer from unauthorized traffic. The Internet Connection Firewall (ICF) is built right into Windows XP, so you don't need to buy any additional software to make your connection more secure. How does the ICF work? It maintains a table of every data request your computer has made and won't allow data to flow onto your machine unless it identifies the data as a response to a request your computer sent earlier.

Note You shouldn't enable the ICF on any computer that doesn't directly connect to the Internet. If you turn on the ICF on a computer that uses Internet Connection Sharing (ICS), it will bring your network to a grinding halt. In fact, the Network Setup Wizard doesn't let you turn on the ICF on a computer that gets its Internet access through ICS.

You can turn on the ICF when you establish your network, but you can always choose to turn it off or back on at a later time.

To enable or disable the ICF, follow these steps:

1. Click Start, choose Control Panel, and then click Network And Internet Connections. Click Network Connections.
2. Click the dial-up or LAN or high-speed Internet connection that you want to protect and then, under Network Tasks, click Change Settings Of This Connection.
3. Click the Advanced tab and then, under Internet Connection Firewall, follow either of these steps:
   - To enable the Internet Connection Firewall, select the Protect My Computer And Network By Limiting Or Preventing Access To This Computer From The Internet check box.
   - To disable the Internet Connection Firewall, clear the Protect My Computer And Network By Limiting Or Preventing Access To This Computer From The Internet check box.

OK, that's the basics of using the ICF. If all you ever do is turn on the ICF and let it do its work, you'll probably be safe. You can go one step further, however, and have Windows XP keep a log of every unsolicited inbound data request (which might represent a hacking attempt) and every successful outbound request your computer makes. By turning on the security logs, you're adding your own intelligence to that of the firewall. If you notice a lot of failed requests from a particular computer, for example, you could contact your Internet service provider (ISP) and report it as potential abuse. Your ISP might not be able to do enough to stop the attacks, but it would have the information in hand in case it was in a position to do something about it.

To enable or disable security logging for the ICF, follow these steps:

1. Click Start, choose Control Panel, and then click Network And Internet Connections. Click Network Connections.
2. Click the connection on which the ICF is enabled and then, under Network Tasks, click Change Settings Of This Connection.
3. Click the Advanced tab and then click Settings.
4. Click the Security Logging tab and then, under Logging Options, select one or both of the following options:
   - To enable logging of unsuccessful inbound connection attempts, select the Log Dropped Packets check box.
   - To enable logging of successful outbound connections, select the Log Successful Connections check box.
   - To disable logging of unsuccessful inbound connection attempts, clear the Log Dropped Packets check box.
   - To disable logging of successful outbound connections, clear the Log Successful Connections check box.
5. Click OK twice.

To view your firewall's security log, follow these steps:

1. Click Start, choose Control Panel, and then click Network And Internet Connections. Click Network Connections.
2. Click the connection on which the ICF is enabled and then, under Network Tasks, click Change Settings Of This Connection.
3. Click the Advanced tab and then click Settings.
4. Click the Security Logging tab and then click Browse.
5. Scroll to pfirewall.log, right-click pfirewall.log, and then click Open.
6. Double-click the log file and view the contents.

Other Firewall Software

If you're running Windows XP, the ICF is probably the only software you'll need. However, if you're running another operating system or if you just want to see what other products are available, you can explore the titles in the following table. Again, I'm just putting out the names of titles from reputable software vendors—no endorsement is implied.

Table 5-2 Firewall Software to Consider

Publisher	Product	Web Site
Internet Security Systems	Black Ice Defender	*http://www.iss.net/solutions/home_office/*
McAfee	McAfee.com Personal Firewall	*http://www.mcafee.com/myapps/firewall/default.asp*
Sygate	Sygate Personal Firewall PRO	*http://soho.sygate.com/default.htm*
Symantec	Norton Personal Firewall 2002	*http://www.symantec.com/sabu/nis/npf/*
Zero Knowledge	Freedom Personal Firewall	*http://www.freedom.net/products/firewall/index.html*
Zone Labs	ZoneAlarm Pro	*http://www.zonelabs.com/*

Divide and Conquer with Security Zones

The Web is a great place, full of information and opportunities to travel, albeit virtually, to places you've only dreamed of visiting. That said, there are some neighborhoods that are safer to visit than others. If you're concerned about what might happen to your computer if you visit certain sites but you just can't keep yourself away because the site's offerings are too good, you can protect yourself by identifying potentially damaging sites to Internet Explorer, which in turn will refuse requests from the site to run any scripts or programs you might not mind being run if another site tried to do the same thing. The flip side is also true—if you want to add a site to a list of sites you trust absolutely, you can crank the security settings all the way down and let the site do whatever it wants. Be sure you trust it, though!

There are four security zones available in Internet Explorer:

- Internet, which is the default zone (Medium security setting)
- Local Intranet, which is for sites on your home or office network (Medium-Low security)
- Trusted Sites, which is reserved for sites that use SSL encryption and that you trust implicitly (Low security)
- Restricted Sites, which is reserved for sites you don't particularly trust (High security)

To add a site to or remove a site from an existing zone, follow these steps:

1. In Internet Explorer, choose Internet Options from the Tools menu.
2. In the Internet Options dialog box, click the Security tab and then click the Web content zone to which you want to add a site.

Note You can't add sites to the Internet zone or the Local Intranet zone. If you don't specify otherwise, Internet Explorer assumes it's an Internet site.

---

3 Click Sites. In the dialog box, follow either of these steps:

- To add a site to a zone, type the address of the site in the Add This Web Site To The Zone box and click Add.
- To remove a site from a zone, click the site to be removed from the Web Sites box and click Remove.

4 Click OK twice.

Key Points

- A good virus-scanning program should check more than the files on your computer; it should also check files on Web sites you visit and files attached to e-mail messages you receive.
- Always make emergency recovery and diagnostic disks so you can try to remove a virus from an infected computer without endangering the other files on your system.
- Never keep sensitive information on your computer, and certainly never give out a password or other access information to someone you don't know.
- If your information is so valuable you can't afford to have it lost or stolen, don't keep it on a computer that's connected to the Internet.
- If you have the choice, buy a hardware router that has a built-in firewall.
- Run the Internet Connection Firewall (ICF) unless you're sharing your Internet access using Internet Connection Sharing (ICS). Remember, the ICF will prevent data from traveling across your network only if ICS is turned off!
- You can change your browser's security settings based on the amount of risk you ascribe to a site.

Chapter 6

Creating User Accounts

Individuals have varying needs. That statement might seem painfully obvious when applied to life in general, but it's even more obvious when you think about using a computer. You put a lot of trust in someone when you let that person use a computer with no restrictions. And, while someone might not try to delete your files or install a program that's really a Trojan horse, you should still make sure that you, and only you and those you trust implicitly, have the ability to break into your computer. My job in this chapter is to bring out the guard dog in you and show you how to create accounts, set strong passwords, customize your users' settings, and then apply all those skills toward the goal of enhancing your system's security.

Creating Accounts in Windows XP Home Edition

One of the great things about Microsoft Windows XP Home Edition is that it lets you create user accounts that really act like the accounts you'll find in business-oriented operating systems such as Microsoft Windows 2000 and Microsoft Windows XP Professional. What that means is that you can limit use of your computer to people who know the password to an account. If they don't know the password, they can't use your machine unless they take your computer home with them, erase the hard disk, and install their own operating system on it. You can also choose to let anyone use your computer without giving the ability to install any new programs or hardware, which is a great option if you have guests over who want to use your computer for a few minutes. Or hours. When you need to get stuff done.

Note Because this is a book about home networking, I'm assuming most of you will be running computers with Windows XP Home Edition. Windows XP Professional has a much more complete tool set for managing how folks use your computer. If you're considering purchasing Windows XP Professional, see the "Do More with Windows XP Professional" sidebar later in this chapter.

Types of Accounts

Windows XP Home Edition recognizes three types of user accounts:

- Administrators, who can change anything about the computer. Administrators (often referred to as *admins*) can install programs and hardware, delete files, change the system settings, or do anything they want to any user's account (including changing the account password or deleting the account altogether).
- Limited users, who can change most aspects of their own account but can't install any programs or change any aspect of another user's account.
- Guest users, who can use any application already installed on the computer but can't change anything, including files, on the machine.

When you run Windows XP Home Edition for the first time, you are asked to create an account for the computer's owner. That account needs to be an Administrator account, for the very good and sufficient reason that if there were no users with the power to add programs or change the computer in any significant way, you'd be stuck with whatever programs and hardware came with the machine. Hey, Minesweeper is a great game, but there's more to life.

If you share a computer and your spouse, partner, significant other, or roommate is the responsible type, you probably can give that person an account with Administrator privileges. After all, you never know when he or she might need to put a program on the computer while you're away. If that person doesn't need to install programs or isn't the responsible type, you should assign him or her a Limited account. Users with Limited accounts are just that: limited. They can run any existing programs, but they can't change anything, delete programs, or accidentally format your hard disk.

The account with the fewest privileges is the Guest account. If you have the Guest account turned on (and it's turned off by default), anyone can fire up your computer and look around. They can run existing programs and save files, but that's about it. If you have friends over who just need to check their e-mail or surf the Web for a while, you can turn on the Guest account and let 'em go to town.

Note The Guest account is turned off by default so you can set up your computer with a password assigned to every account. If you need to be reminded of why protecting your computer is so important, reread Chapter 5, "Making Your Network More Secure."

To turn the Guest account on or off, follow these steps:

1. Log on to an account with administrator privileges (such as the account you created when you set up your computer), click Start, and then choose Control Panel.
2. Click User Accounts, click Guest, and follow either of these steps:
   - If the Guest account is turned off, click Turn On The Guest Account to let users without accounts use your computer.
   - If the Guest account is turned on, click Turn Off The Guest Account to require anyone who wants to use your computer to have an account.

Creating an Account

Adding user accounts to your Windows XP Home Edition computer is quite easy; in fact, the act of creating an account takes no more than a few clicks of the mouse and typing one word. Don't worry, though. You can do quite a bit to tailor the account to your or your friends' needs once it's set up.

To create an account in Windows XP Home Edition, follow these steps:

1. Log on to an account with administrator privileges (such as the account you created when you first set up your computer), click Start, and then choose Control Panel.
2. Click User Accounts and then click Create A New Account.
3. Type a name for the account in the Type A Name For The New Account box and click Next.

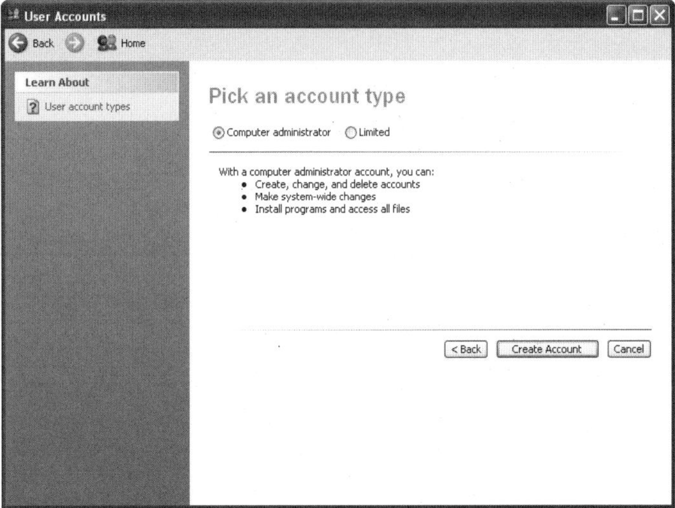

4 In the User Accounts dialog box, follow either of these steps:

- Select Computer Administrator to create an account that will allow the user to install new programs, make systemwide changes, and create or delete accounts.
- Select Limited to create an account that will let the user change his or her own settings and view any files he or she has created, but not to change any other accounts or affect the system as a whole.

5 Click Create Account and then click Close.

Important Safety Tip: Give Yourself Two Accounts! One of the ways that worms (discussed in Chapter 5, "Making Your Network More Secure") operate is to find a computer that will both let them onto the hard disk and allow them to disgorge their payloads, which are usually programs that will take over your computer and use it for no good. Of course, those programs need to be installed on your computer, which is something that only an Administrator can do. You don't need to be logged on as an Administrator at all times; in fact, you should log on to an Administrator account only when you need to install a program, add or change another account, or put in some new hardware.

So give yourself two accounts: one with Administrator privileges and another with Limited privileges. Log on as an Administrator only when you need to change your computer by adding a program or hardware, and use your Limited account for your general computer use. That way, the vast majority of the time you'll be logged on to an account that is much less open to abuse from Internet bad guys. I say "much less likely" because there's no such thing as a foolproof security system, but this approach can't hurt.

Managing User Passwords in Windows XP Home Edition

After you've created an account, the first thing you want to do is assign a password to it. I can't stress enough how vitally important it is to give each account a password. There are a refreshingly large number of neighborhoods where you can leave your front door unlocked and feel safe, but the Internet isn't one of 'em.

Add a Password to an Account

If you are going to visit friends who have a computer running Windows XP Home Edition, you actually don't ever have to tell them your password over the phone or in an e-mail message. As Administrators, they don't need to know what your password is because they can change it to anything they like on their own! The simplest way to create an account with a password is for them to sit with you and let you type in your password when they create your account, but if they'll be gone when you get there, they can set up an account without a password and let you fill it in when you get there.

To add a password to an account, follow these steps:

1 Click Start, and then choose Control Panel.

> **Note** If you want to change the password of an account other than your own, you will need to be logged on as an Administrator.

2 Click User Accounts, click the account to which you want to add a password, and then click Create A Password.

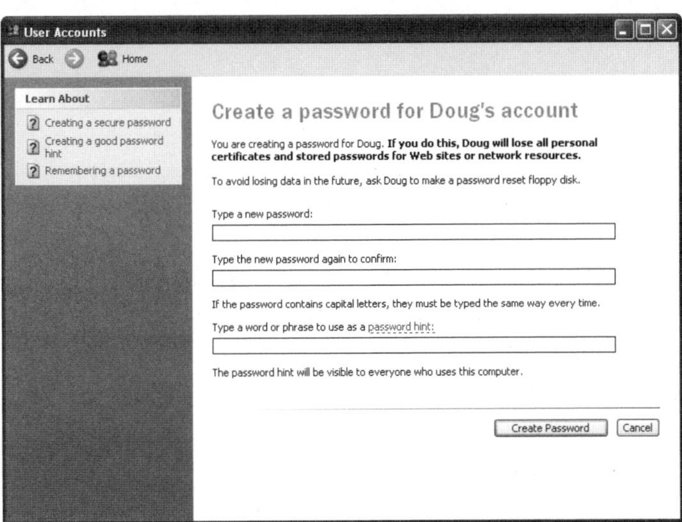

3 Type the password in the Type A New Password box and then confirm it by retyping it in the Type The New Password Again To Confirm box.

4 In the Type A Word Or Phrase To Use As A Password Hint box, type a hint that will help you guess your password should you forget it.

Note Anyone who uses this computer will be able to see your password hint, so the hint should jog your memory, not tell you flat out what your password is or be so obvious that anyone could guess it.

5 Click Create Password and then click Close.

Making a Password Strong

The whole reason you add a password to an account or a network connection is to protect it from unauthorized use while still allowing you to get in and do your work in no more time than it takes to type in eight (or more) characters. You might have heard horror stories about the password that was so good no one could remember it, but there are a thousand more stories of the password that protected your network because the evildoer trying to get into your account couldn't guess your password.

You can usually build passwords out of upper- and lowercase letters, numbers, and some collection of symbols such as !, @, #, $, %, &, ~, *, and /. The best passwords are long, totally random strings of characters, but humans have a hard time remembering random strings of anything unless they can build a story to establish a connection. For example, the password 50%omfhN$ might be remembered as "fifty percent of my friends have NO money," but that's an example I made up to fit my point.

Note I often have difficulty remembering my #%@*&! password.

If you're not willing to go totally random, there are a few guidelines you can follow to make your passwords harder to guess:

- Set passwords that are eight characters or longer.
- Change your passwords at least two or three times a year, and monthly is even better than that.
- Make sure your password is not a dictionary word, or the conjunction of two or three short dictionary words. That goes for non-English words as well, and for symbols substituted for letters. Substituting "0" for "o" and "$" for "s" doesn't make your password appreciably harder to guess.

- Don't use anything directly related to any personal information, such as your birthday, a family member's name, a pet's name, or your ham radio call sign.
- Mix upper- and lowercase letters with at least one number and one symbol (if allowed).
- Don't use the same password for every account! Make as many different ones as you can and, at the very least, make sure the password for your Administrator account on your main computer is unique.
- Do not, under any circumstances, write down your passwords! As I mentioned in Chapter 5,"Making Your Network More Secure," some unscrupulous folks take jobs as janitors just to get information about a company, or your kids might use your password to bypass any controls you've put in place if you put the opportunity in front of them. (Oh, I guess you can keep a list in a safe deposit box, but nowhere else, OK?)

If you have trouble remembering a lot of passwords, use a trick I picked up from a coworker of mine at a defense contractor in McLean, Virginia: use the same eight characters as a base you never write down, but follow the constant code with a random string you can write down. For example, if your constant sequence were zhu#9R2, you could write down a list of password suffixes like this:

ISP	8u#D47
Online Baking	j9%!Qb
Administrator	i0~2lrn

Once you add the suffixes to your base, the actual passwords would be:

ISP	zhu#9R28u#D47
Online Baking	zhu#9R2j9%!Qb
Administrator	zhu#9R2i0~2lrn

Somebody could grab your wallet and do all kinds of violence to your credit cards, but they still probably couldn't get into your e-mail account.

There are a few reasons your passwords need to be both lengthy and non-dictionary words. If someone wants to get into your account, that person will do his or her best to download the password list from your Internet service provider (ISP) and use password guessing programs anyone can download from the Web to try to "crack" your password. Or, if the hacker manages to get a program onto your computer, he or she will be able to track your keystrokes and determine your passwords from that record. With computers being as speedy as they are today, those programs can go through an enormous number of possibilities in a very few minutes. A slow program might try 10,000 passwords a minute, which means that in ten minutes it could work its way through a huge dictionary, and it wouldn't take that much longer to work through all the combinations with one or two numbers added as well. On the other hand, if you throw special characters, different cases, and numbers into the mix, your passwords will stand up to the usual cracking programs and be much, much harder to guess, even if the miscreant knows something about you.

Change Your Password

Once you've added a password to an account, you can, and should, change it frequently. I recommend changing your password two or three times a year, but a lot of corporate administrators set up their networks so that everyone with an account has to change their password on the first day of every month. And don't try to cheat by just switching between two passwords, because the systems are set up so you can't use a password twice.

Note If you never change your password, an attacker needs to get lucky only once.

To change your account password, follow these steps:

1 Click Start, and then choose Control Panel.

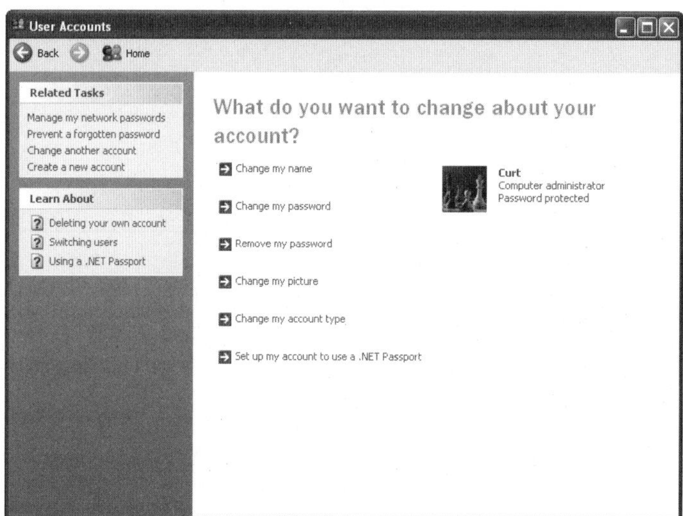

2 Click User Accounts, click the account for which you want to change a password, and then click Change My Password.

3 Type your existing password in the Type Your Current Password box and then type your new password in the Type A New Password and Type The New Password Again To Confirm boxes.

4 In the Type A Word Or Phrase To Use As A Password Hint box, type a hint that will help you guess your password should you forget it.

5 Click Change Password and then click Close.

Change Another User's Password

When I worked for that defense contractor in Virginia, I had a colleague whose Air Force Reserves unit got called up. He was going to be gone for at least two months and would not, under any circumstances, be using his account at the company while he was on active duty, so the system administrator changed his password to a random string and left it that way until my friend got back. None of his files were changed, but neither he nor anyone else could get at them while he was away. If you have a roommate or friend who is going to be gone for an extended period of time, or if you want to hold files hostage for his or her share of the rent, you can change another user's password without deleting his or her account.

To change another user's password, follow these steps:

1 Log on as an administrator, click Start, and then choose Control Panel.

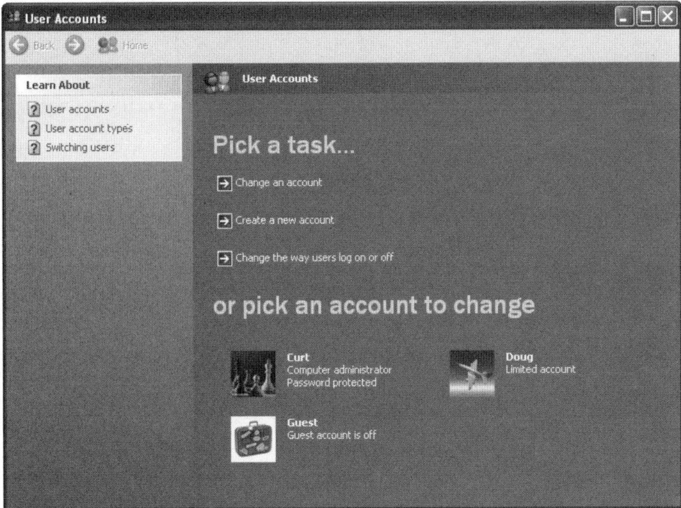

2 Click User Accounts, select the account you want to change, and then click Change The Password.

3 Type the new password in the Type A New Password and Type The New Password Again To Confirm boxes.

4. In the Type A Word Or Phrase To Use As A Password Hint box, type a hint that will help you guess the password should you forget it.
5. Click Change Password and then click Close.

Remove a Password

I debated whether to put instructions on how to remove an account's password in this book, but you might have a good reason for doing so at some point. I will remind you, however, that an Administrator account should *always* be protected by a password.

To remove an account password, follow these steps:

1. Click Start and then choose Control Panel.
2. Click User Accounts, select the account for which you want to delete the password, and then click Remove My Password.
3. Type your password in the To Verify Your Identity, Type Your Current Password box.
4. Click Remove Password and then click Close.

Note When you remove a user's password, you also delete any passwords or other security information your Web browser stored for that user.

Change the Name of an Account

Is there anything more embarrassing than spelling someone's name wrong on a wedding invitation? Spelling a name incorrectly when you're assigning an account on your computer isn't in that league of faux pas, but it's still a bother. You can change the name associated with an account quickly, giving you time to smooth everything over with your esteemed (or maybe just steamed) colleague.

To change the name of an account, follow these steps:

1. Log on as an administrator, click Start, and then choose Control Panel.
2. Click User Accounts and then click the picture representing the account you want to change.
3. Click Change The Name, type a new name for the account in the Type A New Name For *Account Name* box, and then click Change Name.

Change an Account Picture

It's a nice touch that Windows XP Home Edition accounts have a picture associated with them. I play a little chess as a hobby, so I was pretty stoked when I saw that Windows XP Home Edition had picked the chess picture for my

Administrator account. My brother, who was out visiting for a while, got the jet plane, but he's a huge soccer fan and asked me to change his picture to something related to soccer. There's a soccer ball in the basic set of pictures, so a few seconds after he asked, he had his wish fulfilled.

To change the picture associated with your account, follow these steps:

1. Click Start, and then choose Control Panel.
2. Click User Accounts, select the account for which you want to change the picture, and then click Change The Picture.

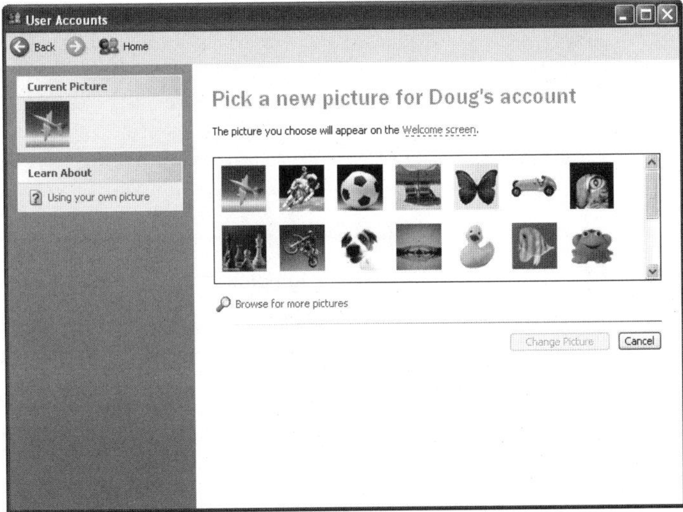

3. Click the picture you want to assign to the account and then click Change Picture.

Note If you would like to choose from pictures available elsewhere on your computer, click Browse For More Pictures and use the Open dialog box to identify the picture you want to assign to the account.

Switching Accounts

I took a slight break during another project I was working on to go visit my brother during the World Cup soccer tournament. We spent a lot of time staring at the screen and screaming for whichever team we wanted to win the match that was on at the time, but we still needed to get things done on the computer. He was working on his doctorate and I was working on another project, so we set up his computer so it faced the television and switched back and forth using it. Because Windows XP Home Edition lets you switch from one user account to another, the fact that only one of us could use the computer at a time didn't mean we couldn't both stay logged on and receive e-mail and such. Logging off and logging back on isn't that much of a hassle, but if you have a lot of Web sites and documents open, it's much handier to just switch users.

To switch from one user account to another in Windows XP Home Edition, follow these steps:

1. Click Start, click Log Off, and then click Switch User.
2. Click the name of the account you want to use, and then, if necessary, type in the password for that account and press Enter.

Note One of the great security features in Windows XP Home Edition is that if the computer's screen saver appears while a user with a password-protected account is logged on to the machine, anyone who wants to use the computer will need to type in that user's password to gain access to the computer. If someone who wants to use the computer without asking turns off the computer to get around the lockout, he or she will still need to log on to the computer when Windows restarts.

Do More with Windows XP Professional You probably know that Windows XP comes in two flavors: Home Edition, which has everything you need to set up a home or small business network, and Professional, which is intended for home-based power users and corporate clients and has everything Home Edition has—plus a lot more. If you're working on a large corporate network or if you want to have a lot more control over your home network, you should check out Windows XP Professional. For detailed information about the differences between Home Edition and Professional, refer to the appendix, "Which Windows Should You Do?"

One difference between Windows XP Home Edition and Professional is that Professional has another type of account: Standard. Standard accounts are available only if you're on a corporate network, but they're only slightly less powerful than an Administrator account and are much more useful to the average employee than a Limited account (which is also available). Here's what you can do in a Standard account:

- Install and uninstall software and hardware, within limits set by an Administrator
- Create, change, or remove your password
- Change your account picture

Another useful item in Windows XP Professional is what's called Automated System Recovery (ASR). The five-second explanation of ASR is that it creates what used to be called a system restore point and makes it possible for you to undo a change that completely hoses your machine or recover from a catastrophic failure such as the disappearance of the hard disk that contains your operating system. Finally—at least for this list—if you're into secure computing, Windows XP Professional lets you encrypt your entire file system to keep prying eyes a long way away from your data.

Creating Accounts in Windows Me and Windows 98 SE

In Microsoft Windows Millennium Edition (Me) and Microsoft Windows 98 Second Edition (SE), the phrase *creating accounts* takes on a different meaning than it does when used in the context of Windows XP. In Windows Me and Windows 98 SE, the computer starts out with no access restrictions—anyone who figures out how to turn on the machine can do whatever he or she wants. What you can do is create a *profile*, using techniques that are very much like how you create an account in Windows XP. Rather than being able to create an Administrator or Limited account, as you can in Windows XP, you are creating a place to hold the user's personalized settings, such as his or her own Favorites list, Documents submenu on the Start menu, and My Documents folder. Everyone with a profile (or anyone who clicks Cancel in the Windows logon box) can change anything on the computer, including deleting any other profile.

Lingo In Windows Me and Windows 98 SE, a profile is a set of personalized settings.

So why are accounts, such as they are, useful in Windows Me and Windows 98 SE? There are two benefits that come to mind. The first benefit is that anyone who logs on to your computer without authenticating him or herself by typing a user name and password won't be able to access your network, though surfing the Web and so on will be possible. The second benefit is that logging on to an account in either operating system identifies the user when you track any changes made to a Microsoft Office document.

The Microsoft Excel spreadsheet in Figure 6-1, for example, incorporates changes from two different users. If the users who made the changes hadn't logged on, the changes would appear to be from the same person.

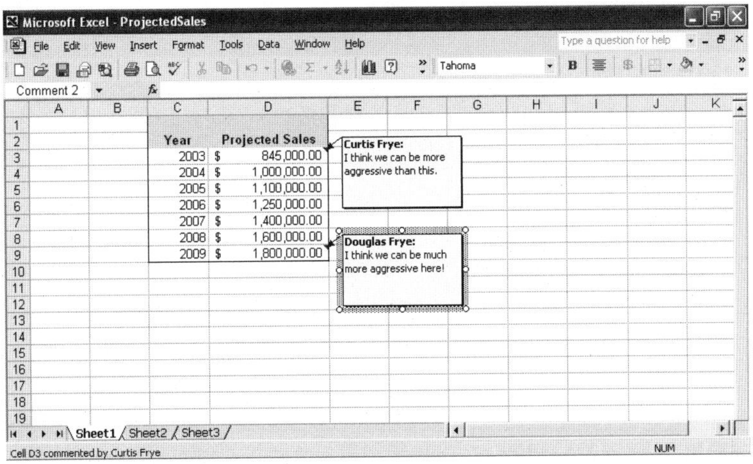

Figure 6-1 When a user logs on to a computer using a specific account, the changes he or she makes are identified in Office programs in which Change Tracking is turned on.

Turning On Multiuser Settings

As I mentioned earlier, both Windows Me and Windows 98 SE come out of the box in "single user" mode, where anyone who turns on the computer can use it. You can prepare either operating system for multiple users by running the Enable Multi-User Settings Wizard, which walks you through creating the first user account.

To turn on multiuser settings in Windows Me and Windows 98 SE, follow these steps:

1. Click Start, choose Settings, and then choose Control Panel.
2. Double-click Users and, in the Enable Multi-User Settings Wizard, click Next.
3. In the User Name box, type the name for the first account you want to create and click Next.
4. Type a password for this account in the Password box, retype it in the Confirm Password box, and click Next.

Note If the passwords you type don't match, the wizard will display a warning message and ask you to retype the passwords.

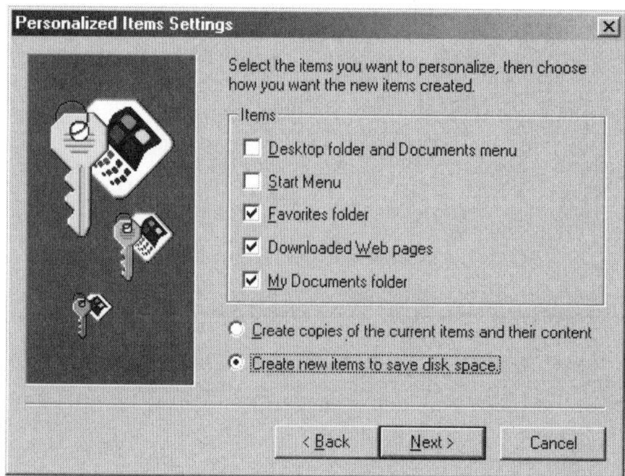

5. Select the check boxes next to the items you want to be personalized for this account, select Create New Items To Save Disk Space to create new versions of the selected items for each user, and click Next.

I've described the items you can personalize for each user profile in the following list.

- Desktop Folder And Document Menu. Selecting this check box means users will only see icons for programs they added themselves on the desktop, and will only see documents they created or edited on the Document menu.
- Start Menu. Selecting this check box means the user's Start menu will display only user-installed programs.
- Favorites Folder. Selecting this check box means users will have a unique list of Internet and Web favorite sites, which are shortcuts they can store in their Web browser and some other programs.
- Downloaded Web Pages. Selecting this check box creates a separate folder where the Web pages you view are stored. If you return to a page that hasn't been changed since the last time you visited it, your Web browser can reload the page from this folder.
- My Documents Folder. Selecting this check box creates a new My Documents folder for the user, so he or she doesn't run the danger of mixing up personal files with those of others.
- Create Copies Of The Current Items And Their Content. Select this option button to copy the selected items (Favorites, and so on) into the new user's profile.
- Create New Items To Save Disk Space. Select this option button to create an empty Favorites list, My Documents folder, and so on.

Note If you want everyone who uses your Windows Me or Windows 98 SE computer to have access to your network, I recommend selecting the check boxes next to the last three items only, leaving the Desktop Folder And Documents Menu and the Start Menu check boxes cleared. When users have their own Desktop Folder And Documents Menu settings, they won't see the network in My Network Places. Of course, that means you can select Desktop Folder And Documents Menu in users' profiles to prevent them from seeing your network. Remember, though, that Windows Me treats everyone as an administrator, so they can change their settings back.

---

6. Click Finish. When you are asked if you want to restart your computer, click No.
7. On the desktop, right-click My Network Places and choose Properties.

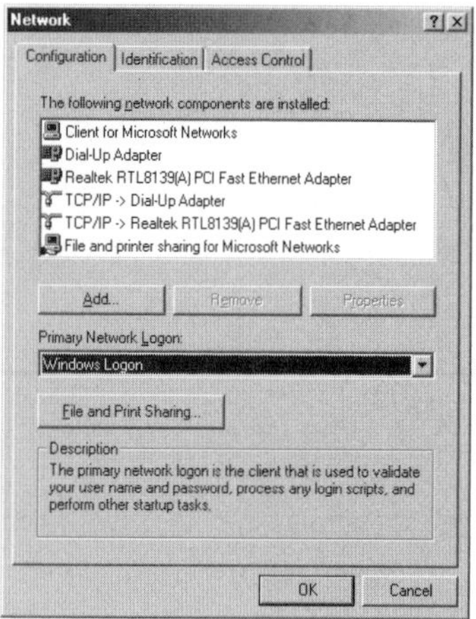

8. On the Configuration tab, click the Primary Network Logon down arrow and select Windows Logon. Choosing the Windows Logon setting means that anyone with an account on your computer will be able to access your network.
9. Click OK and restart your computer.

Creating User Accounts in Windows Me and Windows 98 SE

Once you've created the first user account in Windows Me or Windows 98 SE, you can set up additional accounts so anyone else who wants to use the computer can save his or her own profile and set the operating system's appearance to personal preferences.

To create a user account in Windows Me and Windows 98 SE, follow these steps:

1. Click Start, choose Settings, and then choose Control Panel.
2. Double-click Users and, in the User Settings dialog box, click New User.
3. In the Add User Wizard, click Next, type the name of the user's account in the User Name box, and click Next.

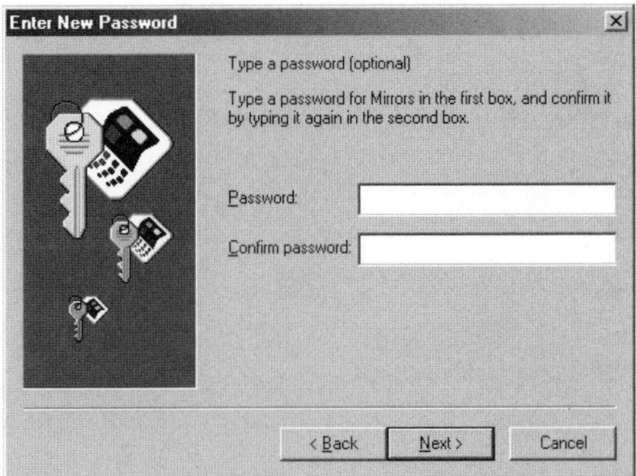

4 Type a password for this account in the Password box, retype it in the Confirm Password box, and click Next.

5 Select the check boxes next to the items you want to be personalized for this account (the last three, unless you don't want the account holder to have access to your network), select Create New Items To Save Disk Space to create new versions of the selected items for each user, and click Next.

6 Click Finish.

Managing User Accounts in Windows Me and Windows 98 SE

Windows Me and Windows 98 SE let you change the settings in your users' accounts, whether you want to change passwords to enhance security or customize the appearance of the computer for each individual who uses the machine.

Manage Passwords in Windows Me and Windows 98 SE

As with any other type of account, choosing strong passwords and changing them regularly improves the security of your system immeasurably. Even though it's less of a concern on Windows Me and Windows 98 SE, where the only practical limitation to a user who uses the computer without an account is that he or she can't access file shares on your home network, it's still a good habit to keep up.

See Also *For more information on choosing effective passwords, see the earlier section, "Making a Password Strong."*

To change an account password in Windows Me and Windows 98 SE, follow these steps:

1 Click Start, choose Settings, and then choose Control Panel.

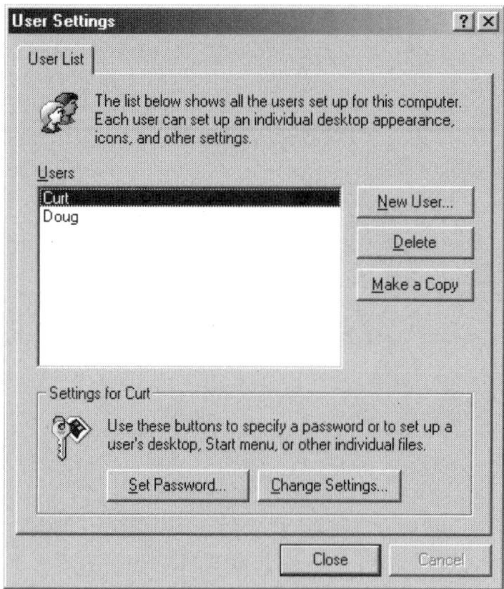

2 Double-click Users, click the account for which you want to change a password, and then click Set Password.

3 Type the account's existing password in the Old Password box, type the new password once in the New Password box, type the new password again in the Confirm Password box, and then click OK.

Note To remove a password from an account in Windows Me or Windows 98 SE, leave the New Password and Confirm Password boxes blank.

Customize an Account in Windows Me and Windows 98 SE

From users' perspective, the primary benefit of having an account on a computer is that they can customize the operating system's appearance to suit their needs. If you've ever worked on a shared machine and had to wade through unfamiliar settings, programs you have no idea how to use, and a list of files in the Documents menu that have bumped all your work off the bottom of the menu, you know how important it is to control your workspace. Here's how you do it.

To change an account's custom settings in Windows Me and Windows 98 SE, follow these steps:

1. Click Start, choose Settings, and then choose Control Panel.
2. Double-click Users, click the account you want to change, and click Change Settings.
3. Select or clear the check boxes next to the options you want to change and click OK.

Copy an Account in Windows Me and Windows 98 SE

Many times when you create an account for a friend, you'll have a good idea what settings you want to assign to the account, in particular the customization settings that let the user get on to your network while still having a personalized working environment. If you have an account that has the settings you want, you can copy those settings to a new account and save yourself the trouble of remembering which check boxes to select and which to clear.

To copy an account in Windows Me and Windows 98 SE, follow these steps:

1. Click Start, choose Settings, and then choose Control Panel.
2. Double-click Users, click the account you want to copy, and click Make A Copy.
3. Type a password for this account in the Password box, retype it in the Confirm Password box, and click Next.
4. Select the check boxes next to the items you want to be personalized for this account (the settings that appear in the wizard for this account reflect the settings of the account you're copying), select Create New Items To Save Disk Space to create new versions of the selected items for each user, and click Next.
5. Click Finish.

Delete an Account in Windows Me and Windows 98 SE

If you have an account on your computer that won't be used any more, perhaps by a roommate who moved out or a visiting relative who is now mooching off some other family member, you can delete it (the account) and continue on with your life.

To delete an account, follow these steps:

1. Click Start, choose Settings, and then choose Control Panel.
2. Double-click Users, click the account you want to get rid of, and click Delete.
3. Click Yes to confirm you want to delete the account and then click Close.

New Technology File System (NTFS): A More Powerful File System

If you ever have trouble managing your hard disks, with their myriad folders and subfolders where you store your files, spare a moment for the poor computer science graduates who have to figure out how your computer will keep track of everything. In fact, keeping track of file locations is just the beginning. Not only does your computer need to have a record of where every file is stored, but it also needs to keep track of all your changes and rewrite files accordingly. The basic tool used to keep track of file locations is the file allocation table (FAT), and it was used to name two of the early, popular file systems: FAT and FAT32.

FAT

Introduced in 1981, FAT is relatively ancient in computer terms. Because of its age, most operating systems, including Microsoft Windows NT, Windows 98, the Macintosh OS, and some versions of UNIX, offer support for FAT. The FAT file system limits file names to no more than eight characters before the period and no more than three after. File names in a FAT file system must also begin with a letter or number; they can't contain spaces, and they aren't case sensitive (meaning that "A" and "a" are read as the same character). Windows 95 offered VFAT, an extension of the FAT standard, which allowed file names of up to 255 characters, allowed the file names to have multiple periods, and preserved the case of your file names (though it's still not case sensitive). One important limitation of both the FAT and VFAT schemes is that they are limited to volumes of 4 gigabytes or less, which means they don't work well for many modern hard disks.

FAT32

As you might guess from the name, FAT32 is an extension of the FAT and VFAT standards. The big advantage of FAT32 is that the file allocation table itself is much larger than it is in the FAT standard, so FAT32 disks can keep track of many times more files than a disk formatted to the FAT standard. Another advantage of the larger file allocation table in FAT32 is that the operating system can divide your hard disk into smaller units.

Asking any file management system to keep track of every bit on a hard disk is out of the question, so these systems break your hard disk into manageable chunks. Because the FAT32 file allocation table has more places to store records of what is in each chunk, hard disks using the FAT32 standard use smaller chunks and store your data more efficiently.

While it's much better than FAT at managing your disk space, FAT32 does have disadvantages. First, it isn't compatible with any operating system other than Windows 98 and the OSR2 version of Windows 95. You can read FAT32 disks from Windows 2000 computers, though. Second, your disk utilities and antivirus software must be FAT32-aware. Otherwise, they could interpret the new file structure as an error and try to correct it, destroying the file allocation table and potentially making the files on your disk unrecoverable.

NTFS

Microsoft introduced the New Technology File System (NTFS) with Microsoft Windows NT 4.0 with the goal of introducing a new file management system that overcame some of the limitations inherent in the FAT and FAT32 schemes. Some of the benefits of NTFS are:

- **Much higher storage capacity** While the FAT system supports volumes of up to 4 gigabytes, NTFS supports volumes up to 16 exabytes. To put the 16 exabyte file capacity of NTFS into perspective, consider that one exabyte is 1,073,741,824 gigabytes. That is, as we say in the industry, a *lot* of vacation pictures.
- **Better fault tolerance** FAT and FAT32 systems keep backup copies of the file allocation table in case something goes wrong, but NTFS actually writes all your changes to a log. That way, if something goes wrong, your operating system can go back over the changes and restore the file to a previous state.
- **Better security** FAT and FAT32-based systems let you use passwords to protect folders against unauthorized users who try to open the folders over your network, but anyone at the computer where the files are stored can get at them. By contrast, NTFS lets you restrict who gets at individual files, not just folders, on a user-by-user basis.

I'd generally recommend changing your file system to NTFS if you want to take advantage of the enhanced features found in that file allocation system. Many of the advanced features in Windows XP Professional, such as the Encrypted File System, also require you to format your hard disk using the NTFS standard.

Table 6-1 summarizes the differences between the NTFS, FAT, and FAT32 file systems.

Table 6-1 Comparing the NTFS, FAT, and FAT32 File Systems

NTFS	FAT	FAT32
A computer running Windows XP or Windows 2000 can access files on an NTFS partition. A computer running Windows NT 4.0 with Service Pack 4 or later might be able to access some files. Other operating systems allow no access.	Access is available through MS-DOS, all versions of Windows, Windows NT, Windows 2000, Windows XP, and OS/2.	Access is available only through Windows 95 OSR2, Windows 98, Windows Me, Windows 2000, and Windows XP.
Recommended minimum volume size is approximately 10 megabytes (MB). Volumes much larger than 2 terabytes (TB) are possible. Cannot be used on floppy disks. File size limited only by size of volume.	Volumes from floppy disk size up to 4 gigabytes (GB). Does not support domains. Maximum file size is 2 GB.	Volumes from 512 MB to 2 TB. In Windows XP, you can format a FAT32 volume up to 32 GB only. Does not support domains. Maximum file size is 4 GB.

To convert the file system on a disk to NTFS, follow these steps:

1. Click Start, and choose Run. Type **convert drivename: /fs:ntfs** in the Open box, and press Enter.
2. In the Command window that appears, answer Yes to the questions that ask if you're sure you want to go through with the change and, if necessary, to attempt to change a drive (called a *volume* in the question) that's in use. If your computer has only one hard disk, or if for any other reason the conversion program can't go through with the change, answer Yes to have the conversion done the next time the computer restarts.
3. When your computer restarts, answer Yes to approve the change.

Key Points

- In Windows XP Home Edition, give Administrator accounts only to folks who really need to make major changes to your computer. Everyone else should get Limited accounts.
- Make two accounts for yourself: one with Administrator privileges and the other without. Use the Administrator account only when you need to change something.
- Good passwords are hard to guess, possible to remember, and change frequently.
- Windows XP Professional lets you do a lot more than Home Edition. If you find yourself limited by Home Edition, try Professional!
- In Windows Me and Windows 98 SE, user accounts are more like profiles; they don't really restrict what a user can do on your computer.
- Users can get on a computer running Windows Me or Windows 98 SE without logging on, but they can't get onto your network.
- When someone has finished using your computer, you should delete that account or at least change the account's password.
- If you want to use the advanced security features available in Windows XP Professional, you should convert your hard disk to an NTFS file management system.

Chapter 7

Getting Your Network to Work for You

Thus far in *Faster Smarter Home Networking* I've shown you how to get your computers ready for networking, set up your network, control who gets access to your computers by creating accounts and assigning passwords that are hard to guess, and even do what was once thought impossible—transfer files between Macintosh and Windows computers. Now that I've laid the groundwork, I can start showing you how to take advantage of your network's power and flexibility to make your life easier. To that end, the first thing I'll show you how to do is to share files on your computer with other users on your network.

My job in this chapter is to show you how to make folders on one computer available to other network users, to protect your folders with passwords, and to make connecting to shared folders as painless as possible.

Sharing Your Folders with Others

Sharing high-speed Internet access is often the attraction that makes folks want to create a home network, but there are real benefits to making files on one computer available to other members of your household. When I was in college, a few of my friends and I started a chain story, where folks take turns writing a page or two of action. The story was on a computer at the central support site, but we could get to that computer from any computer lab on campus (well, except for the lab in the business school, but that is a totally separate issue). Some friends of mine wrote their holiday letter the same way, by putting the file in a shared folder on their home network and letting everybody have a go at writing their own section. It worked pretty well, and, because everyone could work on it at their own pace and on their own time, it ended up getting done early and without too much gnashing of teeth.

Sharing Folders in Windows XP

The folks who developed Microsoft Windows XP figured that sharing folders would be something you'd like to do, so they put everything you need to share a folder in My Computer. In fact, all you need to do to start the process is click the folder you want to share and then click Share This Folder. If it were any easier, the operating system would hand deliver the folder for you.

Note When you type a name for the shared folder, you won't change the name of the folder on your computer, only the name by which the folder is identified over the network.

To make a folder accessible to others in Windows XP, follow these steps:

1 In My Computer, navigate to the folder you want to share and then, in the File And Folder Tasks panel, click Share This Folder.

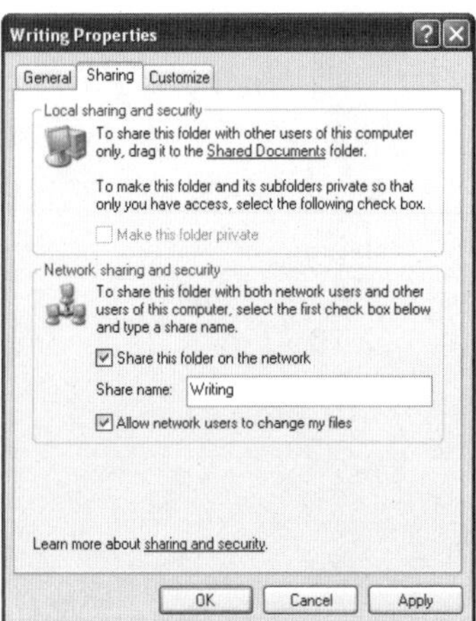

2 On the Sharing tab of the Properties box, select the Share This Folder On The Network check box.

3 In the Share Name box, type a name for the folder as it will appear to other users on the network.

4 Click OK. If you're asked whether you're sure you want to share your folder, click Yes.

After you click OK, the folder icon will change to that of a folder with a hand below, indicating that the folder is a shared resource.

Note Windows XP Professional lets you limit which users, or groups of users, can view or modify a file.

Sharing Folders in Windows Me and Windows 98 SE

Just as you can share a folder in Windows XP, you can share folders in Microsoft Windows Millennium Edition (Me) and Microsoft Windows 98 Second Edition (SE). In the older two operating systems, however, you can choose whether you want to let users modify your files or just look at them. Because Windows XP Home Edition uses accounts to restrict unauthorized users from getting at the files on your computer, the designers left the ability to limit access by password or membership in a user group to Windows XP Professional.

See Also *For more information on restricting access to a folder, see the section later in this chapter entitled "Too Much of a Good Thing: Restricting Access to a Folder."*

When you first create a home network, computers running Windows 98 SE and Windows Me don't assume you want to share the files on that computer with anyone on your network. So, to make your files available, the first thing you need to do is to turn on file and printer sharing.

To turn on file and printer sharing in Windows Me or Windows 98 SE, follow these steps:

1 Click Start, choose Settings, and then choose Control Panel.

2 Click Network.

3 On the Configuration tab, click File And Print Sharing.

4 Select both the I Want To Be Able To Give Others Access To My Files check box and the I Want To Be Able To Allow Others To Print To My Printer check box.

5 Click OK.

After you've made it clear you want to share your files and printers, you can go ahead and share a folder.

To make a folder accessible to others in Windows Me or Windows 98 SE, follow these steps:

1 Right-click the folder you want to share and choose Sharing from the shortcut menu.

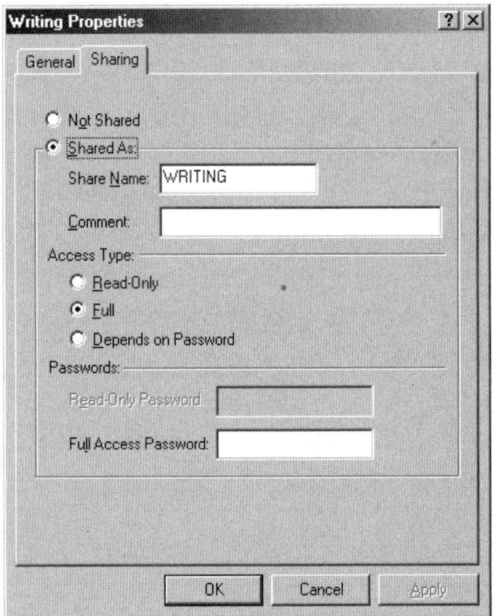

2 On the Sharing tab of the Properties dialog box, select Shared As.

3 In the Share Name box, type the name you want displayed to users who view the folder over your network. In the Comment box, you can type a comment that will appear when someone hovers the mouse pointer over the folder.

4 In the Access Type section, perform either of these steps.

- Select Read-Only to allow anyone to read your documents but not to modify them.
- Select Full to allow anyone to read, edit, or delete your documents.

5 Click OK.

After you click OK, the folder icon will change to that of a folder with a hand below, indicating the folder is a shared resource.

Sharing Your Music and Pictures in Windows XP

Because it was obvious to the Windows XP designers that folks were using their computers as far more than word processors and Web browsers, you have several tools at your disposal for enjoying music and images. For example, you can use Microsoft Windows Media Player to copy music from a CD to the hard disk on computers running Windows XP. You can also use the built-in tools of Windows XP to view and manage your images, such as pictures you take with a digital camera or that you create on your own with a graphics program.

Note Remember that music you store on your computer may be copyrighted, which limits what you can do with the files. Windows Media Player Help provides information about how the program deals with licensed recordings. To view that information, choose Help Topics from the Help menu. On the Search tab, type **license** in the Search box, and then double-click Understanding Licensed Files.

To make your music available to other users of your network, follow these steps:

1 Click Start and then choose My Computer.

Note If for some reason My Computer doesn't appear on your Start menu, you can open it by clicking Start, clicking All Programs, clicking Accessories, and then clicking Windows Explorer. In Windows Explorer, click My Computer.

---

2 Double-click Shared Documents and then double-click Shared Music.

3 If you haven't already saved the file to this folder, do so now to make it available to other users of your network.

To make your pictures available to other users of your network, follow these steps:

1. Click Start and then choose My Computer.

> **Note** If for some reason My Computer doesn't appear on your Start menu, you can open it by clicking Start, clicking All Programs, clicking Accessories, and then clicking Windows Explorer. In Windows Explorer, click My Computer.

2. Double-click Shared Documents and then double-click Shared Pictures.
3. If you haven't already saved the file to this folder, do so now to make it available to other users of your network.

> **Note** Windows Me and Windows 98 SE have no specific folders set aside for sharing your pictures and music, but you can create shared folders with names such as Shared Pictures and Shared Music to keep the naming scheme consistent.

Displaying Your Entire Network

I hate to admit it, but I'm horribly absent-minded. No less than five or six times a day I'll walk into a room and be totally unable to recall what in the world I meant to do when I walked through the door. The trick that works for me, and for a lot of other people who have the same difficulty, is to go back to where I was before and see if something in the room triggers a memory that will put me back on track.

It can be the same way with networks. If you save a file in a remote location, as you'll learn to do later in this chapter, you might need to scout around a bit to find it. The Microsoft Office programs (Microsoft Word, Excel, Access, PowerPoint, and FrontPage) make it easier for you by remembering the last couple of files you opened, but you might be cranking out a report and have pushed the name of the file you want off the bottom of the list. If you need to look around a bit, or if you're just curious to see what your network looks like from 20,000 feet, you can view the entire network at once and hone in on what you want.

Displaying Your Network in Windows XP

Viewing your entire network in Windows XP can be done with two clicks of the mouse. From that overhead view, you can move around your network, viewing folders and files at will.

To display your entire network in Windows XP, follow these steps:

1. Click Start and then choose My Network Places.

> **Note** If you don't see My Network Places on the Start menu, you can open it by clicking Start, clicking All Programs, clicking Accessories, and choosing My Computer. Then, on the Other Places panel, click My Network Places.

2. Click View Workgroup Computers in the Network Tasks list.
3. Double-click any of the computers or devices in the Workgroup dialog box to display their contents or properties.

> **Note** The Workgroup dialog box contains any printers, computer-based faxes, and other computers on your network. Do note, however, that computers without sharing enabled will not appear in the dialog box.

Displaying Your Network in Windows Me or Windows 98 SE

Viewing your entire network in Windows Me or Windows 98 SE takes a few more steps than it does in Windows XP, but there is nothing tricky to the process. And, just as you can do in Windows XP, you can explore your network at will by moving around in the Entire Network window.

To display your entire network in Windows Me or Windows 98 SE, follow these steps:

1. Double-click My Network Places (Windows Me) or Network Neighborhood (Windows 98 SE), and double-click Entire Network (see Figure 7-1).
2. Double-click the name of the network in the Entire Network dialog box and then choose any of the computers or devices in the dialog box to display their contents or properties.

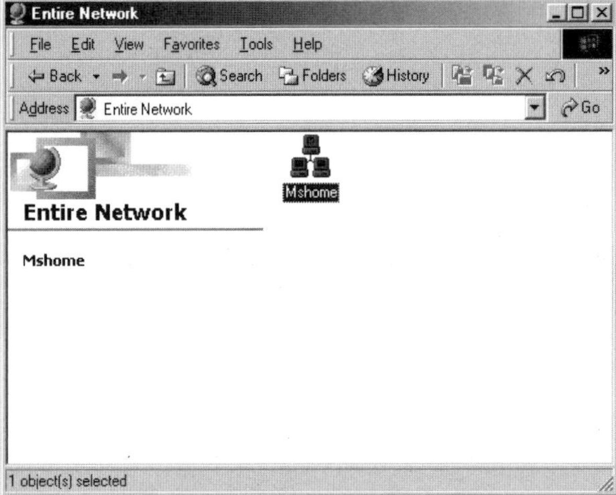

Figure 7-1 Clicking Entire Network in Windows Me lets you see any networks to which your computer belongs.

Opening Folders on Other Computers

Once you remember where the file you want to open resides in your network, your next task is to open the folder. The quickest way to open a shared folder on another computer is to open My Network Places in Windows XP and Windows Me or Network Neighborhood in Windows 98 SE and navigate to the folder you want to open. From within most programs, such as Microsoft Word, you can also use the Open dialog box to navigate to the shared folder, as shown in Figure 7-2. Again, you open either My Network Places or Network Neighborhood, which you'll find on the same directory level as My Computer, and navigate to the folder with the file you want to open.

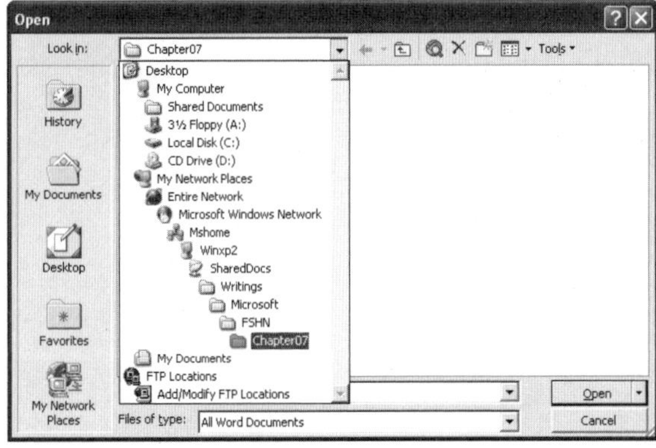

Figure 7-2 Microsoft Word's Open dialog box displays My Network Places.

Opening Folders in Windows XP

When you work in Windows XP, you can find the other computers on your network by displaying My Network Places, which you can open directly from the Start menu. Once you're in My Network Places, you can move to any computer on your network and open any shared folder.

To open folders on other computers on your network from Windows XP, follow these steps:

1 Click Start and then choose My Network Places.

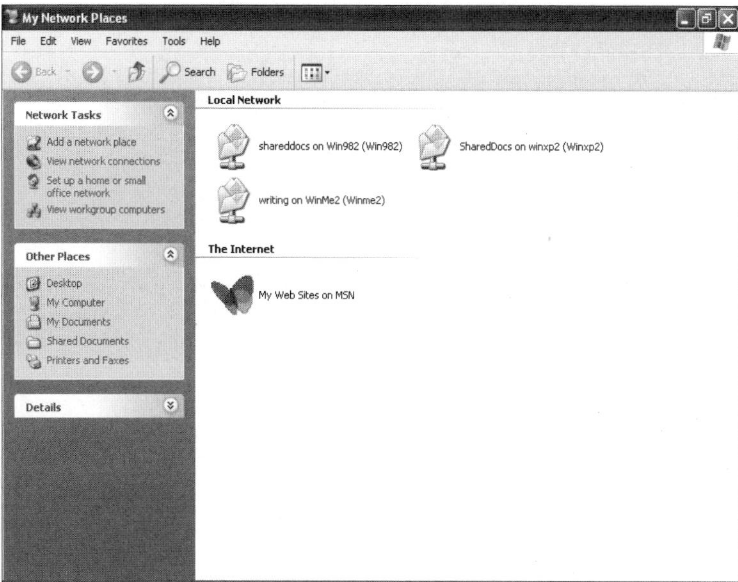

2 Double-click the icon representing the shared folder you want to open. If necessary, you can navigate within the dialog box to open subfolders within the shared folder.

Opening Folders in Windows Me and Windows 98 SE

On computers running Windows 98 SE, the magic words you need to know to open folders on other computers are *Network Neighborhood*. When you double-click the Network Neighborhood icon, which appears on your desktop, you can view the shared folders available to you on your network. Windows Me uses the same name for its network representation as Windows XP: My Network Places.

To open folders on other computers on your network from Windows Me or Windows 98 SE, follow these steps:

1. Double-click My Network Places (Windows Me) or Network Neighborhood (Windows 98 SE) and double-click the folder you want to open.
2. Navigate within the dialog box to select the folder and file you want to open. If necessary, you can navigate within the dialog box to open a subfolder within the shared folder.

A Name for Everything: The Universal Naming Convention

One of the nuances of working with home networking with older operating systems such as Windows Me and Windows 98 SE is that you sometimes need to tell Microsoft Windows the network address of the computer or shared folder you want to open. (You'll see one way network addresses can be used in the next section, "Getting the Lay of the Land: Mapping Drives.") Just as C:\MyDocuments\Resume.doc is the name of a file on your hard disk, you can use the *Universal Naming Convention (UNC)* to specify a computer, shared resource, or file on your network to which you want to connect.

Lingo The Universal Naming Convention (UNC) is the standard format for specifying the location of a file, folder, printer, or other shared resource on a networked computer.

UNC addresses are of the form \\server\share\path\filename, but only the server element (the name of the computer) is required. For example, on a computer named DEN, you could display all shared resources for that computer by typing the UNC **\\DEN** into Microsoft Windows Explorer, My Computer, or Microsoft Internet Explorer. If there were multiple shared folders on that computer, you could open one of the folders by appending its name to the UNC after a backslash and the name of the computer. If you had a shared folder named Stories, for instance, the UNC for that folder would be \\DEN\Stories.

The path element of a UNC refers to the subfolders a program must navigate to open a file or find a resource. For example, if you had a 2002 subfolder inside your Stories folder for stories written during 2002, the UNC for that subfolder would be \\DEN\Stories\2002.

On any computer on your network, click Start and choose Run. In the Open box, type the UNC of a computer on your network and click OK. If one of your computers were named Win98, for example, you would type **Win98**. When you click OK, Windows displays the shared resources for the computer you named.

UNCs are helpful when you need to specify the computer, folder, or file you want to open, and they're especially handy if you're having trouble with your network and don't see one of your computers in My Network Places (Windows XP and Windows Me) or Network Neighborhood (Windows 98 SE). After you've checked your cables to make sure your computers are physically connected to your network, you can see if your network is still functioning by attempting to display a computer's shared resources using a UNC.

To test a computer's network connection by connecting to the computer using a UNC, follow these steps:

1. Click Start and choose Run.
2. In the Open box, type the UNC of the computer you want to open. If the computer's name is LIVINGROOM, for example, the UNC would be \\LIVINGROOM.

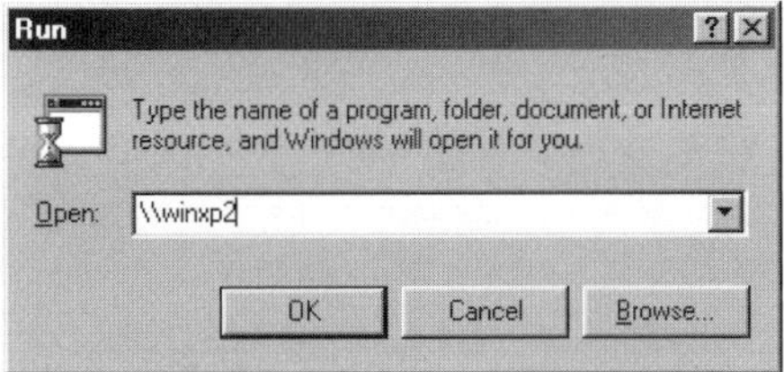

3. Click OK. If the shared folder appears in a new window, the connection is fine.

What can cause a computer to suddenly drop off your network? If your computer turns off its hard disks after 20 minutes or so, the computer might not be detected when the computer serving as the focal point in the network checks it. You might also have made a change to a computer or disconnected from and then reconnected it to the network. Network changes can take anywhere from 5 to 15 minutes to take effect, so your network might not have been updated since your last change.

Getting the Lay of the Land: Mapping Drives

If you're like me, you've probably found that you use files in one or two folders a lot more than you use files in other folders. While you can dig through My Network Places or Network Neighborhood to open those folders, you can make those folders available in My Computer or Windows Explorer by assigning a drive letter to the shared folder. Just as your hard disk is assigned the drive letter C and your floppy disk drive is assigned the drive letter A, you can assign, or map, an unused drive letter to a shared folder elsewhere on your network.

When you map a drive letter to a folder, the folder appears in My Computer on the same level as your hard disk, floppy disk drive, and CD-ROM drive. Figure 7-3 shows how My Computer displays a mapped drive in Windows 98 SE. Once you've mapped a network drive on your computers, you can browse the network drive like any other drive by double-clicking it in My Computer or Windows Explorer.

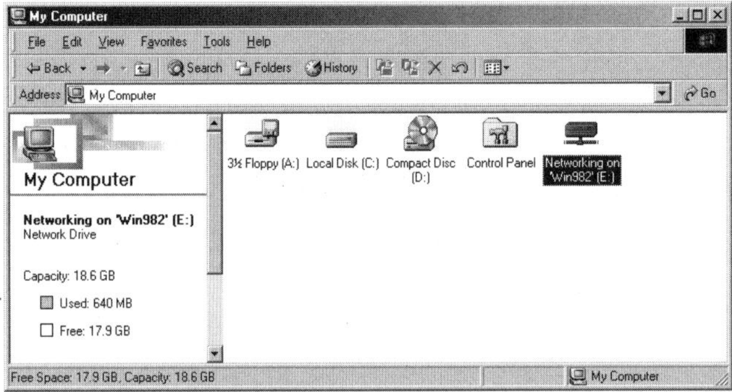

Figure 7-3 A mapped network drive appears in My Computer on the same level as the hard disk drives, floppy disk drives, and CD-ROM drives, making it easier for you to find it and the files it contains.

Note When you map a drive, the drive appears only on the computer from which you mapped the drive, not on every computer on your network.

Map a Drive in Windows XP

With the focus on home networking you find in Windows XP, you won't be surprised to find that the commands to map a drive letter to a shared folder are found in My Computer.

To map a drive in Windows XP, follow these steps:

1. Click Start and choose My Computer.
2. Choose Map Network Drive from the Tools menu.

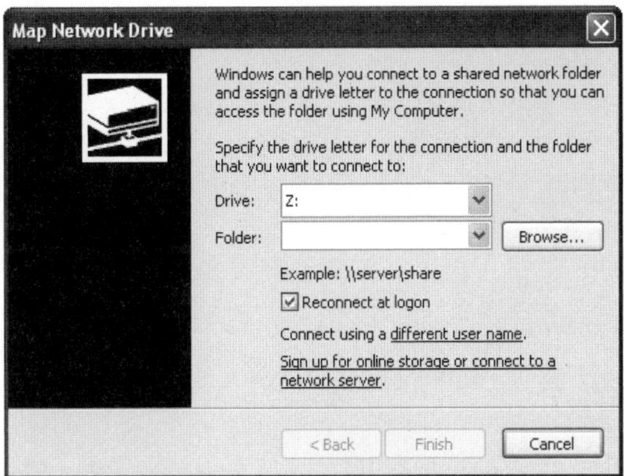
Map Network Drive
Windows can help you connect to a shared network folder and assign a drive letter to the connection so that you can access the folder using My Computer.
Specify the drive letter for the connection and the folder that you want to connect to:
Drive: Z:
Folder:
Browse...
Example: \\server\share
Reconnect at logon
Connect using a different user name.
Sign up for online storage or connect to a network server.
< Back
Finish
Cancel

3 If desired, click the Drive down arrow and select a letter other than the default to assign to the network drive you are creating.

4 Click Browse, and in the Browse For Folder dialog box, select the folder you want to establish as a network drive. You could also type the UNC of the folder.

5 Click OK. If you want to reconnect to the network drive whenever you turn on your computer, select the Reconnect At Logon check box.

6 Click Finish.

Map a Drive in Windows Me or Windows 98 SE

Just as you can do in Windows XP, you can map a network drive in either Windows Me or Windows 98 SE. The program you need to run is Windows Explorer, which you can find on the Start menu. Once you've run Windows Explorer, however, you can map the drive in the exactly the same way you would in Windows XP.

To map a drive in Windows Me or Windows 98 SE, follow these steps:

1 In Windows Me, click Start, choose Programs, choose Accessories, and then choose Windows Explorer.

2 In Windows 98 SE, click Start, choose Programs, and then choose Windows Explorer.

3 Choose Map Network Drive from the Tools menu.

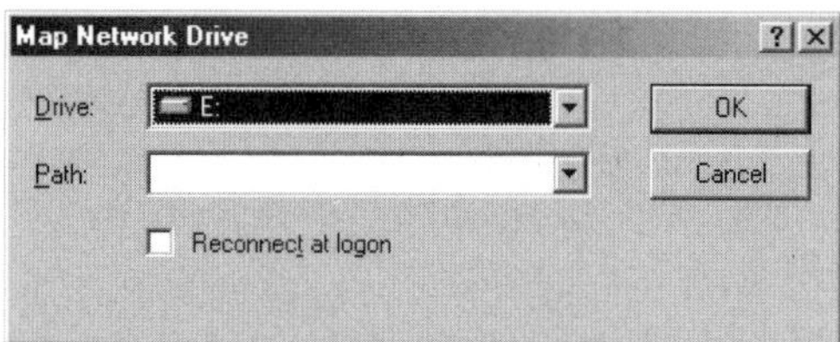

4 In the Map Network Drive dialog box, click the Drive down arrow and select the drive letter you want to assign to the shared folder.

5 In the Path box type the UNC of the folder you want to map as a network drive.

6 If you want to bring up the shared folder as a drive every time you log on to your computer, select the Reconnect At Logon check box.

7 Click OK.

Note If the computer hosting the shared folder you have mapped to a drive letter is turned off when you attempt to connect, you'll get an error message stating the folder is unreachable. If that happens when you are in the middle of editing a document and an attempted save fails, don't try to wait it out. Save the file on the hard disk of the computer you're working on and transfer a copy to the network drive when it's available.

Disconnecting from a Mapped Drive

Every time you turn off your computer, you are disconnected from the network. But not to worry! If you select the Reconnect At Logon check box when you map the drive, you'll be reconnected each time you log on. If you want to disconnect from a drive while you're still logged on to your computer, you can do so quickly. To disconnect from a mapped drive in any operating system, open My Computer, right-click the drive from which you want to disconnect and choose Disconnect.

Too Much of a Good Thing: Restricting Access to a Folder

Not every file is meant for everyone's eyes, whether you want to keep your personal letters personal or you want to share a project you're working on with only one or two other folks on your network. Windows XP uses a different style of access restrictions than Windows Me and Windows 98 SE; while you can set passwords for individual folders in Windows Me and Windows 98 SE,

Windows XP relies on the presence of accounts to restrict access to the computer as a whole, rather than restricting access to individual folders.

Restricting Access to a Folder in Windows XP

The first level of defense against unwanted users reading or manipulating your files is the requirement for every user who uses your computer to have an account. And yes, the Guest account you read about in Chapter 6, "Creating User Accounts," is turned off by default for a reason—there's no use setting up accounts if someone can get onto your computer and poke around without a password.

So, if you can't actually set a password for a folder in Windows XP, how do you make your files secure over a network? The trick is to move the folder you want to protect into the My Documents folder set aside for your account's files. The My Documents folder for each user is private, and while you can share it, it's better to create a different directory where you keep your public files. Because most programs save files to your My Documents folder as a default, you might accidentally make a file public when you wanted to keep it private.

To restrict access to a folder in Windows XP, follow these steps:

1. Click Start, choose My Computer, and navigate to the folder to which you want to restrict access.
2. In the File And Folder Tasks panel, click Move This Folder.
3. In the Move Items dialog box, click the hard disk on which Windows is installed (most likely that will be C), click Documents And Settings, click your user name, and then click My Documents.
4. Click Move.

To allow users to view the documents in a folder but not to change them, follow these steps:

1. Click Start, choose My Computer, and navigate to the folder to which you want to restrict access.
2. In the File And Folder Tasks panel, click Share This Folder.
3. On the Sharing tab of the Properties dialog box, clear the Allow Network Users To Change My Files check box.

Restricting Access to a Folder in Windows Me or Windows 98 SE

Every writer wants to be read, whether you're a science textbook writer trying to make a quick buck recycling electrons or a science fiction writer trying to become the next big name in the field. If you're a fiction writer who wants feedback but isn't so keen on letting other folks edit your work without your supervision, in Windows Me and Windows 98 SE you can password-protect a folder in such a way that users on your home network can read your work but not edit or delete it. You can also require users to enter a password to gain full access to the folder (meaning others can do anything they want with the files), or set two passwords to let some users read what you've written and others to modify or delete it.

See Also *For more information on creating strong passwords, see the section in Chapter 6 entitled "Making a Password Strong."*

To restrict access to a folder in Windows Me or Windows 98 SE, follow these steps:

1. In My Computer or Windows Explorer, right-click the folder to which you want to restrict access and choose Sharing.

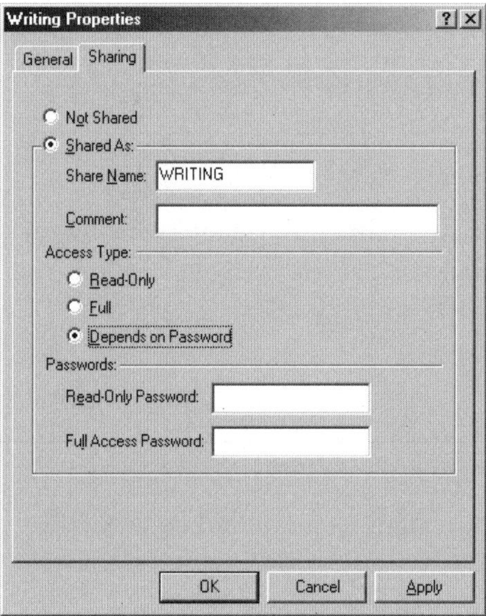

2. On the Sharing tab of the Properties dialog box, follow any of these steps to password-protect your shared folder:

- Select Read-Only and type a password in the Read-Only Password box to require users to type in a password to be able to read but not delete or modify the files in the protected folder.
- Select Full and type a password in the Full Access Password box to require users to type in a password to be able to read, modify, and delete the files in the protected folder.
- Select Depends On Password and type passwords in both the Read-Only Password and Full Access Password boxes to set two levels of protection for the files in the protected folder.

3 Click OK.

Note Setting the same password for Read-Only and Full access would be rather pointless, don't you agree?

Letting Others See a Removable Drive

As I mentioned earlier in the book, universal serial bus (USB) technology lets you move hard disks, CD-ROM drives, and other items from computer to computer. One of the most useful USB items I've found is the CD recording drive. With a CD recording drive, you can make backup copies of your important files in a few minutes without worrying about whether the files are too big to fit on a floppy or whether you've stored the backups on a computer that you might not be able to get to when you're away from home. Of course, a CD recording drive also works as a regular drive; you can drop a CD into the tray and play music or read files from it. When you share a removable drive, whether it's a removable hard disk, a CD drive, or a CD recorder, you let other users on your network see the contents of the CD in the drive and read or manipulate them. It's important that you understand that there are risks involved in making those files available to anyone on your network. In fact, Windows XP displays a warning message asking if you're sure you want to expose your drive to the network. If you do want to make your drive available, you can do so easily.

Sharing Removable Drives in Windows XP

The procedure for sharing a removable drive in Windows XP is very much like what you need to do to share a folder. In fact, you use the same Sharing And Security command to turn on sharing and set the share name for your drive.

To let others see a removable drive in Windows XP, follow these steps:

1 Click Start and choose My Computer.

2 Right-click the CD-ROM drive you want to share and choose Sharing And Security.

3 On the Sharing tab of the Properties dialog box, select the Share This Folder On The Network check box.

Note If you try to share the hard disk on which your computer's operating system is installed, the Properties dialog box will appear with a message that sharing the root drive isn't recommended. If you want to go ahead and do it anyway, click the If You Understand The Risk But Still Want To Share The Root Of The Drive link to continue.

---

4 Type a name for the drive in the Share Name box and click OK.

You can now view the files on the removable drive as if it were any other shared folder on your network.

Sharing Removable Drives in Windows Me and Windows 98 SE

Just as the steps you take to share a removable drive in Windows XP are what you do to share a folder, you use your folder sharing skills to share removable drives in both Windows Me and Windows 98 SE. If you're at all worried about whether you should just let your fellow network users read your files but not change or delete them, you can always limit what they can do. Simply follow the instructions described earlier in this chapter, in the section "Too Much of a Good Thing: Restricting Access to a Folder."

To let others see a removable drive in Windows Me or Windows 98 SE, follow these steps:

1 Right-click the folder you want to share and choose Sharing.

2 On the Sharing tab of the Properties dialog box, select Shared As.

3 In the Share Name box, type the name you want displayed to users who view the folder over your network. In the Comment box, you can type a comment that will appear when someone hovers the mouse pointer over the folder.

4 In the Access Type section, perform either of these steps:

- Select Read-Only to allow anyone to read your documents but not to modify them.
- Select Full to allow anyone to read, edit, or delete your documents.

5 Click OK.

Accessing and Manipulating Files on Other Computers

Part of the beauty of creating a home network is that, for the most part, you can treat files and folders on other computers as if they were on your own computer. If you're in the living room and want to watch a show while you check how your bids are progressing in an online auction, or if you need to retrieve the backup copy of an essay you stored on your roommate's computer because you accidentally deleted the copy on your computer, you can reach out and touch those other computers without hesitation.

Copying and Moving Remote Files

In Windows Me and Windows 98 SE, you can move or copy a file on a network the same way you do when you want to copy or move a file on your own computer. In My Computer, copy the file (or cut it, if you want to move the file and delete the previous copy), navigate to the directory where you want the file to go, and paste the file into its new home. You can also copy and move remote files in Windows XP, but the procedure is different than in Windows Me and Windows 98 SE. Because Windows XP is relatively new, I'll describe that procedure in detail.

To copy and move files on other computers in Windows XP, follow these steps:

1 Click Start, choose My Network Places, and navigate to the file you want to copy or move.

> **Note** If you need to open My Network Places, click Start, choose All Programs, choose Accessories, and choose Windows Explorer. Then click My Computer, and click My Network Places on the Other Places panel.

2 Click the file you want to copy or move and do one of the following.

- In the File And Folder Tasks list, click Copy This File and use the controls in the Copy Items dialog box to select the location to which you want to copy the file.

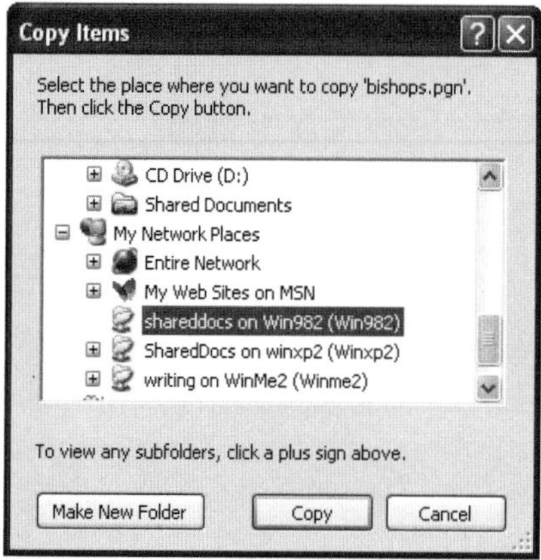

- In the File And Folder Tasks list, click Move This File and use the controls in the Move Items dialog box to select the location to which you want to move the file.

3 Click OK.

Deleting Remote Files

Just as you can copy and move files to and from other computers on your network, you can delete any files that aren't protected. But be careful! When you delete a file on another computer, the file doesn't go to the Recycle Bin—it's gone for good. Because deleting files on other computers is permanent, you might instead create a new To Be Deleted folder on the other computer and move any files you think should be deleted to that folder. Be sure to send the owner of the file an e-mail or instant message so he or she knows the file is in there!

To delete a remote file, follow these steps:

1 Locate the file you want to delete by performing either of these steps:

- In Windows XP or Windows Me, click Start, choose My Network Places, and navigate to the folder with the file you want to delete.
- In Windows 98 SE, double-click Network Neighborhood and navigate to the folder with the file you want to delete.

2. Right-click the file you want to delete and choose Delete.
3. Click Yes.

Opening Remote Files

Whenever you want to read or edit a file that's stored on another computer on your network, you can move to the folder where the file is stored, open it, and get to work.

To open a remote file, follow these steps:

1. Locate the file you want to open by performing either of these steps:
   - In Windows XP or Windows Me, click Start, choose My Network Places, and navigate to the folder with the file you want to open.
   - In Windows 98 SE, double-click Network Neighborhood and navigate to the folder with the file you want to open.
2. Double-click the file you want to open.

Saving Remote Files

I'll talk in some depth about making backup copies of your files in Chapter 11, "Maintaining Your Home Network," but for now let me make the point that saving second or third copies of important files to other computers on your network, or to a removable hard disk or CD recorder, will save you a lot of grief in the long run. Ever since I managed to wipe out five pages of writing by saving the wrong version of a college term paper two hours before it was due, I've been quite diligent about keeping several copies of anything I'd hate to have to do over. You should, too.

To save a file to a remote location, follow these steps:

1. In the program you used to create your file, choose Save As from the File menu.
2. Click the Save In down arrow and double-click one of these.
   - My Network Places in Windows XP or Windows Me
   - Network Neighborhood in Windows 98 SE
3. Navigate to the folder in which you want to save the file and click Save.

Resolving Naming Conflicts

One of the nice things about the Windows family of operating systems is that you can give your files and folders long, descriptive names that make it easy to identify the file or folder and its contents. You can use that flexibility to avoid naming conflicts among files on computers in your home network and in files you send to others.

As a hypothetical example, consider the lonely computer book author sitting in front of the (OK, my) computer in my pajamas at 3:00 a.m., desperately trying to finish those last few paragraphs so I can turn in the chapter that never seems to end (in this book, that would be Chapter 4) before my editor gets to the office later that morning. My editor, Jenny, has more than just my book on her plate—at last count, she was working on at least five different projects, with more on the way as the new publishing season heats up. As such, my sending her an e-mail message with an attachment named Chapter04.doc doesn't help her much. Sure, it's attached to my message and she knows when it comes in that it's for this book, but if she were to save the file into the wrong directory or try to put it into the same directory as another file named Chapter04.doc, she could be in for trouble. Likewise, after the technical editor and copy editor have had their way with the chapter, she'll need to send it back to me so I can make any changes they've requested.

Keeping the same name for the file throughout all of these changes would be silly and confusing; so we use a system that takes advantage of both the ability to give our files long names and how inexpensive hard disk storage space is these days. Whenever Jenny sends me an edited version of a file, she'll change the file's name to something like Chapter04_jb01.doc, which retains the original file name and indicates she has edited the document.

Note We use underscores instead of spaces so the file name is all one word, which is still necessary for some e-mail systems. For most e-mail systems, spaces in file names are perfectly valid, but it's better to be safe than sorry.

You don't need to use a system as formal as what I use with my editors at Microsoft Press, but the next time you let the family collaborate on your holiday letter, you might want to have each person change the name of the file so you can easily identify the most recent version of the document.

Turning Off File Sharing

As a general rule of network security, you should never make any resource, whether it's a folder, printer, or otherwise, available over the network for one minute longer that you need to. If the project you were working on with your family is complete, you can turn off sharing for the folder where the files are stored so you can finish things off. I also turn off file sharing if I'm going on vacation but want to leave my network running so the guy who feeds my cats can use the Internet while he's here.

To turn off file sharing for a folder in Windows XP, follow these steps:

1. Right-click the folder you no longer want to share and choose Sharing And Security.
2. On the Sharing tab, clear the Share This Folder On the Network check box and click OK.

To turn off file sharing for a folder in Windows Me or Windows 98 SE, follow these steps:

1. Right-click the folder you no longer want to share and choose Sharing.
2. On the Sharing tab, select Not Shared and click OK.

Key Points

- If you're working with others on a project, putting the files for that project in a shared folder can save you lots of time and energy.
- It's okay to share music and pictures that are yours to share, but make sure you're not infringing on someone's copyright when you do it.
- You create a shortcut to a frequently used shared folder by mapping that folder to a drive letter on your computer.
- You can work with files in shared folders just as you would if they were stored on your own computer.
- If you don't want folks to work with documents in your shared folder as if they were stored on your own computer but you do want to make them available to authorized users, you can add password protection.
- You can share a removable drive, such as a hard disk or CD-ROM drive, but remember that anyone on your network (or anyone who can get onto your network) will have access to it.
- Remember that Windows Me lists your network resources in My Network Places, not Network Neighborhood.

Chapter 8

You Need Only One Printer

If you don't have a home network and you want to print a document on a printer that's not connected to the computer you're using, you're in very much the same predicament as when you want to transfer a file from one computer to another. You need to copy the file to a disk (if it'll fit), carry the disk to the computer with the printer attached (if no one else is using it), and print your document (if the software you need is installed on that computer). When you put printers on your network, you can print to any one of them just as easily as to any other. Stay in your chair, select a printer, and print the file. It's that simple.

My job in this chapter is to show you how to hook up a printer to a computer, and then to share the printer so others on your network can see it. Your other networked computers need to have the software drivers to control the printer as well, but you can install them quickly. I'll then show you how to use your printer effectively by password-protecting it (if desired), turning off sharing, or removing the printer from your network altogether.

Expanding Your Family: Putting a Printer on Your Home Network

Not having a computer network hurts two types of people: innocent bystanders (for example, someone whose computer is connected directly to a nice printer) and you. If you've used computers in your home or office without the benefit of a network, you've probably wished that the really good printer, the expensive laser printer or the color ink jet model, were attached to your computer so you didn't have to copy all your files to disk or CD-ROM and then get in line to use the computer with the nice printer.

Location, Location, Location: Placing the Printer

When it comes to setting up a home network, Microsoft Windows operating systems treat printers as just another network element, equal to computers and shared drives. You can add printers to any computer on your network and share them with everyone else on your network.

When you're choosing which computer to connect a printer to, keep in mind that everyone in the house will want to print to it, and that the printer should be ready whenever it's needed. To that end, you should locate the printer near a computer that is always on and that is in a high traffic area, one that won't disturb you when you're trying to sleep or get work done.

Adding a Printer to a Computer

There are two things you need to do to share a printer over a home network. The first step in the process is to connect the printer to a computer on your network. Adding printers to computers is something folks have been doing since the very earliest days of computing, so it should come as no surprise that Windows operating systems have wizards to step you through the process.

Note You should always purchase Plug and Play-compatible printers—they're set up to work with Windows and make installation a snap. Plug and Play printers are identified as such on the box, so if you're in doubt you can just read the package.

To install a printer on your computer, follow these steps:

1. Log on to your computer using an account with sufficient permissions to install new hardware (that is, with an administrator account in Windows XP).
2. Set up your printer, plug it in, and connect it to one of your computer's universal serial bus (USB) or parallel ports. When you do, your computer will recognize that new hardware has been connected and run the New Hardware Wizard.

Note If you aren't using a Plug and Play printer, you'll need to follow the instructions that came with your printer to start the installation process. Most of the time, you'll have an installation CD-ROM or floppy disk you can pop into a drive.

---

3 Insert the CD-ROM or floppy disk that came with your printer into the appropriate drive, select Install The Software Automatically, and click Next.

> **Note** Again, if your printer came with different directions, follow those directions!

4 The New Hardware Wizard will search your computer's drives for software to run the printer. When the computer finds the software, it will copy the files it needs and run any additional installation software that came with the printer.

> **Note** The installation software might ask you to print a test page to be sure that the printer heads are aligned properly and that the ink or toner cartridges are disgorging their contents freely. I always print a test page during printer installation and directly after so I can be sure my programs interact properly with the printer.

5 When the last page of the New Hardware Wizard appears, click Finish.

Tell the Host: Sharing Is a Virtue

Once you have connected your printer to its host computer and printed a test page, you need to let the host know you want to share the printer with the rest of the network. If you're running Microsoft Windows XP, you don't need to do anything; whenever you add a printer to your network, any computer running Windows XP will sense the newcomer, sniff it to see what it's about, and add the printer to its list of available resources. For computers that don't run Windows XP, there are a few more steps, but it's not too much pain for quite a lot of gain.

> **Note** You might need to have your printer's installation disk on hand for Windows to copy the drivers to your computer.

Sharing the Printer Wealth in Windows XP

To let others use your printer over the network when the printer is connected to a Windows XP computer, follow these steps:

1 Click Start and choose Settings.

2 Click Printers And Other Hardware.

3 Click the icon representing the shared printer and then, in the Printer Tasks list, click Share This Printer.

4 On the Sharing tab of the printer's Properties dialog box, click Additional Drivers.

5 Select the Intel Windows 95, 98 And Me check box, and click OK to let anyone using a computer with one of the listed operating systems to print to the printer you just shared.

Sharing the Printer Wealth in Windows Me and Windows 98 SE

As is the case on computers running Windows XP, sharing a printer on computers running Microsoft Windows Millennium Edition (Me) and Microsoft Windows 98 Second Edition (SE) is a straightforward operation. I did want to put the instructions in their own section because the steps you follow are slightly different in these older operating systems, but there's nothing tricky about it. It's just a matter of knowing which menu items to choose to show the printers available to your computer.

To let others use a printer connected to a computer running Windows Me or Windows 98 SE, follow these steps:

1 Click Start, choose Settings, and then choose Printers.

2 Right-click the printer you want to share and choose Sharing.

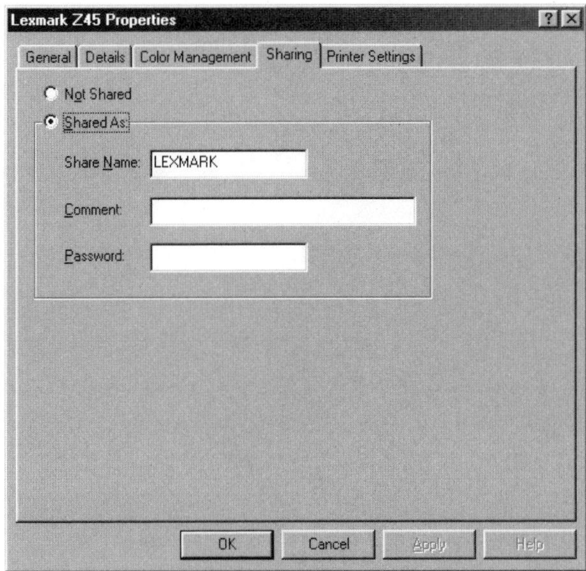

3 Select Shared As, type a name for the printer in the Share Name box, and type a comment for the printer in the Comment box.

4 Click OK.

Detecting a Network Printer from Windows Me and Windows 98 SE Computers

One handy manifestation of the focus on home networking found in Windows XP is that Windows XP computers all know how to detect printers that are connected to other Windows XP computers on your network. Unfortunately, Windows Me and Windows 98 SE don't have that same capability. No, they need to be told. But only once, so they're way ahead of kids, spouses, and significant others in that respect.

To add a printer to the list of available printers on a computer running Windows Me or Windows 98 SE, follow these steps:

1 Click Start, choose Settings, and then choose Printers.

2 Double-click Add Printer.

3 Click Next, select Network Printer, and then click Next.

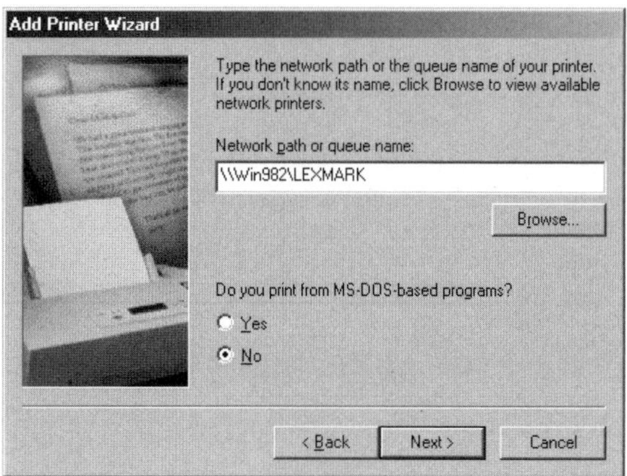

4 Type the Universal Naming Convention (UNC) of the printer in the Network Path Or Queue Name box, and click Next.

5 Type a name for the printer in the Printer Name box, select the Yes option button in the Do You Print From MS-DOS-Based Programs section, and click Next.

> **Note** If you don't need to print from any programs that run in an MS-DOS window, you can select the No option button.

6 Select Yes to print a test page and then click Finish.

Printing to a Network Printer

After you add a printer to your network and have ensured that every computer knows the printer exists, you can use that printer regardless of where you are on your network. If you're in the den and want to print out a letter on the laser printer in the living room, all you need to do is identify the laser printer as the instrument that will bring your deathless prose to the world.

To print to a network printer, follow these steps:

1 Choose the Print function in the program you're running, usually by choosing Print from the File menu. In most programs, including Microsoft Word, you'll see a dialog box that lets you choose the printer you'll use to print your document.

> **Note** In many programs, clicking the Print toolbar button will print the entire document to the active printer without letting you change anything. Choosing Print from the File menu or using the equivalent menu command in your program will usually open the dialog box and let you change things.

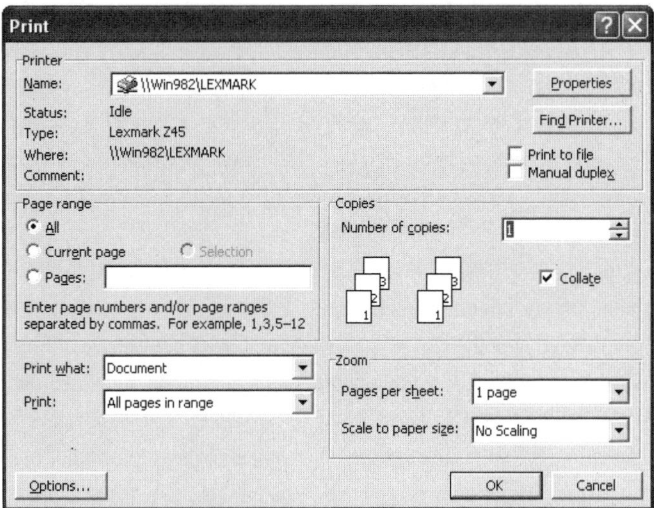

2 Click the Name down arrow and select the printer you want to use to print this document.

3 Choose the pages to print by following any of these steps:

- Select All to print the entire document.
- Select Current Page to print only the page where the insertion point is located.
- Select Pages to print only the pages you define in the text box next to the option button.
- Select a portion of the document and choose Selection to print only the highlighted portion of your document.

Note Word 2002 lets you highlight noncontiguous parts of your document, so the Selection printing option is particularly useful in that program.

---

4 Type the number of copies you want to print in the Number Of Copies box.

5 Click OK.

Note The printing options available to you will vary based on the programs and printers you use to print.

When Network Printing Goes Wrong When I worked for a defense contractor in McLean, Virginia, I spent a lot of time writing and editing presentations for some folks who were trying to develop new business areas for the company. One reason that work was cool was that I got to see some things other folks didn't get to see, but it also meant that I got to play with one of very few color printers in the company. Back in 1993, every full-color printed page cost about $3, so mistakes were, shall we say, frowned on.

The company had a great network, but the software to print to the color printer existed only on three computers on "Rug Row," the part of our main building that housed our executives and had nicer carpet than the rest of the buildings. So I got to use those computers early in the morning, late at night, and whenever folks were out of the office and someone higher up the pecking order didn't lay claim to the printer.

The real problem, however, was that the computer I used to compose and edit the presentations did not have the same font set as the computers I used to print the presentations in color. The differences were obvious on the printed page, what with changed letter sizes, different line breaks, and even a few characters (dashes, quotation marks, and accented letters) that were represented as completely different characters. The moral of the story? Always examine your documents closely before you print them on a new printer or a new computer, both by moving through the electronic version of the document and by printing test pages from throughout the document.

Making Your Printers Dance and Sing

Sharing a printer over a network is a lot like sharing an Internet connection—you can create a hard copy of any document from any computer in the house. If you have a wireless network and a laptop computer, that means you can print anything from anywhere. That sort of flexibility is what brought me into home networking for the first time, and the minor inconvenience of having to get up off the sofa and wander over to the printer on my bookshelf to pick up my document is nothing more than a reminder that printers still can't hand you the printout directly. I'll drop a note in the Microsoft Suggestion Box to see if there's any way that capability can be added to the next version of Windows, but for now you should plan on spending at least a few seconds a day away from the sofa.

Changing the Default Printer

When you have more than one printer available to a computer, one of those printers will be designated as the *default* printer.

Lingo The default printer is the printer a computer will use to print a document unless you specify otherwise.

If you work from home and have a black and white laser printer you use for printing letters and a color ink jet printer you use to print photographs and Microsoft PowerPoint slides, you want to be sure you know to which printer you're sending a document. The price difference between color and black and white documents isn't as big as it used to be (remember, in 1993 it cost my employer $3 to print a page on a color laser printer), but it's still embarrassing to walk into your living room expecting to pick your report out of the laser printer and discover you just sent 50 pages of plain text to a color printer you just installed.

To change the default printer on a computer running Windows XP, follow these steps:

1 Click Start, and choose Control Panel.

2 Click Printers And Other Hardware.

3 In the Pick A Task list, click View Installed Printers Or Fax Printers, right-click the printer you want to assign as the default printer, and choose Set As Default Printer.

4 After you confirm that you want the printer to be the default printer, a check mark appears next to the printer, indicating it is the default printer on that computer. Close the printer window.

To change the default printer on a computer running Windows Me or Windows 98 SE, follow these steps:

1 Click Start, choose Settings, and then choose Printers.

2 Right-click the printer you want to assign as the default printer, and choose Set As Default. After you confirm that you want the printer to be the default printer, a check mark appears next to the printer, indicating it is the default printer on that computer. Then close the printer window.

Password-Protecting a Printer

Remember what I said about color printers being less expensive to use than they were a few years ago? It's true, but it doesn't mean you need to let just anyone use your color printer whenever they want to. When I was a kid I thought cats were cool and would spend hours drawing them with my crayons and colored pencils. I have no doubt that if I'd had access to a color printer, I would have spent many hours and many dollars worth of supplies printing page after page of kitty pictures.

You can avoid indiscriminate or unknowing use of a printer by protecting that printer with a password. When you password-protect a printer, anyone who sends a job to that printer will need to type in a password to convince the printer to do it. Adding a password will keep out the casual user and might also alert you to the fact that you are indeed sending 50 pages of text to the color printer.

Note Protecting a printer with a password is possible only in Windows Me and Windows 98 SE.

To password-protect a printer in Windows Me or Windows 98 SE, follow these steps:

1 Click Start, choose Settings, and then choose Printers.

2 Right-click the printer you want to protect and choose Sharing.

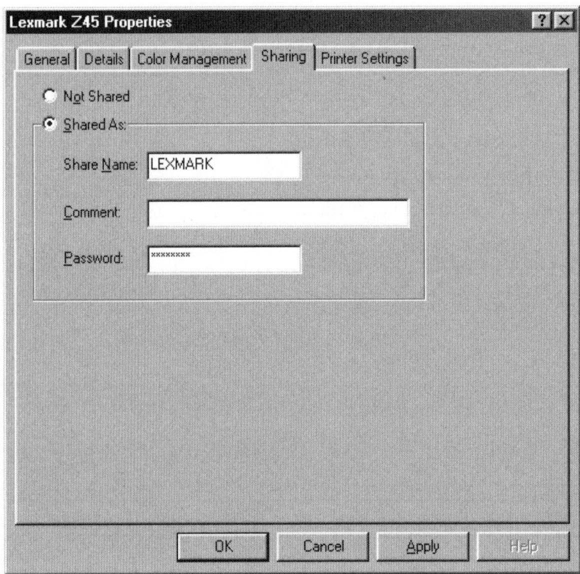

3 Type a password in the Password box and click OK.

Deleting a Printer

As with all manner of computer equipment, printers come and go. I personally have gone through five printers since I bought my first computer, but every time I bought a new printer I made sure the old one went to a good home. Of course, because I wasn't using the printer any longer, I deleted it from my system so I wouldn't try to print to it by accident. I've spent time standing next to a new printer, wondering why my document wasn't printed, when all the while my computer was searching in vain for the printer that used to be there.

Note When you delete a printer, you remove just the pointer to it in the system. Unless you run any deinstallation software that came with the printer, the drivers will remain on your computer. Leaving the drivers on your computer won't hurt anything, so don't worry about trying to remove them. If you leave the drivers on your computer and later decide to reconnect the printer to your computer, you probably won't need to reinstall the drivers.

To delete a printer from a computer running Windows XP, follow these steps:

1. Click Start, and then choose Control Panel.
2. Click Printers And Other Hardware.
3. In the Pick A Task list, click View Installed Printers Or Fax Printers.
4. Right-click the printer you want to delete, choose Delete, and then, in the message box, click Yes.

To delete a printer from a computer running Windows Me or Windows 98 SE, follow these steps:

1. Click Start, choose Settings, and then choose Printers.
2. Right-click the printer you want to delete, choose Delete, and then, in the message box, click Yes.

Note Sometimes when you turn off a computer, or if a printer cable comes loose, the computer will lose track of one or more printers connected to it. You can tell a printer is installed but not active if the printer icon is in the Printers tool in Control Panel but is gray rather than black. If that's the case, delete the printer, unplug it from the computer, and then plug it back in. Windows will recognize the new hardware and reinstall it, using the drivers you put on the computer when you first installed the printer.

Turning Printer Sharing Off

I like to say that there are no irreversible computer networking decisions. Whatever you, the network creator, choose to do, you might also choose to undo. Sharing printers is no exception. Allow me to paint you a picture, one that is probably all too familiar. It's early morning, and you've been up all night working on a project you absolutely have to hand in today. Your job, your promotion, your boat, your very well-being is on the line. And you can't get at the printer because someone else is printing the large-print version of *War and Peace*. You can make sure this never happens to you by turning off printer sharing. Yes, it's selfish. Yes, your roommate or family might not understand, but it will save you from grief. Just be sure to turn sharing back on when you're done.

To turn off printer sharing for a computer running Windows XP, follow these steps:

1. Click Start, and choose Control Panel.
2. Click Printers And Other Hardware.
3. In the Pick A Task list, click View Installed Printers Or Fax Printers.
4. Right-click the icon representing the shared printer, choose Sharing, and then, on the Sharing tab, select the Do Not Share This Printer option button.
5. Click OK.

To turn off printer sharing on a computer running Windows Me or Windows 98 SE, follow these steps:

1. Click Start, choose Settings, and then choose Printers.
2. Right-click the printer you want to stop sharing and choose Sharing.
3. Select Not Shared, and then click OK.

Making Remote Printing Painless

In the home networking world, there are few things more horrifying than when you print a document, your computer says everything is fine, but nothing comes out of the printer. But don't despair! There are a few things you can check to clear up most of your printing problems.

- Check the printer itself to ensure it has power, paper, and either ink or toner. You should also look out for any error lights or messages on the printer. If the printer isn't responding, either press the Reset button (if it has one) or try turning it off and back on—the printer might just have gotten stuck in a process and needs your help to start over.
- Check every wire you can get your hands on. One of the most common causes of network printing problems is that someone moved a printer or unplugged it and forgot to reconnect it.
- Check the Printers And Other Hardware tool in Control Panel to make sure the printer is active. If a printer is dimmed in Printers And Other Hardware, it is inactive. To activate it, you need to delete the printer, unplug it, and plug it back in.

- Check to make sure the proper printer drivers are installed on the host computer and on the computer from which you are trying to print. If the drivers are installed, try deleting them and reinstalling them. You should also visit the manufacturer's Web site to ensure you have the most recent drivers for your printer.
- In the Printers And Other Hardware tool in Control Panel, right-click the printer and choose Open to display any pending jobs for the printer. If a job is listed but it isn't going through, consider deleting the print job to free up the printer. You can delete a job by right-clicking it and choosing Delete.
- Bear in mind that your network might just be slow, whether because of your shared Internet access or because the computer to which your printer is connected was conserving power until you contacted it about printing your document. On my little network I have had to wait a minute or two for a job to go through, so do give your printer some time to get on the job.

Key Points

- Windows treats printers as any other network component, meaning you can share them, protect them, or remove them from the network at any time.
- Attaching a printer to a computer on your network is sufficient if all of your computers run Windows XP, but if you have computers running Windows Me or Windows 98 SE on your network, you'll need to run the Add A Printer Wizard on those computers so they'll know about the network printer.
- Printing to a network printer is no different than printing to a printer that's attached to your computer. If you want to use another printer on your network, just select that printer using the Name down arrow in your program's Print dialog box.
- If you find yourself using the same printer all the time, you can set it as your computer's default printer.
- In Windows Me and Windows 98 SE, you can protect a printer by requiring anyone who wants to use the printer to type in a password.
- You can always turn off printer sharing if you have an important job or remove it from your network entirely if you're going to replace the printer with a new one.

Chapter 9

Communicating Across Your Network

One aspect of networks that makes them worth having is that they let you talk with individuals from around the world as easily as you can talk with someone in the next room. While conversing with someone on the other side of the world is a great thing to be able to do, you shouldn't overlook the benefits of being able to contact someone on the other side of the house without yelling. And, in the case of Microsoft Windows Messenger and Microsoft MSN Messenger, which are client programs you use to connect to the .NET Messenger service, you can exchange pleasantries (and files) with up to four friends no matter where they are on the globe.

Regardless of whether you're using Windows Messenger, which comes with Windows XP, or the free MSN Messenger program you can download for Windows 98 Second Edition (SE) or Windows Millennium Edition (Me), you can engage your buddies in rollicking text, voice, and video conversations. And what's so great about the two .NET Messenger programs is that they're compatible—you can have a text chat with anyone who uses either of the two programs.

My job in this chapter is to show you how to set up Windows Messenger and MSN Messenger; to create a Contact list so you can keep track of when your friends are online; to communicate with your contacts by text, voice, and video; to share programs across the Internet; and to customize both Windows Messenger and MSN Messenger so they put your best face forward online.

Outdo E-mail with Instant Messaging

I could (and sometimes do) go on and on about the virtues of electronic mail. It's there whenever you need it. You can communicate with anyone, anywhere. You can leave and come back to it at any time. Yep, nothing but benefits. Well, maybe there are some drawbacks: You're not in a real conversation. And, if your e-mail gets held up at a computer along the way, or your server hiccups, or the people you're trying to reach don't have their program set to check their mail every hour or less, you may not be able to get in touch with them. It's at times like these that you would love to send your colleague a message and engage him or her in a real-time conversation, preferably by voice, but typing back and forth in a shared window wouldn't be too bad either.

Enter the *instant message*, a direct communication between two or more individuals. Instant messaging is a direct descendant of Internet Relay Chat (IRC), which was an early form of the chat rooms you also find on the Internet today. In fact, IRC was such a well thought-out communication platform that it's still used to provide chat services and as the backbone technology for some online games.

Lingo An instant message is a text note you send to another user of an online service such as .NET Messenger.

I'll talk about chat rooms and games in Chapter 10, "Playing Games on Your Home Network," but it's important to distinguish instant messaging from a chat room. A chat room is an electronic area where anyone can join an ongoing conversation. The rooms are usually limited to discussions on a particular topic, but in most cases there's no direct supervision. Instant messaging (yep, the noun has been "verbed") entails a private conversation between two people, plus (in the case of MSN Messenger and Windows Messenger) up to three others you invite to join the conversation. It's like having your own private chat room, and you can talk about whatever you want, as shown in Figure 9-1.

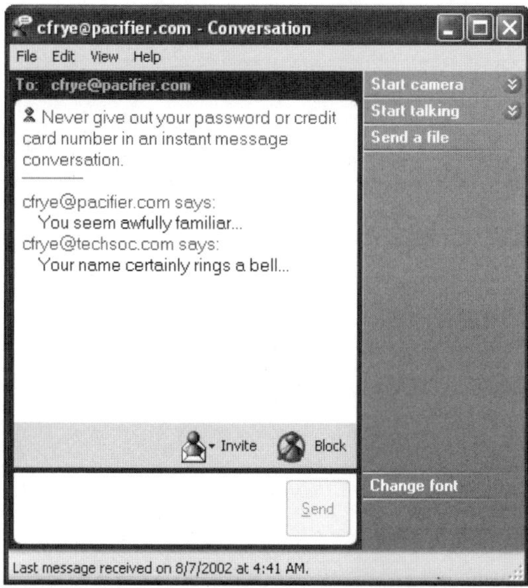

Figure 9-1 The author sends himself an instant message. He thinks.

Note You can check the status of the .NET Messenger service by visiting the service's status page at *http://messenger.microsoft.com/support/status.asp*.

WITW? What All Those Initials Mean Practically no one types as fast as they talk, and very few folks type as fast as they'd like. When you're sending an instant message without the benefit of sound or video, you need to type as quickly as you can. Over the years, users of bulletin board systems (BBSs), chat rooms, and instant messaging services have developed a number of *initialisms* to represent common phrases and save wear and tear on their fingers. Table 9-1 on the next page lists a number of common initialisms you'll probably run into online.

Lingo What's an initialism? An initialism is a series of letters that is not pronounced as a word, as compared to an acronym, which is an initialism pronounced as a word. An abbreviation, by contrast, is the first few letters of a word, followed by a period.

Chat room and instant message users have developed lots of abbreviations and initialisms over the years, so this list is nowhere near exhaustive. If you're not sure of what something means, don't be afraid to ask!

Table 9-1 Common Initialisms

Initialism	Translation
AFAIK	As Far As I Know
ASAP	As Soon As Possible
BBL	Be Back Later
BRB	Be Right Back
CYA	See Ya (Later)
EG	Evil Grin (also <eg>)
F2F	Face to Face
FYI	For Your Information
FWIW	For What It's Worth
G	Grin (also <g>)
GTG	Got to Go (or Good to Go)
HTH	Happy to Help
IMNSHO	In My Not So Humble Opinion
IMO	In My Opinion
IMCO	In My Considered Opinion
IMHO	In My Humble Opinion
IMS	I'm Sorry
IOW	In Other Words
IRL	In Real Life
LOL	Laugh Out Loud
OIC	Oh, I See
OTOH	On the Other Hand
OTTOMH	Off the Top of My Head
PAW	Parents Are Watching
ROFL	Rolling on Floor Laughing
S	Smile (also <s>)
SNERT	Snot-Nosed Egotistical Rude Teenager
TIA	Thanks in Advance
TY	Thank You
U2	You, Too
WAYD	What Are You Doing?
WITW	What in The World?
WTG	Way to Go

To take advantage of the free .NET Messenger service, you'll need to sign up for a .NET Passport. A .NET Passport is an identity you create that lets you register once for a wide variety of sites that use the Passport to identify visitors. When you set up your .NET Passport, you're required to give only your e-mail address and a password so you can access the system securely. What's more, any information you do provide is encrypted before it's transmitted over the Internet, and sites that use the .NET Passport as their sign-in identifier sign an agreement to put safeguards in place to protect your personal information.

See Also *You can get a lot more information on the benefits of having a .NET Passport by visiting* http://www.passport.com.

To set up a .NET Passport in Windows XP, follow these steps:

1. If necessary, on the taskbar, click the Show Hidden Icons button to display all the icons on the taskbar, and click the Windows Messenger icon—the featureless, roly-poly green person.
2. Click Next to move past the first page of the .NET Passport Wizard, select the Yes option button to indicate you have an e-mail address, and click Next again.
3. If you don't have an e-mail address, select the No option button and go through the steps to create an account.
4. Type your e-mail address in the E-Mail Address box, and click Next.
5. Type your password in the Password box, and type it again (to verify the spelling) in the Retype Password box. Select the Save My .NET Passport Information In My Windows XP Account check box if you want Windows to submit your Passport sign-in information whenever it's requested, or clear the check box if you'd rather type in your password whenever it's requested. Click Next to continue moving through the wizard.

   If you're concerned about your computer's security, you might consider clearing the check box and typing in your password whenever it's requested. If you feel your security is adequate, you can have Windows provide your sign-in information automatically.

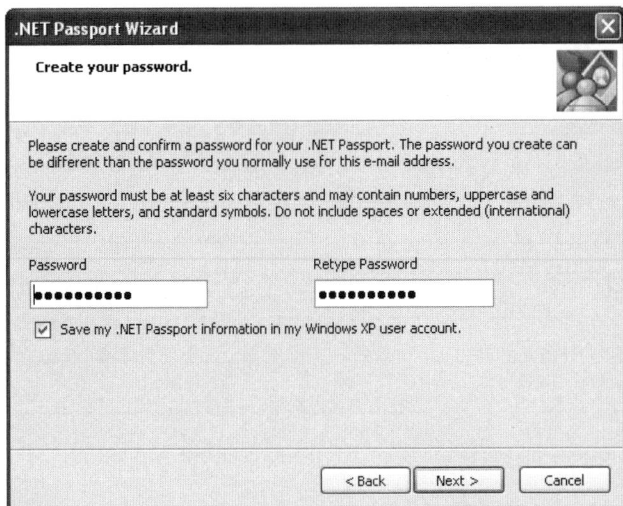

6 Click the Select A Secret Question down arrow and select a question from the list. Type the answer to the question in the Answer box, and click Next.

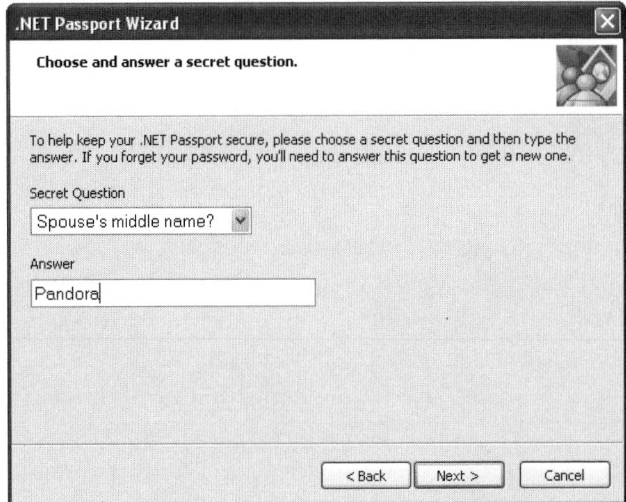

Note You might consider using a fake question for your secret question, such as choosing a question asking for your mother's maiden name, when in fact the answer is the maiden name of a coworker.

7. Click the Country/Region down arrow and select your country or region. Click the State down arrow and select your state (or province, county/region, *Land*, *kraj*, or prefecture, as appropriate for your place of residence), and then (if appropriate) type your ZIP code in the ZIP Code box. Click Next.
8. Click the I Accept The Agreement option button to accept the End User Licensing Agreement, and click Next.
9. Select the Share My E-Mail Address check box if you want Windows to send your e-mail address to every Passport Partner site you visit, and select the Share My Other Registration Information check box to send your other information to every Passport Partner site you visit. (For U.S. residents, "other information" comprises your country, state, and ZIP code.)

Note You can get more information on how Passport partners handle your personal information by clicking the Tell Me More About .NET Passport, Privacy, And Security link.

---

10. Click Next to move to the final wizard page, and click Finish to finish the wizard. The .NET registration system will send an e-mail message to the address you provided in the .NET Passport Wizard. Follow the steps in the message to finish setting up your .NET Passport.

Note If you don't follow the instructions in the e-mail message, the phrase *E-mail Address Not Verified* will appear next to your online identity in Windows Messenger.

To set up a .NET Passport in Windows 98 or Windows Me, follow these steps:

1. Visit *http://www.passport.com/*, and click the Register For Your Free .NET Passport Today! button.
2. Type your e-mail address in the E-Mail Address box. Type your password in the Password box, and verify it by typing it again in the Retype Password box.
3. If you want to share your registration information with Passport member Web sites, select the Share My E-Mail Address check box.

Note You can get information on how your personal information will be used by clicking the Tell Me More About .NET Passport, Privacy, And Security link.

---

4 Read the Terms Of Use and licensing agreement, and click I Agree to accept its terms. Click Continue on the confirmation Web page to return to the Passport site.

Starting to Use Windows Messenger

If you have Windows XP, once you have a .NET Passport, you can sign in to the Windows Messenger service and begin interacting with your fellow subscribers.

Important If you're using Windows 98 SE or Windows Me, you'll need to use MSN Messenger instead of Windows Messenger. Skip ahead to the section "More Backwards Compatibility: MSN Messenger," later in this chapter.

Signing In to Windows Messenger

If you want Windows to remember your password and sign you in whenever you run Windows Messenger, select the Sign Me In Automatically check box in the sign-in dialog box. In general, you should do this only if you believe your computer is completely secure. I don't select the Sign Me In Automatically check box on any computers that don't run Windows XP because that's the only operating system that controls who can log on to my computer.

To sign in to Windows Messenger, follow these steps:

1 On the taskbar, double-click the Windows Messenger icon and click the Click Here To Sign In link.

2 Type your password in the Password box, and click OK.

Setting Up a Contacts List

After you log on to the Windows Messenger service, you can create a list of other subscribers that you want to keep track of while you're signed in to the service. After you create your Contacts list, your friends will be broken down into two groups: those who are logged on to Windows Messenger, and those who aren't. You'll be able to interact with your buddies using text, voice, and video, but first you have to let Windows Messenger know who the folks you want to talk to are.

A box appears whenever a contact signs in to the service, letting you know that a particular friend is online.

To set up a Contacts list in Windows Messenger, follow these steps:

1. On the taskbar, double-click the Windows Messenger icon.
2. On the Windows Messenger toolbar, choose Tools, and click Add A Contact. In the Add A Contact dialog box, select the By E-Mail Address Or Sign-In Name option button and click Next.

> **Note** You can search for a contact whose e-mail address you don't know by choosing the Search For A Contact option button and clicking Next. You'll see a form into which you can type what you do know about the person you're trying to contact. After you click Next, you'll see a list of .Net Messenger subscribers who chose to share their information and who meet your search criteria. If the person you want has a .NET Passport, you'll be able to add him or her as a contact.

3. Type your contact's e-mail address in the box and click Next.

> **Note** You're notified when someone else adds you to his or her contact list. If you don't want to interact with that person, you can always block him or her from sending messages to you. You'll find out how later in this chapter.

Conversing Using Windows Messenger

Okay…the stage is set. You're online, your conversation partner is online, you've got some nice smooth jazz on the stereo, the lights are down low, and there's an animated image of a flickering candle on your screen. It's time to get down to the serious business of communicating! But how? Windows Messenger lets you choose the best way to converse with your contacts—by typing, by voice, or by video.

Talking by Typing

The classic way to communicate over the Internet is through text, whether you do so by sending an e-mail message or by sharing a chat session on a server. In Windows Messenger, you initiate a conversation with one of your contacts by double-clicking the name of the contact, the practical upshot of which is that the two of you share a Conversation window.

The people you're trying to contact will see a box appear on their screens, letting them know that you're trying to get in touch with them, as shown in Figure 9-2. They'll have the opportunity to accept or reject the call, and don't be concerned if it takes a few minutes for them to respond. I hop up from the computer quite a bit to get drinks, put the cat out, make a sandwich, let the cat in, answer the door, and pet the cat while I'm waiting.

Figure 9-2 When a contact initiates a conversation with you, Messenger displays the text of the message and whom it's from.

Note You can begin typing on the next line (that is, add a line break to the text you send) by pressing Shift+Enter.

To begin a text conversation with another Windows Messenger participant, follow these steps:

1. Sign in to Windows Messenger, and then, in your Contacts list, double-click the name of the contact you want to talk to.

   Note If your Contacts list isn't showing, you can display it by double-clicking the Windows Messenger icon on the taskbar.

2. Type your message in the lower window of the Conversation window. Press Enter when you're ready to send your message.

   Note To add more people to your conversation, in the I WantTo section of the Windows Messenger dialog box, click Invite Someone To Join This Conversation. Click the name of the contact you want to invite, and then click OK.

Talking by Talking (and Typing)

I'm a big believer in the power of the human voice. It's hard to be subtle when you're sending a string of letters over a wire to someone else who's reading them on a screen. Handwriting is much better, but communicating by speaking makes it possible to discern the little differences in inflection and tone that make all the difference. To strike up a voice conversation over Windows Messenger, and in the process avoid long-distance phone charges, you'll need a modem that transmits data at 33.8 Kbps (kilobits per second) or faster, a microphone, and speakers.

Note As with most things, you'll find that the more money you spend on your microphone, the better sound quality you get. If you plan to do a lot of voice messaging, I recommend spending at least U.S.$40 on a combination microphone and headset.

To add voice communication to your Windows Messenger conversation, follow these steps:

1. Sign in to Windows Messenger, and begin a conversation with one of your contacts.
2. If this is the first time you're having a voice conversation using Windows Messenger, click Start Talking to run the Audio And Video Tuning Wizard. Work your way through the wizard to set up your microphone and speakers so they'll work properly with Windows Messenger. The wizard will run only once. After the wizard runs, Windows Messenger will alert your contact that you want to initiate a voice conversation.

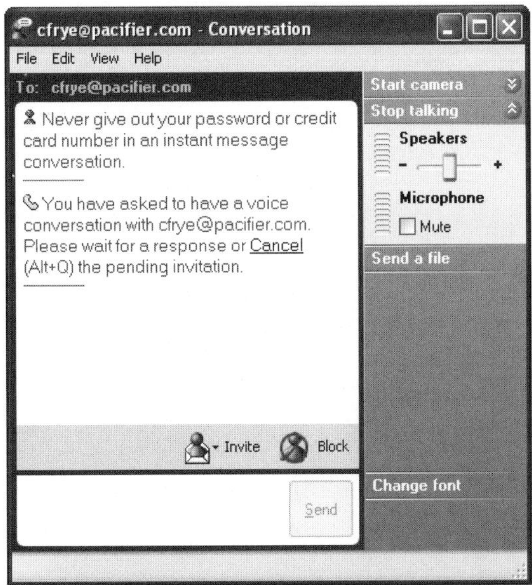

3. Use the horizontal Speakers slider to control your speaker volume, and select the Mute check box if you want to turn off your microphone. (Clearing the Mute check box will turn your microphone back on.) When you're done talking, click Stop Talking to end the voice portion of your conversation.

Talking Face to Face, Sort Of

Talking to someone else over your Internet connection for no extra charge is great, but adding video of yourself and the person with whom you're communicating makes things that much closer to being in the same room. To establish a video connection, you'll need a high-speed Internet connection, if at all possible, and a Web camera, which you can buy from any medium-size or larger computer store for as little as U.S.$30. It is possible to send video over the Internet at speeds as low as 33.8 Kbps, but you'll get a choppy, grainy image. Even so, it's better than nothing, and you do get to see the face of your friend on the other end of the conversation.

Here are some tips that will help you get a stable, communications-friendly video image:

- If possible, put the light behind the camera and facing you. If the light is behind or above your head, your face won't be lit and the camera will get a shocking dose of illumination whenever you move your head enough to uncover the light. Side lighting is also better than back lighting.
- Plug your camera directly into the USB port on your computer instead of attaching it to a hub. It isn't supposed to make much of a difference, but it can.
- Sit in front of a solid, light-colored background so you stand out better.
- Don't move too much! If you watch the news, you'll notice that the newscasters stay stock still while they read their copy.
- Sit on the tails of your coat so the fabric doesn't bunch up around your shoulders. Lumpy shoulders look *really* bad on camera.

To add video images to your conversation, follow these steps:

1. Sign in to Windows Messenger using your .NET Passport, and start a conversation with someone on your Contacts list.
2. Click Start Camera to notify your contact that you want to exchange video images.
3. If you don't see the video, speakers, and microphone controls, choose Show Sidebar from the View menu.
4. When you're done sending video, click the Options down arrow and select Stop Sending Video. Your image will freeze, but your contact will still send you video. To end the conversation entirely, click Stop Talking.

Sending Files

One helpful aspect of Windows Messenger is its ability to send files directly to the person with whom you're conversing without having to get into your e-mail program, dig out the file, send the message, and then return to Windows Messenger. Whenever I'm discussing a writing project with a coauthor using Windows Messenger, I appreciate the ability to write an update, take a screen shot, or send the correct version of a file instead of the older version I sent the first time. I always put the Send A File feature to good use.

To send a file to someone with whom you are having a conversation in Windows Messenger, follow these steps:

1. In the Conversation dialog box, click Send A File Or Photo.
2. In the Send A File To dialog box, click the file you want to send and then click Open. A notice that you're attempting to send a file appears on your contact's screen, and he or she will have the opportunity to accept or reject the file.

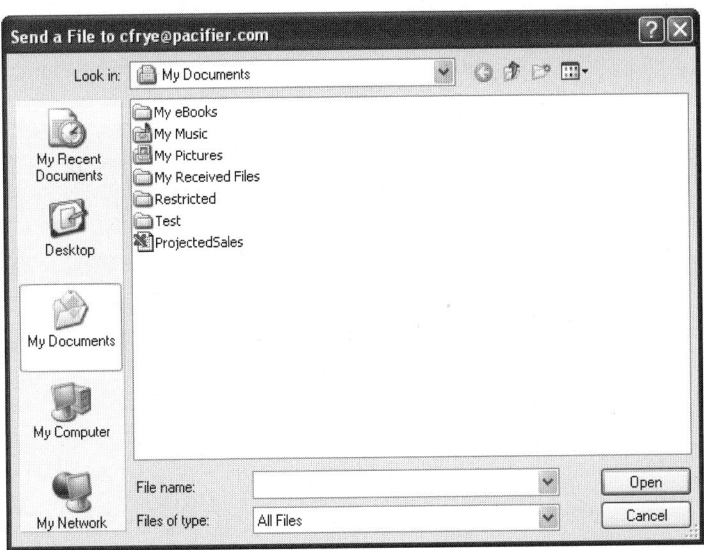

Note You can send a file to any contact by right-clicking his or her name, choosing Send A File Or Photo, selecting the file you want to send, and clicking Open.

Setting Up a Shared Whiteboard

When I worked in the Washington, D.C. area, I always enjoyed the design brainstorming sessions we had for the projects we worked on. Our meeting rooms always had erasable whiteboards on three walls and bulletin boards with enough thumb tacks to last until the end of time on the fourth wall. We never did get one of those fancy electronic whiteboards, which you could share over a network connection with colleagues around the world, but you can do something very similar in Windows Messenger.

Microsoft Paint, a freehand graphics program included with the Windows operating system, can also be made to function as a shared graphics program. If you want to collaborate on a design with some colleagues using Windows Messenger, you can fire up the whiteboard version of Microsoft Paint and get to work. When you're done, you can save your work to a file you can print, edit, and include in other documents.

Note You should make sure everyone who will work with you in Paint has his or her screen set to the same resolution. If you don't, the image will be distorted on the screens of participants with a different resolution than your computer.

To set up a shared whiteboard, follow these steps:

1. Start a Windows Messenger conversation with everyone with whom you want to share the whiteboard.
2. Click Invite and choose To Start Whiteboard. After your contacts click Accept, a Sharing Session window appears. In the bottom part of that window, you'll see the whiteboard application, which is a version of Microsoft Paint.

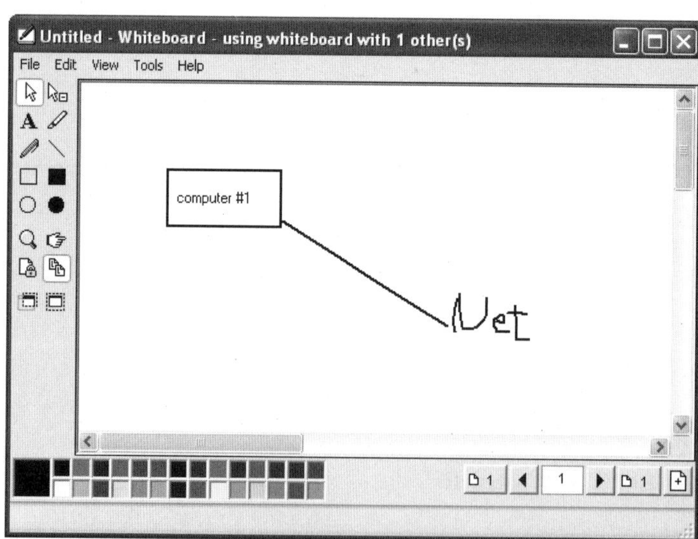

3 Use the tools in Microsoft Paint to create your document together, and choose Save from the File menu to save your work.

4 Click Close in the Sharing Session window to end your whiteboard session.

Letting Others Control a Program

Wouldn't it be neat if you could share programs other than Microsoft Paint using Windows Messenger? It would be, and it is. As long as you have an application installed on your computer, you can let other participants in a Windows Messenger conversation with you take a shot at controlling the program. They don't even need to have the program installed on their computer! You retain control over who gets to "steer," but if someone has an idea that's hard to explain in words, or if someone has been nominated to make a change, you can give that person control of any program.

Note I don't recommend sharing control of a program over anything less than a high-speed connection. There's a lot of data being passed to and fro, and people may just become frustrated because their screens take so long to be updated.

Displaying the Same Program on Everyone's Computer

The first step in collaborating within a program is to identify the program you want to share. It's actually a pretty straightforward process—you start a conversation, identify the program you want to share, and everyone agrees to display it on their screens.

Note The other participants in the conversation don't need to have the shared application installed on their computers.

To display the same program on everyone's computers, follow these steps:

1 Click the contact you want to share with, and then click Start Application Sharing in the I Want To panel. After your contact clicks Accept, he or she will see a Sharing Session window.

2 When everyone has chosen either to accept or reject the sharing invitation, the Sharing dialog box will appear on your computer. Select the program you want to share and click Share.

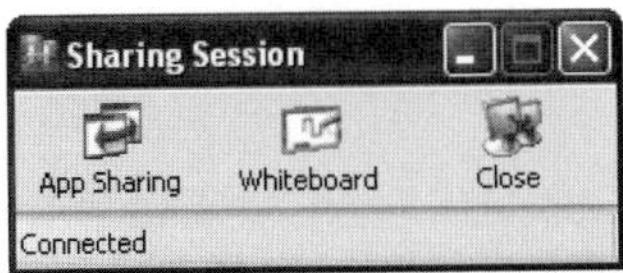

Letting Other Participants Control a Program on Your Computer

Once the shared program is running and everyone can see it, you can turn your colleagues loose and let them request control of the program. You, or the person controlling the computer on which the shared program is running, has the final say over who gets to sit in the driver's seat. You can allow anyone who wants control to take it immediately, determine on a case-by-case basis who will get to control the program, or take control yourself and not let go.

To let other participants control a program on your computer, follow these steps:

1. Invite your conversation participants to share an application, and click the application you want to share.
2. Click Allow Control to let other participants ask to control the application, which they can do by double-clicking the application window. When you see a request, click Accept to allow the transfer of control to take place, or click Reject to block it.

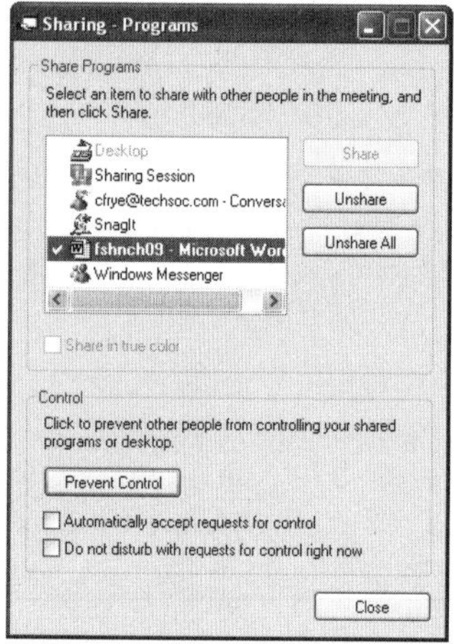

You can manage control transfer requests by doing any of the following:

- Select the Automatically Accept Requests For Control check box to let anyone take control at any time.
- Select the Do Not Disturb With Request For Control Right Now check box to reject any requests for control.
- Click the Prevent Control button to prevent any attempt to take control of the application.
- Click Close to close the application. Be sure to save your work first!

Making Windows Messenger Dance and Sing

Windows Messenger takes just a few minutes to set up, but you'll probably find yourself using it for hours on end. Since you've already paid for your Internet access, you can talk as much as you want at no additional charge. To close out this section, I've included instructions on how to set up Windows Messenger just the way you like it.

- To prevent someone on your Contacts list from participating in a conversation with you, right-click the contact and choose Block.
- To change how you are identified in Windows Messenger, click your name in the Contacts list and choose Personal Settings. Type your name as you would like it to appear in the My Display Name box.
- To temporarily block messages while giving the person attempting to contact you a reason why you aren't accepting messages, click your name from the Contacts list and choose one of the reasons listed. If you select Appear Offline, you will be listed as being offline, but you will still be able to see if anyone on your Contacts list is online. You won't, however, be able to send any messages until you change your status.

Note You will be marked as Away whenever your screen saver turns on.

- To prevent Windows Messenger from running whenever you start Windows, choose Options from the Tools menu, click the Preferences tab, and clear the Run This Program When Windows Starts check box.
- To control what information other Windows Messenger subscribers can see, choose Options from the Tools menu and use the controls in the Options dialog box to determine what others will be able to see.

See Also *You'll see how to get help over the Internet using Windows Messenger later in this chapter.*

More Backwards Compatibility: MSN Messenger

I mentioned earlier that Windows Messenger is available only with Windows XP, but that doesn't mean that folks with computers running Windows 98 SE or Windows Me are left out of the conversation. Not at all. Microsoft developed MSN Messenger, which lets the owners of older operating systems interact with

Windows Messenger users! When you fire up MSN Messenger, you sign in to the same service used by Windows Messenger owners. In fact, when you're online, you can't tell if someone is running MSN Messenger or Windows Messenger. MSN Messenger isn't as full-featured as Windows Messenger, but, cross my heart, it's still a great program.

Setting Up MSN Messenger

Windows Messenger comes with Windows XP, but you need to go to the Microsoft Web site to get your copy of MSN Messenger. Once you've found the program's home page, which is *http://messenger.microsoft.com* (that was easy), you can select the language in which you want the program documented and install it over the Internet. The program is about 1.5 megabytes (MB), so over a high-speed connection it will transfer to your computer in well under a minute. If you use a regular modem to connect to the Internet at 56 KBps or so, you'll need to set aside about 15 minutes to bring the program down to your computer. Once the installation program is ready to go, you'll be up and messaging in no time flat.

To download and set up MSN Messenger, follow these steps:

1. In Internet Explorer, type **http://messenger.microsoft.com** in the Address box and press Enter. Click the MSN Messenger link to move to the download page.

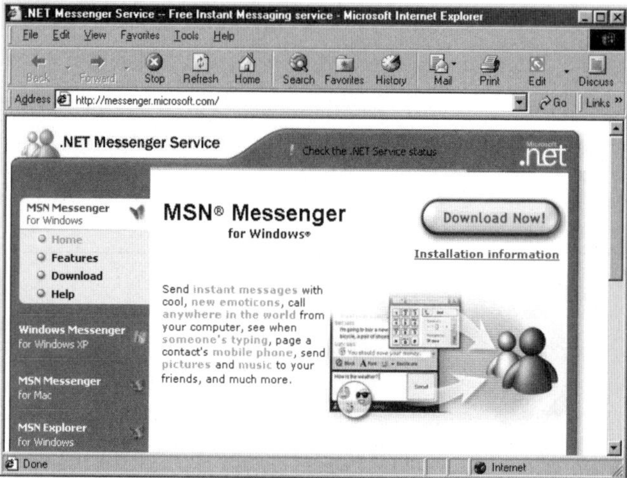

2. Click Download Now to begin installing MSN Messenger on your system. In the File Download dialog box, select the Run This Program From Its Current Location option button and click OK.

3 Click Yes twice to indicate you want to continue installing Messenger on your computer and to accept the End User Licensing Agreement. When you do, the installation program will install Messenger onto your computer.

4 Click the Click Here To Sign In link.

5 In the Sign In To .NET Messenger Service dialog box, type your user name in the Sign-In Name box, type your password in the Password box, and click OK.

Creating a Contacts List

After you're connected to the Messenger service, you can have MSN Messenger keep its electronic eyes out for your friends. When you add someone to your Contacts list, MSN Messenger lets you know if he or she is signed in to the system or not. And, if a contact signs on while you're on, a box will appear, indicating that your friend is online and available for chatting!

To add a contact to your Contacts list, follow these steps:

1 Start MSN Messenger and then, in the I Want To section of the program window, click Add A Contact.

2 Select the By E-Mail Address Or Sign-In Name option button and click Next.

3 Type the contact's e-mail address in the box and click Next.

Note If the person you want to contact doesn't have a .NET Passport, MSN Messenger will send the person an e-mail message describing the process for getting one.

---

4 Click Finish to close the wizard, or click Next to add another contact.

Initiating and Receiving Contacts

Starting a conversation with one of your friends is extremely straightforward—you tell MSN Messenger you want to send an instant message, and then identify the contact you want to send it to. "Sending an instant message" in MSN Messenger is the same as "starting a conversation" in Windows Messenger, so don't be confused if you use one or the other depending on which computer you use to sign in.

To initiate a contact with MSN Messenger, follow these steps:

1. Start MSN Messenger and click Send An Instant Message.
2. Click the contact to whom you want to send the instant message, and click OK.

What to Do Once You're in Contact

After you've started a conversation with one of your contacts, you can send your friend a file, run your e-mail program from within MSN Messenger to send the person an e-mail message, or change the typeface MSN Messenger uses to display the text of your conversation. Each of these capabilities makes it easier for you to interact with your friends and colleagues using the Messenger service.

Note As always, you should be sure that your virus-checking software knows to check every incoming file. You don't want to receive any virus-laden files from your contacts, and you would never forgive yourself if you accidentally spread a virus from your computer because you forgot to check what you were sending.

To interact more fully with your MSN Messenger contacts, start a conversation with a contact, and then follow any of these steps:

- Click the Send A File Or Photo link to display the Send A File dialog box. Select the file you want to send and click Open.
- Click the Send E-Mail link to run your default e-mail program. Your contact's e-mail address will be put on the To line for you.
- Click Font to open the Font dialog box. Click the type face and size you want MSN Messenger to use to display your text.

Note There is an older messaging service named Microsoft NetMeeting, but someone signed in to a NetMeeting server can't interact with someone using Windows Messenger or MSN Messenger. It's much better to have everyone use one of the Messenger programs to communicate, especially now that there is a Messenger program available for every current operating system.

Starting a Voice Conversation in MSN Messenger

Just as you can use Windows Messenger to speak with someone else who is running Windows Messenger, you can use MSN Messenger to speak with someone else running that program as well. All you need to do is start a conversation with one of your contacts and then add your voice to the equation.

Note The big limitation on using MSN Messenger to establish a voice conversation is that you can converse only with other MSN Messenger subscribers. It would be nice if you could reach out with your voice to Windows Messenger users, but you'll need to let your fingers do the talking.

To start a voice conversation in MSN Messenger, follow these steps:

1. Initiate a conversation with a contact, and choose Start Talking from the Actions menu.

   Note The first time you try to initiate a voice conversation with another contact, MSN Messenger will run the Audio Tuning Wizard to calibrate your microphone and speakers. If your system gets out of balance later, you can always run the wizard again by choosing Audio Tuning Wizard from the View menu.

2. After your contact accepts the voice conversation, you can begin talking. When you're done, close the Conversation window.

Getting Help in Windows XP Through Remote Assistance

Knowing a bit about computers is a great thing for cementing friendships. Yep, barely a week goes by when one of my friends doesn't call me up and ask me how to do something or other in Microsoft Windows or one of the Microsoft Office programs. Most of the time I can help them out—no problem. I mean, I know Excel and Word backward and forward; and without even looking at a computer screen I can walk my friends through pretty much anything. Plenty of times, however, I have no idea what they're talking about, whether it's because they are using a program I'm not familiar with, are attempting to use a feature for the first time and don't have the vocabulary to describe what they see, or it's late at night, their project is due in the morning, and they're in desperate need of a gallon of coffee. Remote Assistance would do the trick even better, however.

Important Remote Assistance is available only if both parties are using Windows XP.

Asking for (and Getting) Remote Assistance

Sometimes you need to see what's on a person's computer screen to help him or her work through a problem. That's where the Windows XP Remote Assistance technology really comes in handy. With Remote Assistance, the person trying desperately to help you do your work can see exactly what's on your screen and guide you by phone or in the built-in Chat window.

To set up a Remote Assistance session, follow these steps:

1. In Windows Messenger, right-click the name of the contact in your Contacts List, and select Ask For Remote Assistance. Windows Messenger will send an invitation to your contact that indicates you want to start a Remote Assistance session.
2. After your contact accepts the invitation, a message box appears indicating he or she is willing to start Remote Assistance. Click Yes to establish the Remote Assistance connection. You'll see a window as shown in Figure 9-3.

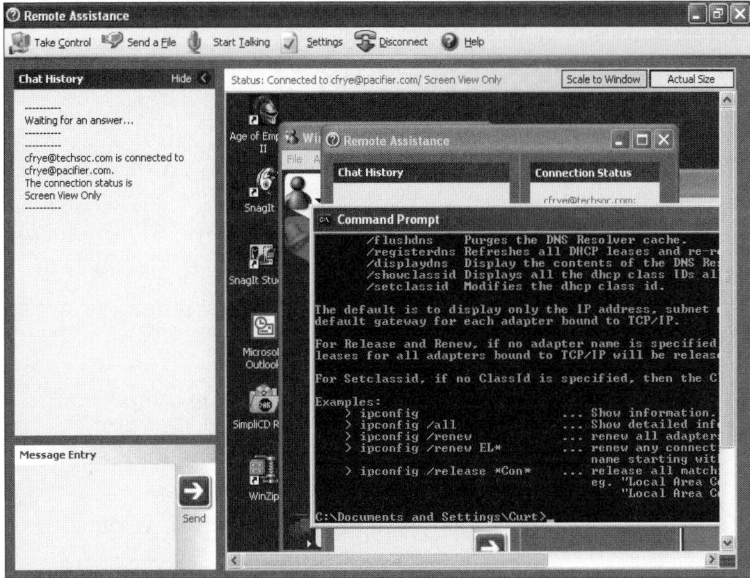

Figure 9-3 When you establish your Remote Assistance connection, you'll see a window indicating the connection has been created.

3 A Remote Assistance dialog box that's similar to yours appears on your contact's screen, but that dialog box contains an image of your screen. Now, whenever you do something (open a file, change folders in My Computer, or whatever), your contact will see it. There's also a Chat window at the left of the Remote Assistance dialog box, which you can either use or close if you're not sending messages.

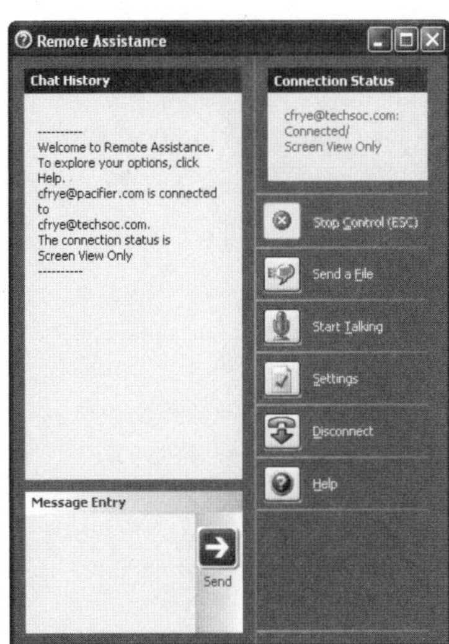

4 Click Disconnect to end the Remote Assistance session.

Letting Your Assistant Control Your Computer

I can't count the number of times I've asked, "Can I drive?" In the context of computer assistance, that usually means I wanted to sit in the comfy chair and control the mouse and keyboard. With Remote Assistance, you can use your mouse and keyboard to share control of the computer of the friend you're helping. He or she can revoke the privilege at any time, though, so play nice.

To let a contact share control of your computer during a Remote Assistance session, follow these steps:

1 Begin a Remote Assistance session using Windows Messenger and have your contact click the Take Control button at the top left corner of the window.

2 In the message box that appears, click Yes to allow your contact to control your computer.

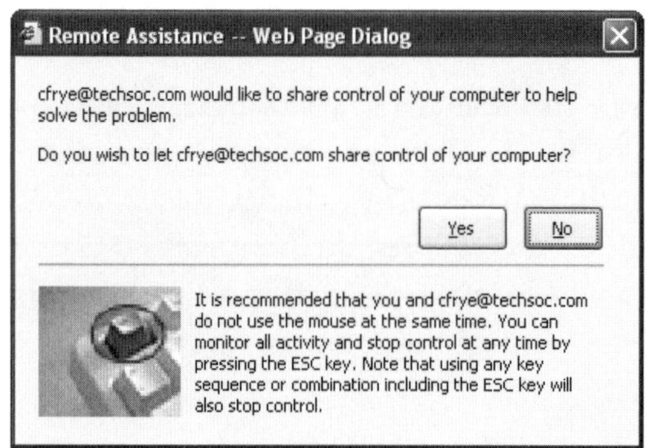

3 Click Stop Control to end your contact's control over your computer.

Note Pressing the Esc key, even if you do it to execute a command, will also end your contact's control over your computer.

---

4 When you're done, click Disconnect to end the Remote Assistance session.

Note The Remote Assistance window has most of the same tools available in Windows Messenger, so you don't have to open another program to communicate with the person you're assisting.

Key Points

- Instant messaging on the .NET Messenger service is a terrific way to use your computer network to have a real-time conversation with up to four friends and colleagues.
- You need a .NET Passport to use the .NET Messenger service, but getting a .NET Passport benefits you beyond simply letting you send instant messages.
- You can add contacts to your Contacts list by putting in their e-mail address, or you can search for their information in the .NET Messenger service database.
- If you want to block someone from contacting you, you can do so quickly.
- If you and your contact use Windows Messenger, you can communicate using text, voice, and video. If you both have MSN Messenger, you can communicate using text or voice. If you use different programs, you can still communicate over the .NET Messenger service by sending instant messages.
- Sharing an application and sending video are tasks you should normally perform only if everyone involved has a high-speed Internet connection.
- Remote Assistance lets the person who's trying to help you see exactly what sort of predicament you're in so they can do something about it.

Chapter 10

It's Playtime! Entertainment in a Networked Environment

I'm a big fan of computer games, whether I'm playing a Swords and Sorcery game with friends from across the country or whiling away a few minutes playing solitaire or Minesweeper on my computer. Games are interesting because they push the envelope regarding what you can make a computer do. Sure, the biggest, newest, and fastest computers can take whatever game designers throw at them, but a lot of ingenuity goes into writing games you can play on any reasonably new computer that you didn't spend two months of salary to buy. And, of course, the games need to be fun.

What's great about playing games over a home network is, once again, flexibility. If you're in the den and want to visit the MSN Zone for a quick game of chess, you can install the program (it takes practically no time at all) on your computer and log on for some fun. With all the free games available at the MSN Zone and other places online, you can have lots of fun without buying games from the store. You can also play games against other folks over your home network, whether the game is hosted by a server, such as the MSN Zone, or is an online role-playing game, such as Microsoft Asheron's Call, or is played over a connection between two computers on your home network. If you're a hardcore gamer, you can also set up your home network so that everyone on the network plays against each other.

If you're more of a conversational type and don't have any specific contacts with whom you can converse on a regular basis, you can try chat rooms or newsgroups to scratch that talkative itch.

My job in this chapter is to show you how to install games on your computer, to tweak a game's settings so it will run well on your computer, to troubleshoot your game and your computer, and to use your Microsoft Xbox gaming console to play games over a broadband Internet connection. I'll also show you how to get into online chat rooms and how to read newsgroup messages.

Installing and Running a Game

Adding a game to your computer is just like adding any other type of program. You choose where you want the program to reside on your hard disk, you choose how much or how little of the program you want to copy to the hard disk and how much you want to run from the CD, and you step through the installation sequence. Once the game is installed, and you've restarted your computer if necessary, you can run the game like any other program. One difference between many games and other programs you'll run, however, is that the game will most likely have an introductory animation that summarizes the game's back story and motivates your play.

Note When you install a game from a CD-ROM, most of the time you'll be able to follow something approximating the following steps to get everything going. You should familiarize yourself with the process using this example, which is based on Microsoft Age of Empires II, but be sure to follow the instructions that came with your game.

To install a game, follow these steps:

1. Insert the game's CD-ROM installation disk into your CD-ROM drive, display the contents of the drive in My Computer, and double-click the setup program (it will probably be named Setup).

Note Many game installation disks have an AutoRun file on them, meaning the setup program will run as soon as your computer recognizes the disk.

2 For a Microsoft game, write down your Product ID number so you can get technical support and upgrades to your game, and then click Next.

3 The installation program will usually suggest a directory where it will install the program. If you want, you can choose to change that directory, but there should be no reason to do so. Take aim; click Continue.

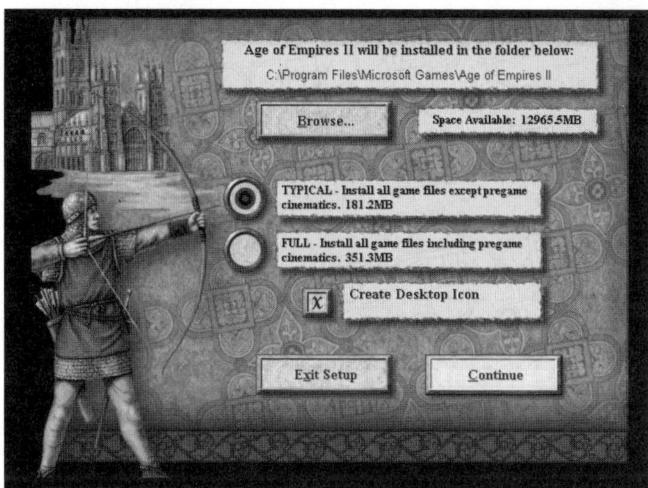

4 If you have sufficient space on your hard disk to install the entire game there, and you are given the option in the installation procedure, do so. (In the case of Microsoft Age of Empires II, you can choose to install everything, or everything except the cinematic sequences at the start of the game.) Click Next to install the game, and then restart your computer.

5 Click I Accept to accept the End User License Agreement.

Note Again, familiarize yourself with the process using this example, which is based on Age of Empires II, but be sure to follow the instructions that came with your game.

To play a game against other online opponents, follow these steps:

1 Run the game, and click MSN Zone (in this case) to play against other human opponents.

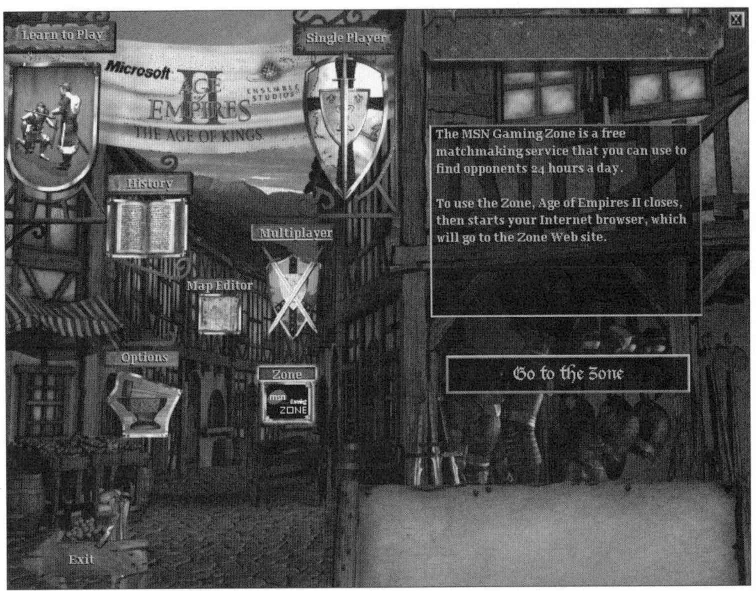

Note You could click Multiplayer if you wanted to play against computer opponents.

---

2 Click the "room" that reflects the skill level you want to join, and sign in with your .NET Passport.

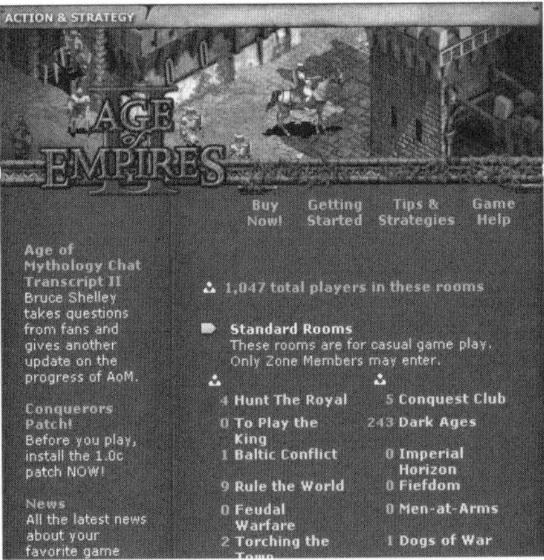

3 Click Join to sign up for a game.

Note The animation you see when you start a game is great to watch once or twice, but after that you'll most likely lose interest. You can usually skip a section of a pre-game, introductory sequence by pressing the spacebar.

Games You Can Play for Free

If you're on a limited budget, and I know I once was, you're probably spending a significant part of your disposable income on your computer equipment and the best Internet connection you can afford. And, no matter how good you get at Minesweeper or Solitaire, you'll know there are better games out there. Without a doubt, there are, and you can play them for free in the Microsoft MSN Gaming Zone.

Note The appearance of the MSN Gaming Zone site might change over time. If these steps are not exactly what you see when you visit the site, look on the navigation bar for links to free games.

To visit the MSN Gaming Zone free games area, follow these steps:

1 Go to *http://www.microsoft.com/games/*.

2 Select Free Games, and click Go.

Note If you're looking for games that are appropriate for younger children, click the Zone Kids link in the navigation pane at the left of the Zone home page, or visit *http://zone.msn.com/hub_kids.asp*.

3. Click the name of the game category you want to view, and then click the name of the game you want to play.

> **Note** Checkers is a good game for learning how to play multiplayer games over the Internet.

4. Some games use a system of "rooms," which in turn are divided into categories depending on how competitive you want to be. Click the room you want to enter, and then click OK.
5. Follow the directions in the installation wizard, if there is one. (Some games you can just start playing in your Web browser.) If you want to add a shortcut to the MSN Gaming Zone to your desktop, click Yes when that message box appears.
6. Click Tutorial to move through an introduction to the MSN Gaming Zone.

> **Note** The tutorial will answer most of your questions about the games and will teach you about the standard procedures used.

7. Click Return to go back to the game room you selected and start playing!

> **Note** Some free games do require you to download additional software or to have a .NET Passport.

Troubleshooting Games

Game programmers want to get every bit of performance they can out of your system so their game looks and plays just that much better than the competition's. They'll implement shortcuts that depend on your having specific types of hardware installed on your computer, ask your video card to keep up with more calculations per second than you or I could do in a lifetime, and try to keep everything on a single CD-ROM, if possible. Well, actually, the days of the single CD-ROM game might well be past us, but we can hope. At any rate, if the game you can't live without playing is asking too much of your computer, there are a number of things you can do to get up and running.

Update DirectX

You might have wondered whether the programmers who write games for your PC have to write every bit of their program from scratch, including device drivers for every possible monitor, sound card, and game controller a gamer might use. Fortunately, they don't. After all, making the basic elements of games work on computers running any operating system from Microsoft Windows 98 to Microsoft Windows XP is a tough enough job without having to write routines to make the monitor, sound cards, and game controllers behave themselves.

One way Microsoft makes it easier for programmers to control video and sound devices running on Windows computers is through Microsoft DirectX. At the core of DirectX are its application programming interfaces (APIs), which act as a kind of bridge for the hardware and the software to "talk" to each other. Because the DirectX APIs take away a lot of the programming work, the game programmers can concentrate on creating better graphics and immersing music and audio effects. You might even find that some of your games run better after you download and install a new version of DirectX—the new software might include instructions that let your video or sound cards operate more efficiently.

Note The programming work to develop a DirectX API for each hardware component has to be done by someone, of course, but the majority of that work is done by the hardware manufacturers. Because manufacturers know their products best, they are in the best position to write APIs that conform to the DirectX standard.

Almost every game is shipped with the lowest version of DirectX the game needs to run, but if you have a later version of DirectX on your computer, whether you installed a game that used that later version or downloaded the software from the DirectX Web site, you shouldn't have any trouble running any of your games. (It's the magic of backward compatibility at work again.)

Because there are so many games and hardware devices out there, however, there is the possibility that you might find that one of your games doesn't work with the newest version of DirectX. If you do have trouble running one of your games after you update your operating system to include the most recent edition of DirectX, you can usually solve the problem by visiting the Web sites of the game's publisher and your hardware manufacturers to download a *patch* that fixes the problem.

Lingo A patch is a software program written to correct a flaw in or extend the capability of another program, such as a game.

To download the most recent version of DirectX, follow these steps:

1. Save all your work, quit any programs you are running, and then go to *http://microsoft.com/windows/directx/downloads/*.
2. Click the link provided to select the most recent version of DirectX available for your operating system.

> **Note** Windows XP comes with DirectX 8.1 installed.

3. In the area representing the operating system running on your computer, click the Select Language down arrow, and select the language of the DirectX package you want to download. Click Go.

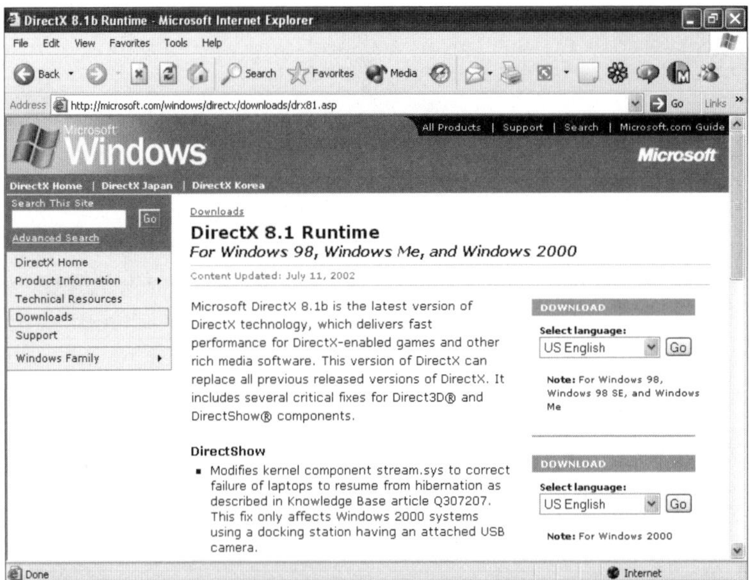

4. Click the link representing the DirectX installation file and then, in the dialog box that appears, click Open. Once you've installed the new version of DirectX, reboot your computer when asked to do so.

Install Game Patches

When you think about all the combinations of video cards, sound cards, operating systems, game controllers, and hard disks you can have in a single computer, the number of systems game programmers have to consider when writing a game is astonishing. While there's no way they can test to be sure their programs works under every possible computer configuration, game developers do their best to ensure their programs will run flawlessly for you. If any bugs do crop up, however, the game's publisher will put aside employee vacations until it can issue a patch to fix the problem.

Note Game publishers will also issue patches to enhance a game, not just to fix a problem. Some patches can be issued to add multiplayer capability to a game, to add new levels or character classes to a role-playing game, or to improve the performance of the game's artificial intelligence engine (the "mind" behind the computer opponent you love to play against).

To download a patch for a game from Microsoft Game Studios, follow these steps:

1 Save your work, quit all the programs you have running, and go to *http://www.microsoft.com/games/PC/*.

2 Click the link representing the game you want to update.

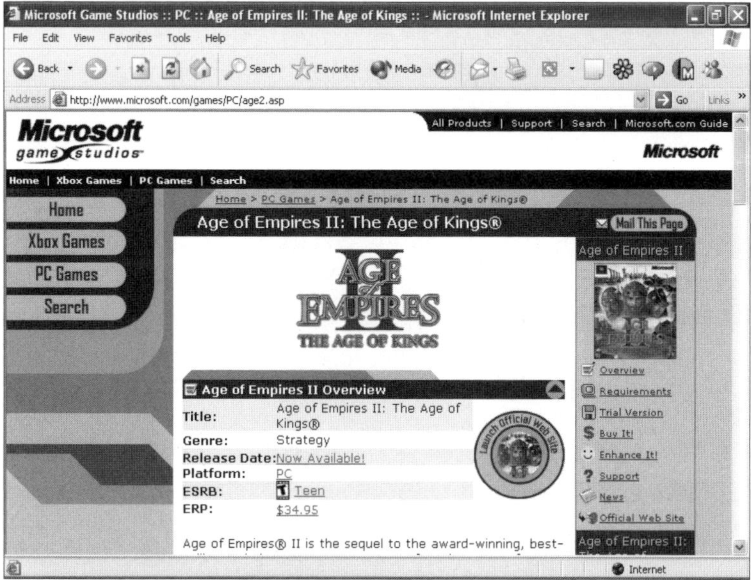

3 Click the Support link to display the technical updates available for the game and then, if necessary, click the link representing the language you want for the patch.

4 Click Open. Follow the directions in the program and, if prompted to do so, reboot your computer.

Note Microsoft Game Studios and many other game publishers make trial version of their games available for you to try before you buy the game. For games published by Microsoft Game Studios, there might be a Trial Version link on the game's home Web page. You may also find a movie that shows the game's artwork and demonstrates game play. Be prepared, though—trial programs and previews are often large (that is, the files are usually more than 10 megabytes [MB]) and will take a while to download if you don't have a high-speed connection.

Update All Device Drivers

Whenever I install a new game on my computer, I always check the Web sites of the game publisher and the manufacturers of my video card, sound card, and game controllers to see if there are any issues I need to know about. Game publishers are usually pretty good about getting in touch with hardware manufacturers when the publisher's quality assurance testers have been running into problems playing the game on computers with the manufacturer's devices. The hardware manufacturers are also very interested in ensuring their stuff works with every game out there, so they have plenty of incentive to work with the publishers to get things right.

Note For a hardware company, there's little worse than getting a reputation in the computer gaming industry as an outfit that puts out hardware that won't run the most popular games.

If you aren't able to find the driver you need by going to the hardware manufacturer's Web site (maybe the drivers aren't there or you can't figure out how to find them), you can always visit a "one-stop shopping" site with drivers for all kinds of hardware. While there are a bunch of sites out there, Microsoft TechNet lists these sites as good places to look:

- Drivers Planet, at *http://www.driversplanet.com/*
- Driver Zone, at *http://www.driverzone.com/*
- Driver Guide, at *http://www.driverguide.com/* (you do need to register to use this site)
- Help Drivers, at *http://www.helpdrivers.com/* (this site offers drivers in English, French, German, and Spanish)
- Windows Driver Search Center, at *http://www.windrivers.com/*

The driver file will usually come with instructions on how to install it, either on the Web page on which you found the driver or in a text file (often named Readme) included with the driver.

Note You can browse or search the support articles available on TechNet by visiting *http://www.microsoft.com/technet/*.

If you are running Windows XP, you can also check for updated device drivers by visiting the Microsoft Windows Catalog site. The Windows Catalog is a collection of device drivers that have been tested by Microsoft and are known to work with Windows XP.

To search for drivers for your hardware devices using the Windows Catalog, follow these steps:

1 Save your work, quit all the programs you are running, and go to *http://v4.windowsupdate.microsoft.com/catalog*.

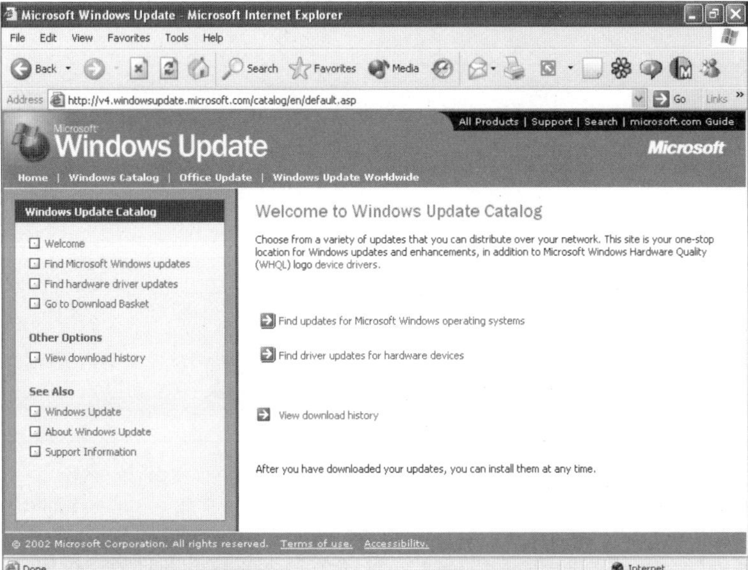

2 Click Find Driver Updates For Hardware Devices.

3 Select the appropriate hardware category from the Hardware Drivers section for the driver update that you want to download.

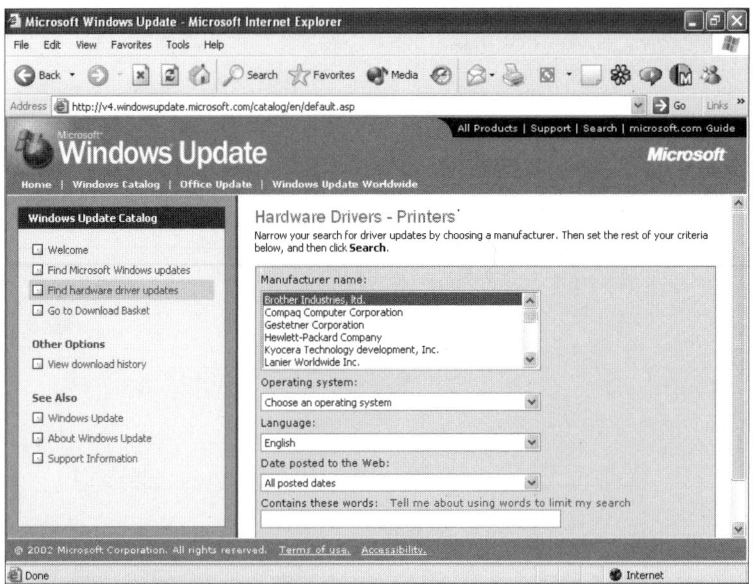

4 Select the manufacturer name, the operating system, the language, and any other items that you want to search for, and then click Search.

5 Select the driver that you want, and then click Add.

6 Click Go.

7 Click Browse to locate the folder in which you want to save the driver, and then click Download Now.

Note Keep in mind that some drivers available on manufacturer Web sites might not have passed Microsoft compatibility testing and could harm your machine, while those in the Windows Catalog are fully certified and safe. Microsoft's Designed for Microsoft Windows XP program addresses this problem; I recommend using hardware products that display the Designed for Microsoft Windows XP logo on the external packaging and on the device itself. If you try to install a driver that has not been approved for use with Windows XP, you will see a warning message asking if you want to continue with the installation. If you do, installing the device driver might not work (annoying) or might cause your computer to malfunction (*very* annoying).

Figuring Out What Hardware You're Running If you've lost the documentation that came with your computer when you bought it, or if you got the computer secondhand and you're not sure what kind of video or sound cards are in there, you can often follow these steps to determine what hardware you have in your computer.

To determine what hardware you're running in Microsoft Windows XP, follow the steps below.

Note If you follow these steps and a question mark appears beside the hardware you have installed, that means Windows wasn't able to figure out what manufacturer made the component you're investigating. If that's the case, you'll need to open the case and eyeball the component yourself. Remember to wear your antistatic wrist strap!

1. Click Start, and then choose Control Panel.
2. In Category view, click Performance And Maintenance and then click System.
3. In the System Properties dialog box, click the Hardware tab and then click Device Manager.

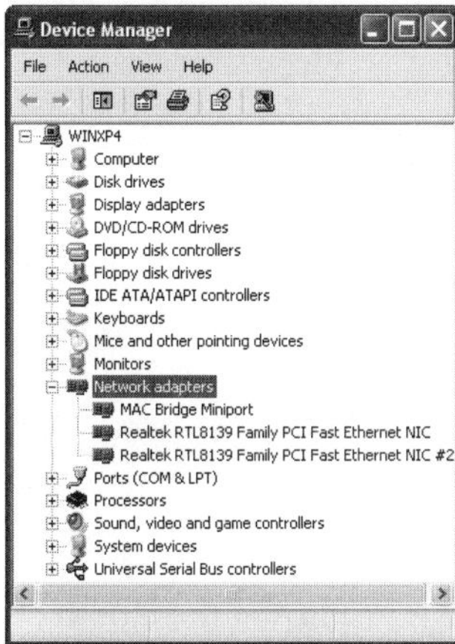

4. Click the Expand control (it looks like a plus sign) next to the category with the device you're investigating. I've chosen to expand the Network Adapters category.
5. Click the device you want to investigate, and then click the Properties toolbar button.
6. Use the information on the General tab of the Properties dialog box to search for an updated driver for the device.

To determine what hardware you're running in Microsoft Windows 98 Second Edition (SE) or Microsoft Windows Millennium Edition (Me), follow these steps:

1. Click Start, choose Settings, and then choose Control Panel.

2 In Control Panel, double-click System. In the System Properties dialog box, click the Device Manager tab.

3 Click the Expand control (it looks like a plus sign) next to the category with the device you're investigating. Click the device you want to investigate, and then click the Properties toolbar button.

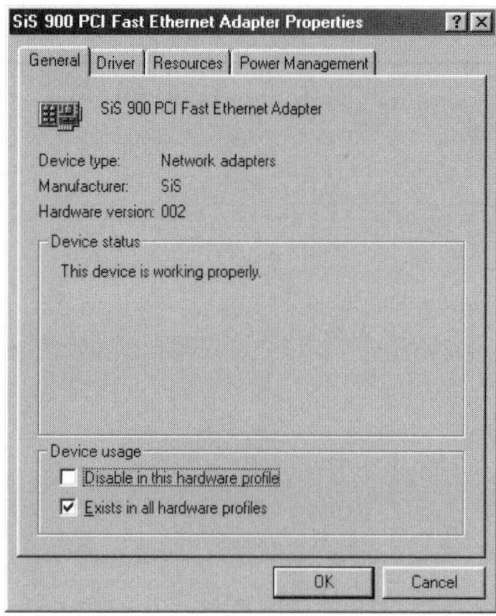

4 Use the information on the General tab of the Properties dialog box to search for an updated driver for the device. Click Cancel to close the System Properties dialog box.

Make Your Games Run More Smoothly

If you're having trouble running your game even after you've installed all the correct device drivers, you might be the victim of a slow CD-ROM drive. In many cases your computer will be able to load the data it needs into your computer's RAM or onto your hard disk before it actually needs it for something that happens in the game, but if your CD-ROM drive is a little older than the rest of your computer, you might need to install the entire game (or as much of it as you can) onto your hard disk.

Most of the time you can improve your computer's performance when it runs any program, not just a game, by purchasing more RAM. A RAM chip is a bit of hardware that acts like a super-fast disk drive, storing recently used files and programs. Have you noticed that when you run a program, close it, and open it right back up, the program starts much faster the second time? That's because the computer wrote the program into its RAM and was able to call it up from memory instead of reading it off of the disk drive.

Note Most games will have the minimum and recommended processor speed, RAM amount, and operating system requirements printed on the bottom or side of the box. The recommended equipment is usually enough to run the game without a hitch, but I've found that for newer games, the RAM recommendations are a little low. In other words, if the game's publisher recommends you have 256 MB of RAM, you might consider going up to 384 MB or 512 MB to be safe. As inexpensive as RAM is these days, it's a worthwhile investment in any case.

Change Your Game's Appearance

If you've upgraded your computer by adding more RAM but you're still not getting the level of game play you'd like, you can usually change some of the game's settings to make the game less processor- and memory-intensive. The downside of simplifying the game's appearance is that it's not as visually and audibly sharp as it might be, but you'll have fewer interruptions while you're playing the game. And that's what matters, right?

Some of the game settings you can change to improve your game's performance include the following:

- Frame rates
- Resolution
- Color depth
- Shadows

Changing the Frame Rate

A game's *frame rate* represents the number of different times your screen is redrawn in a second. The term comes from the movie industry, where the illusion of motion is created by running a strip of film through a projector at a particular rate. Most feature films are displayed at a rate of 24 frames per second, for example. On a computer, and on the new digital projectors you'll find in newer cinemas, you can adjust the frame rate to match the needs of your hardware. It's no fun to play a game that looks great but runs for only a few seconds before it has to read more video from memory or that moves so slowly that you have plenty of time to see the goblin draw its sword, run toward you, and wind up in super slow motion as if it were the climactic battle scene of a feature film. Sure, that sort of thing works great if it's the last scene of a movie, but that's no way to go through an entire game.

Lingo A game's frame rate is the number of times per second the screen is refreshed.

Of course, when you're in a movie theater that can afford digital projection equipment, you can be sure the equipment will be up to projecting however many frames per second the film's creators demand they project. If you try to run the newest, hardware-busting game on your two-year-old computer, you might have some trouble getting everything to be displayed correctly. If you change the frame rate so your screen is updated fewer times per second, you'll get a slightly less "realistic" image on your monitor, but the game can be played more smoothly.

Changing Resolution

Another setting you can change to improve a game's performance is the *resolution* at which the game is rendered. Actually, there are two ways you can change the resolution at which a game is presented. The first change to a games "resolution" you can make is in the number of polygons the computer uses to represent the objects on your screen.

Lingo A game's resolution is the number of polygons used to draw an object on the screen.

You see, most of the images you see on your screen during actual game play aren't drawn by hand and animated the same way they would be in a cartoon. Instead, the characters and objects on your screen are built from literally thousands of triangles, each one shaped and colored according to rules developed for that individual character. As a character or object moves, the program ascertains how you or your character within the game would see an object and redraws it accordingly. If you reduce the number of polygons used to draw each character or limit the total number of polygons used on screen at one time, you can improve your game's performance.

Note I bet now you're starting to get an idea as to why frame rate is so important. In a game with a lot of monsters or objects, calculating and redrawing everything on the screen soaks up a lot of your computer's memory and processing power.

Another way you can improve your game's performance is to change your screen resolution in terms of the number of *pixels* (colored dots) displayed on your screen. Many older monitors are set to a resolution of 800 × 600 pixels, but most newer monitors are meant to run at a resolution of 1024 × 768 pixels. Large monitors can easily display legible (and quite beautiful) images at resolutions of

1280 × 1024 pixels or higher, but if your monitor is 19 inches in diagonal or less, you should consider sticking with either of the two lower resolution settings unless you have eyes like an eagle.

Lingo A pixel is a colored dot used to create images on a monitor, television, or other display device.

In any case, if your game is running slowly or there are strange video artifacts on your screen (characters in two pieces, for example), you should try reducing your screen resolution. If that doesn't work, you may need to update your video card drivers or replace your video card (which may be overheating or failing in some other way) to fix the problem.

Note Many games have a minimum screen resolution at which the game will run. Most of the time you'll find the minimum resolution on the box right next to the minimum and recommended hardware configuration to run the game.

To change your computer's screen resolution in Windows XP, follow these steps:

1. Click Start, and choose Control Panel.
2. Click Appearance And Themes, and then click the Change The Screen Resolution.

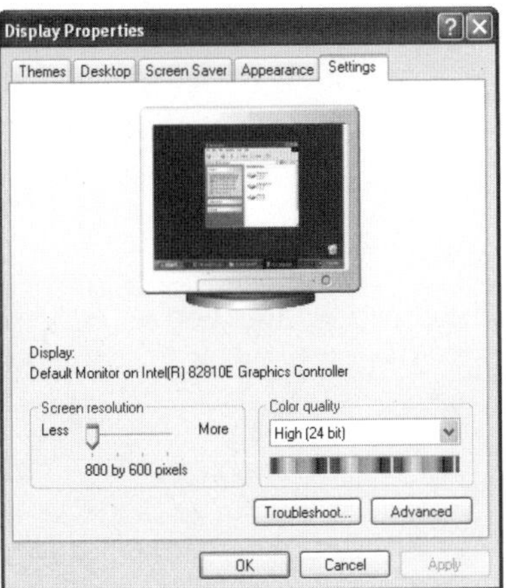

3. Drag the Screen Resolution slider to the setting you want for your monitor, and then click OK.

4. If you want to keep your settings, click Yes in the message box that appears. If you don't want to keep the settings, you can either let the 15-second timer run out or click No.

To change your computer's screen resolution in Windows Me or Windows 98 SE, follow these steps:

1. Click Start, choose Settings, and then choose Control Panel.
2. Double-click Display and then, in the Display Properties dialog box, click the Settings tab.
3. Drag the Screen Area slider to the resolution you want for your monitor, and click OK twice.
4. If you want to keep your settings, click Yes in the message box that appears. If you don't want to keep the settings, you can either let the 15-second timer run out or click No.

Changing Your Monitor's Color Depth

Part of what makes a game so attractive to its players is the range of colors used to depict the characters and objects on the screen. Of course, when you have your monitor set to use millions of colors, you're asking your computer's graphics card to make a lot of decisions about how to draw the game on the screen. You can usually reduce the number of colors used in the game from somewhere in the game's setup feature, but you can also change the number of colors displayed on your monitor to see if that affects your game's performance. It may be that the game's settings take precedence, but it's good to try it anyway.

To change the number of colors displayed on your monitor in Windows XP, follow these steps:

1. Click Start, and then choose Control Panel.
2. Click Appearance And Themes, and then click Change The Screen Resolution.
3. Click the Color Quality down arrow, select the setting you want for your monitor, and click OK.
4. If you want to keep your settings, click Yes in the message box that appears. If you don't want to keep the settings, you can either let the 15-second timer run out or click No.

To change the number of colors displayed on your monitor in Windows Me or Windows 98 SE, follow these steps:

1. Click Start, choose Settings, and then choose Control Panel.
2. Double-click Display, and then, in the Display Properties dialog box, click the Settings tab.

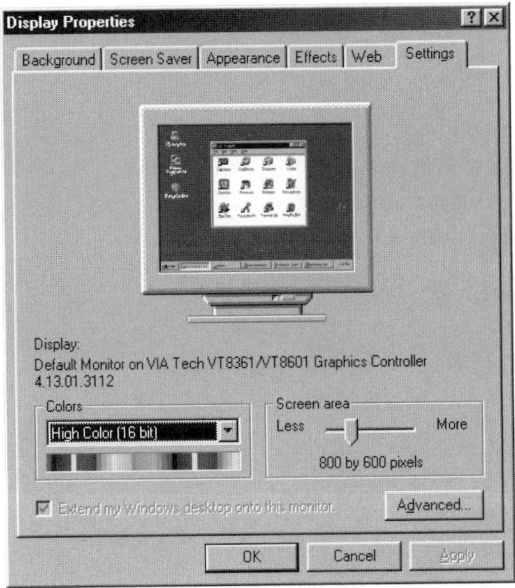

3. Click the Colors down arrow, select the color depth you want for your monitor, and click OK.
4. If you want to keep your settings, click Yes in the message box that appears. If you don't want to keep the settings, you can either let the 15-second timer run out or click No.

Running Games in 256-Color Mode

Some games are so graphics-intensive, or, paradoxically, so old, that the programmers limit you to running the game with only 256 possible colors for each pixel. While any games that need to run in 256-color mode should be programmed to change your monitor's color depth when you run them, the change routine might not work for your monitor. If that's the case, in Windows XP you can change the program's properties so the operating system knows to make the change whenever you run the game and to change back to your previous color setting when the game stops running. (This option doesn't exist in Windows Me or Windows 98 SE.)

Note The Compatibility tab is available only for programs or games located on your computer's hard disk. If you run the game from a floppy disk, CD-ROM, or over a network, you can't change the game's color mode.

To set a game to run in 256-color mode in Windows XP, follow these steps:

1. In My Computer, navigate to the directory with the program's icon, right-click the game or other program that you want to run in 256 colors, and then click Properties.
2. Click the Compatibility tab.

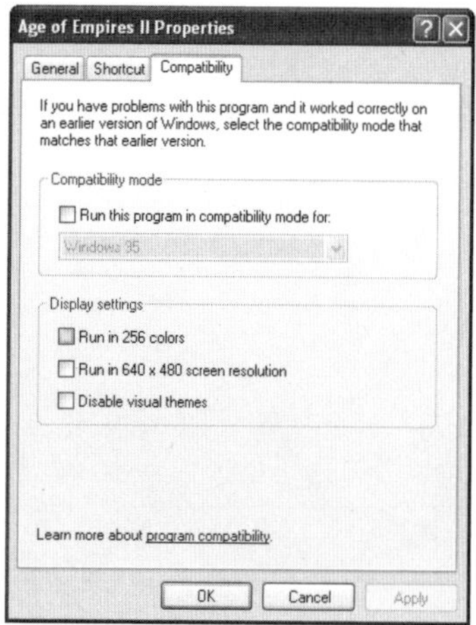

3. Select the Run In 256 Colors check box, and click OK.

Note The two other check boxes on the Compatibility tab let you change the behavior of your game in other ways. If your game appears in a small window in the middle of the screen, for example, you can make that window larger by selecting the Run In 640×480 Screen Resolution check box. Selecting the Disable Visual Themes check box, on the other hand, will often allow an older game to draw its window on the screen correctly.

Adding or Eliminating Shadows

When you play a lot of computer games, you develop a bit of a refined palate for what makes a game enjoyable. While game play is still the most important element in most players' minds, there should be some eye candy on the screen to keep your attention as well. Well-developed characters are one way to get a gamer's attention, but another way to make a game more attractive than its competitors is to handle shadows well. It's kind of a geek thing, but when you're trying to attract a sophisticated audience, shadows are important to get right in a game because shadows are hard to do well.

Think about it: You're depicting a room with the standard four walls, two of which have some torches on them and another that has a sizable fireplace. That's three separate light sources to contend with when you're drawing the shadows for the characters and objects on the screen! Sure, developers could just use the strongest light source as the source of your shadows (a trick many early game programmers used), but pride of workmanship argues against that approach these days. So, if your game is running slower than you'd like, or if the game programmers botched the job and the shadows make the game uglier, you can always turn off shadows until you are in a position to run the game on a more powerful computer. The steps you follow to turn off shadows will vary from game to game, but the Setup or Options item on your game's main menu is always a good place to look.

Why Is There an Ethernet Port on the Back of My Xbox?

You should have heard the groan when I told my editor that I'd bought an Xbox. I'm sure Jenny, my Microsoft Press editor, thought there was no way I'd ever get everything in on time with a high-caliber game machine in my entertainment center, but I've been pretty good so far.

Note At the defense contractor I worked for in McLean, Virginia, it was okay to have games on your computer, but your high scores couldn't be very good.

As much fun as it is, the Xbox became a lot more fun when the Ethernet port on the back of the Xbox came into play. You can probably guess what it's there for, but I'll tell you anyway: If you have a high-speed Internet connection, you'll be able to go head-to-head against Xbox game players from all over the world, not just the friends who come over to your place and eat all of your snacks. The network is called Xbox Live, and you can get more information about it by visiting the Xbox Live Web site at *http://www.xbox.com/LIVE/*.

Talk a Lot, Talk a Little More: Chat Rooms

In Chapter 9, "Communicating Across Your Network," I told you all about the .NET Messenger service, which lets you exchange instant messages, share applications, and even provide remote assistance if you and a friend are both running Windows XP. One limitation of the .NET Messenger service, however, is that you can have a maximum of only four other folks in your chat with you. In most cases that's more than enough, but if you have a lot of friends who are scattered around the globe, you might want to get a room with a few more chairs, figuratively speaking. Alternatively, you might want to go online and discuss a favorite topic (sports, astronomy, astrology, travel, and so on) with whomever's there. You can do all those things in a *chat room* on the MSN Chat Service.

Lingo A chat room is an online space where many users can participate in an ongoing conversation about a particular topic.

Chat Rooms: Subject Matter and Language Considerations Earlier in this book I told you that at times the Internet can be very much akin to the Wild West, where the law wasn't established and folks did more or less as they pleased. In the case of chat rooms, which have been around since the 1970s on private bulletin board systems, many users feel free to exercise their right to free speech by discussing topics and using language that not everyone will be comfortable with. It's a fact of the Internet (well, at least on chat services where the rooms aren't moderated by human operators who watch out for unacceptable behavior) that you may run into topics of conversation or language that makes you uncomfortable, or that you don't feel is appropriate for your children.

I don't have kids, so I won't pretend to tell you what to do regarding chat rooms, but I do feel it's okay for me to ask you to pay careful attention to the subject matter of the chat rooms available to you and your family and to impose whatever restrictions you feel appropriate.

Chatting It Up in Windows Messenger

If you have Windows XP installed on your computer, you're just a few short steps away from chatting with your soon-to-be buddies. As with MSN Messenger on Windows Me and Windows 98 SE, you'll need to download an add-in, but it takes no time at all to get going.

To take part in an online chat in Windows Messenger, follow these steps:

1. In the I Want To section of the Windows Messenger window, click Go To Chat Rooms. If this is your first time using the chat service, you'll be asked to download an add-in for Windows Messenger. Click Yes, and then click the Click Here To Download This Add-In link.

> **Note** Whenever you click Go To Chat Rooms after you've set up your nickname and installed the add-in, you'll go directly to the MSN Chat main page, which has a list of chat rooms.

2. Click Download Now.
3. Click Open, and then click Yes to accept the licensing agreement.
4. Click OK to clear the message box indicating the add-in was successfully installed.
5. In the I Want To section of the Windows Messenger window, click Go To Chat Rooms.

Chatting It Up in MSN Messenger

For those of you who have Windows Me or Windows 98 SE installed on your computers, you can use MSN Messenger to visit the MSN Chat Service and start yakking. You do need to install a bit of additional software so MSN Messenger knows how to display the chat rooms and their contents, but it's a quick download and then off you go!

To take part in an online chat in MSN Messenger, follow these steps:

1. Sign in to the .NET Messenger service, and click Go To Chat Rooms in the I Want To section of the MSN Messenger program window.
2. If this is your first time entering a chat room, you will be asked to choose an MSN nickname. Type your desired nickname in the box, or select the option button next to one of the suggested nicknames, and click Save.

> **Note** Whenever you click Go To Chat Rooms after you've set up your nickname and installed the add-in mentioned later in this procedure, you'll go directly to the MSN Chat main page, which has a list of chat rooms.

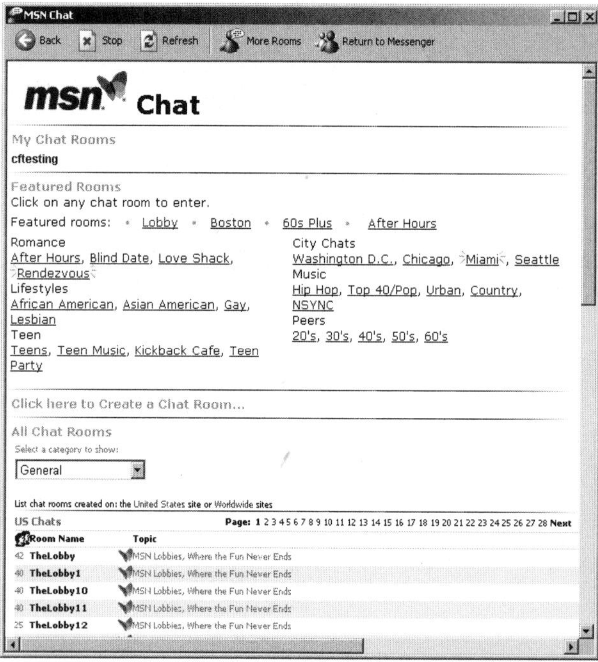

3. Click the name of one of the featured categories to display the chat rooms in that category, or click the Select A Category To Show down arrow in the All Chat Rooms section to display rooms where specific ranges of topics are being chatted about.
4. From the list of rooms that appears, click the name of the one you'd like to enter.
5. If this is your first time entering an MSN chat room, MSN Messenger will begin to download the MSN Chat Control software. To continue the download, you may need to click Yes in a confirmation dialog box.
6. You can participate in the ongoing conversation by typing your message in the text box at the bottom of the chat window and pressing Enter.
7. You can exit the chat room by clicking Exit at the top of the chat window.

Creating Your Own Chat Room

If you're planning a large gathering of friends online, and I've been part of a few of them, you may want to retire to a private electronic space where the hoi polloi can't barge in and ask what everybody's up to. Once you've created the chat room, all you need to do is send your invitees the name of the chat room and the time you want 'em to show up. Do remember to tell them which time zone the time is based on—it's embarrassing when someone in California shows up three hours late for a chat scheduled on New York time.

To create your own chat room in MSN Chat, follow these steps:

1 In the I Want To section of either MSN Messenger or Windows Messenger, click Go To Chat Rooms.

2 Click the Click Here To Create A Chat Room link.

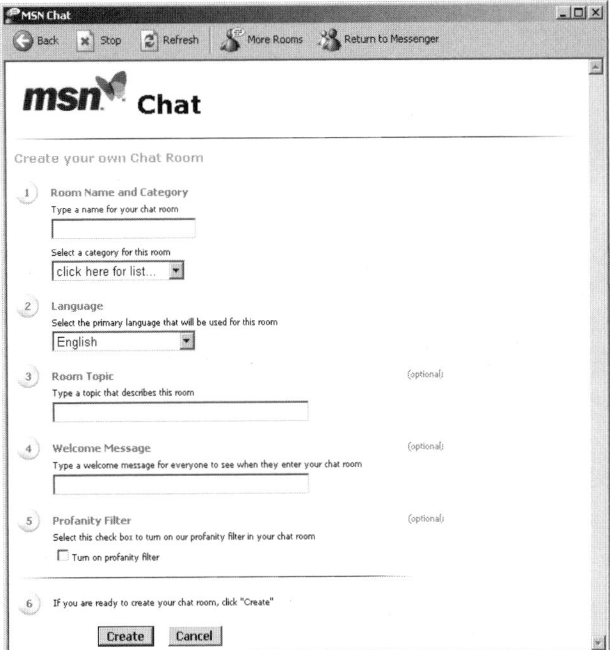

On the Create Your Own Chat Room page, follow these steps to set up your chat room:

1 Type the name for your chat room in the Room Name And Category box.

2 Click the Select A Category For This Room down arrow, and select a category for your chat room.

Note If you want to make your room private, select Unlisted from the Select A Category For This Room list.

3 Click the Language down arrow, and choose the primary language for your chat room.

4 Type the topic of your chat room in the Room Topic box.

5 Type a welcome message for everyone to see when they enter your chat room in the Welcome Message box.

6 If you want to filter out profanity, select the Turn On Profanity Filter check box.

7 Click Create. On the Code Of Conduct page, read the code of conduct for MSN Communication Services and click Yes, I Agree. When you do, the MSN Chat service will create your chat room.

Note You can have your friends and family join your unlisted chat room by clicking the Join A Chat link, typing in the name of the chat room, and pressing Enter.

Exchanging Ideas in Newsgroups

Chat rooms are all about communicating in real time—when you type something, the other folks in the room where you typed your message see it immediately. This characteristic of chat rooms means there's a free-flowing dialog, which seems confusing at first but it makes sense after a few minutes. A newsgroup, on the other hand, contains a series of discreet messages that are displayed in the order they were posted and are arranged by the contents of each message's subject line. Figure 10-1 shows what a newsgroup in the Microsoft Community looks like.

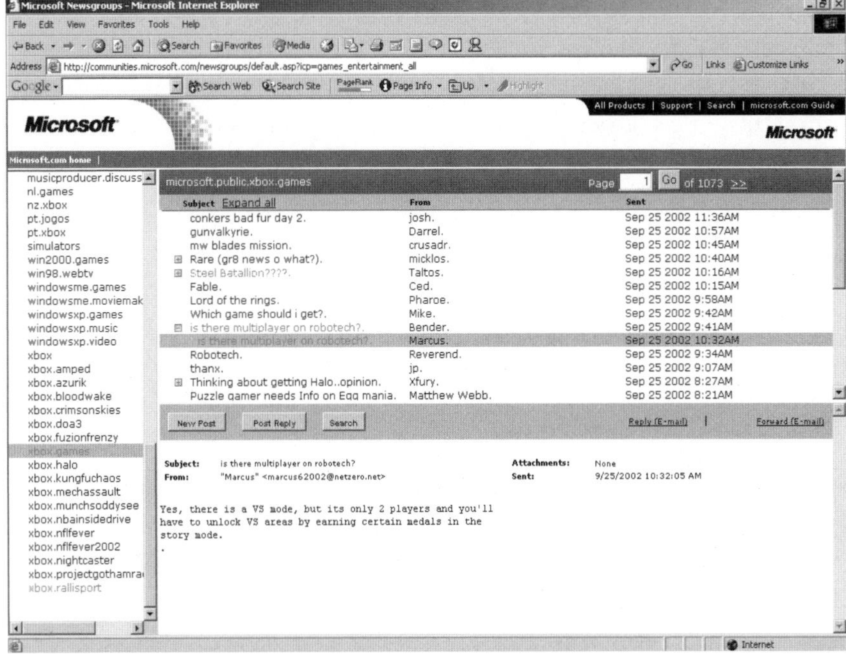

Figure 10-1 This newsgroup has quite a few messages on topics relating to Microsoft Xbox games; you can see the subject, author, and time each message was posted.

In newsgroup parlance, an individual message in a newsgroup is called a *post*, and a series of messages made up of a post and the responses to it is called a *thread*.

Lingo A post is an individual message in a newsgroup. You can also use the term as a verb, as in: "I'll post a response after dinner." A thread is a series of posts made up of an initial post and all the responses to that post.

One look at Figure 10-1 and you can see how easy it is to follow the conversation in a newsgroup. Not only are the posts identified by subject, but the responses are right there for you to see as well.

Note It's a good idea to at least scan the subjects of the last few days' worth of posts in any newsgroup you join. If you were going to ask a question, it's possible someone else asked it already and the answer is there for you!

Viewing Microsoft Community Newsgroups

One of the ways Microsoft helps its customers is by making newsgroups available for folks to ask questions and provide answers for their fellow users. You can find those newsgroups in the Microsoft Community, available at *http://communities.microsoft.com/*, and you need just a Web browser to visit.

To view Microsoft Community newsgroups, follow these steps:

1. Visit *http://communities.microsoft.com/* and click Newsgroups in the left pane of the page.
2. Click the name of the subject area you want to explore.

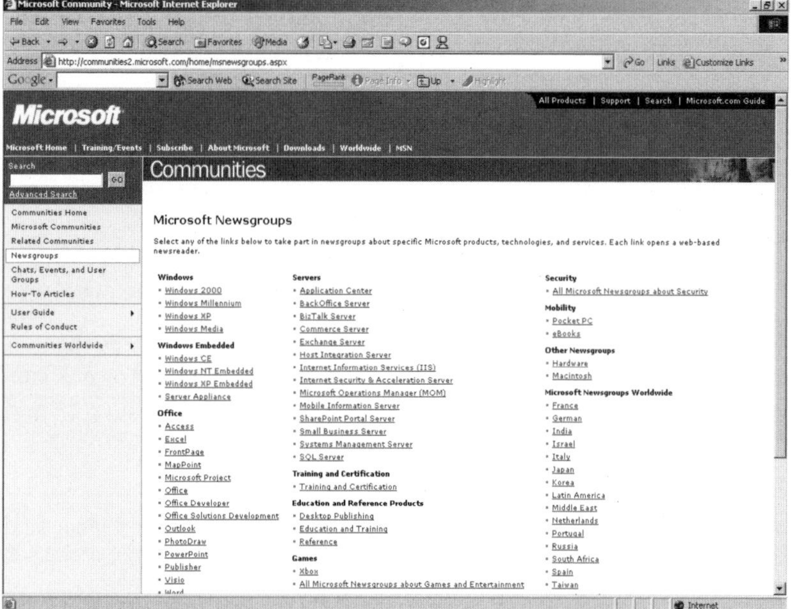

3. Under the topic you want to read about, click the Use Web-Based Reader Link to display the contents of the newsgroup.

> **Note** Note that a list of related and popular newsgroups appears in the left pane of the screen. You can click any of the names to view the corresponding newsgroup.

4. Follow any of these steps to read the posts in the newsgroup:

   - Click the subject line of the post you want to read. Your Web browser will display the text of the post in the bottom section of the page.

- Click the Expand icon (it looks like a plus sign) next to a post to display the responses to that post. You can contract an expanded thread by clicking the Contract icon (it looks like a minus sign) next to the first post in a thread.

Note You can also click the Expand All link in the Subject header to expand every thread.

- Click the two right arrows to move to the next page of posts, click the two left arrows to move to the previous page of posts, or type the page you want to visit in the Page box and click Go.

Giving 'Em a Piece of Your Mind

Once you've familiarized yourself with the newsgroup and its contents, you may very well have something important to say. Whether it's the answer to a question from another user or an opinion, you can compose and post a message in a flash!

To start a new thread, follow these steps:

1 Open the newsgroup in which you want to start your new thread, and click New Post.

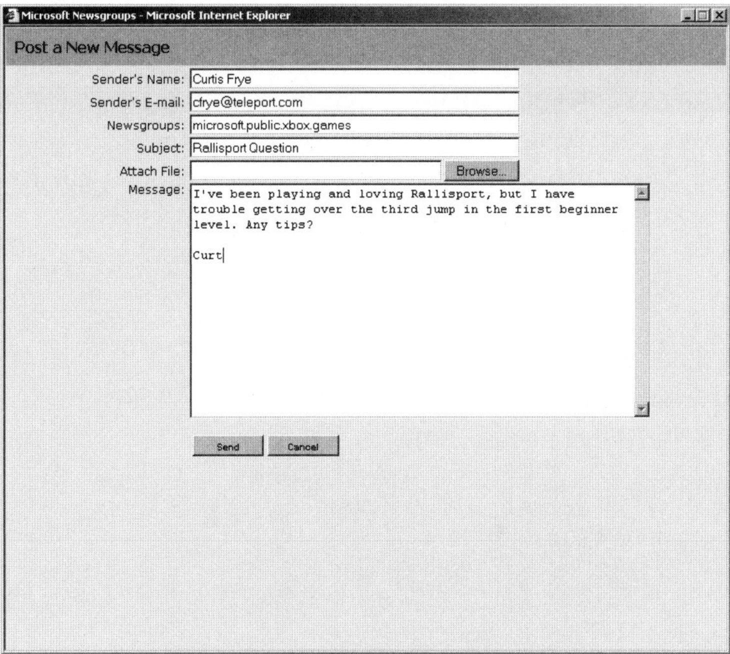

2. Type your name in the Sender's Name box, your e-mail address in the Sender's E-mail box, and the subject for your post in the Subject box.
3. Type the body of your post in the Message box, re-read it carefully to be sure your meaning comes across, and click Send.

To post a follow-up to an existing article, follow these steps:

1. Click the article to which you want to respond and click Post Reply.
2. Type your name in the Sender's Name box, and type your e-mail address in the Sender's E-mail box.
3. The article to which you're responding appears in the Message box. Edit the post so just the previous author's name and the part of the post to which you're responding appear, and type your response in the Message box.
4. Click Send to post your response.

Note If you'd rather respond directly to the person who authored the post, you can display the post and click the Reply (E-mail) link in the subject header of the post, which should launch your e-mail program. If it doesn't, you can always copy the original author's e-mail address from the post and create a new message manually.

Reading Usenet Newsgroups in Outlook Express

The newsgroups you can find through the Microsoft Community aren't the only newsgroups in the world. In fact, there are plenty of other groups out there on Usenet, a network of computers that uses the Internet to transmit news articles around the world to subscribers. It's free to read the newsgroups, but many Internet service providers choose to pay for a reliable message feed.

There are seven major official hierarchies for Usenet newsgroups, and one that's just as relevant but isn't "official":

- **comp** for computer-related discussions
- **misc** for discussion topics that don't fit elsewhere
- **news** for news about Usenet
- **rec** for fun and games
- **sci** for scientific issues
- **soc** for social and cultural issues
- **talk** for general chitchat about the group's subject matter
- **alt** the wild side of Usenet, where the groups center on controversial and fringe topics, and free speech is rampant

There are quite a few other hierarchies around, including *microsoft*, for Microsoft-related newsgroups, but the first seven on the list are the official ones. The alt.* groups were formed in protest to restrictions on content in the official hierarchies (the third alt group was alt.rock-and-roll, so you can probably guess what the first two were), and many, if not all, of these groups are available from most Usenet services. Some family-friendly services do exclude the alt groups from their feed, and alt groups that feature large files are often excluded to reduce the load on a provider's servers.

Caution As with chat rooms, there is the potential for the language in and subject matter of newsgroups to offend some users, and not everything will be appropriate for children.

To prepare Outlook Express for newsgroup reading, follow these steps:

1 Start Outlook Express, right-click the News icon in the Folders pane, and click Properties.

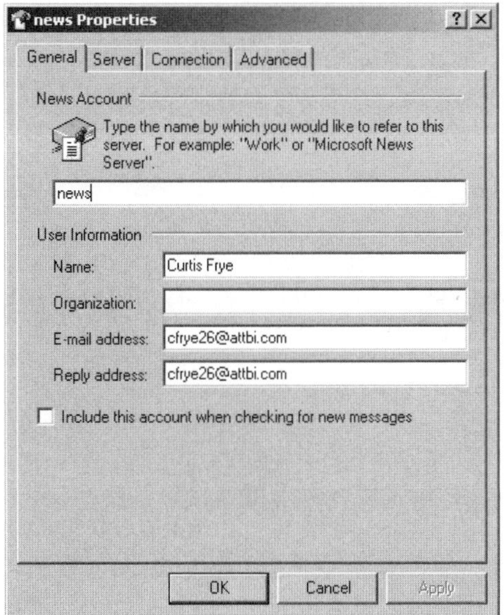

2 On the General tab, type your name in the Name box, your e-mail address in the E-mail Address box, and the e-mail address to which you would like replies addressed in the Reply Address box.

3 Click the Server tab, and type the address of your Internet service provider's news server (such as netnews.microsoft.com) in the Server Name box.

4 Click OK.

5 Click Newsgroups to begin downloading a list of the newsgroups available on your Internet service provider's news server.

Note If you have a slow connection, downloading the list of groups can take a few minutes.

---

6 Click OK.

To subscribe to one or more newsgroups, follow these steps:

1 Start Outlook Express, click the name of your news server in the Folders pane, and click Newsgroups.

2 On the All tab of the newsgroups list, click the name of a group to which you want to subscribe, and click Subscribe. When you subscribe to a group, a marker appears next to the group's name.

Note There are more than 30,000 newsgroups on Usenet, so you might want to limit the groups that are shown by typing a word in the Display Newsgroups Which Contain box.

---

3 Click OK.

To read posts in a subscribed newsgroup, follow these steps:

1 Start Outlook Express, and, if the names of your subscribed newsgroups aren't displayed in the Folders pane, click the Expand control next to the name of your news server (the control looks like a plus sign).

2 Click the name of the group you want to read, and then click the subject line of the post you want to read. Outlook Express will display the text of the post in the bottom section of the page.

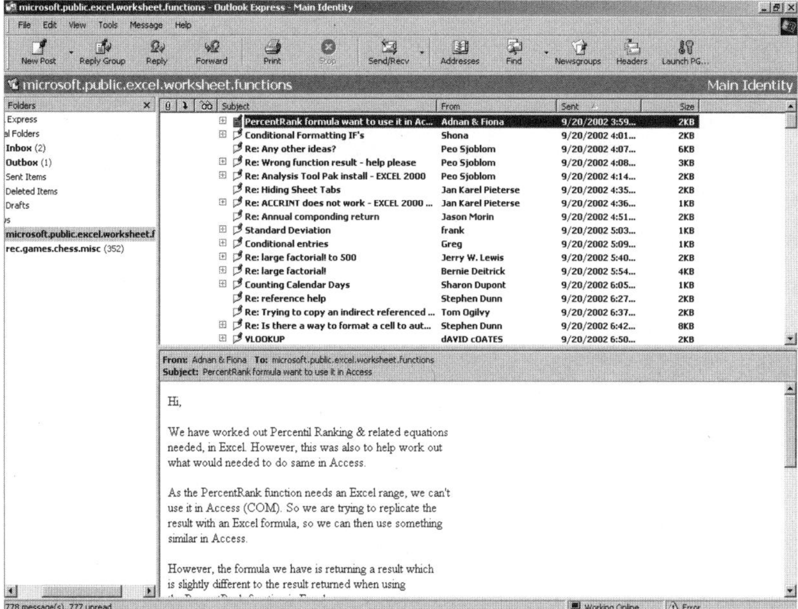

3 Click the Expand icon (it looks like a plus sign) next to a post to display the responses to that post. You can contract an expanded thread by clicking the Contract icon (it looks like a minus sign) next to the first post in a thread.

To respond to a post in Outlook Express, follow any of these steps:

- To respond with a follow-up post to the newsgroup, click the post to which you want to respond, click Reply Group, and click Send.
- To respond to the author using e-mail, click the post to which you want to respond, click Reply, compose the message in Outlook Express, and click Send.
- To send a copy of the post to someone by e-mail, click the post you want to forward, and click Forward. In your default e-mail program, type the e-mail address of the recipient, and click Send.

Key Points

- Be sure your computer meets the minimum hardware and operating system requirements before you buy a game.
- You should always install a game in the directory the Setup program suggests, unless there's a very good reason not to (such as an existing directory with the same name).
- Game publishers, hardware manufacturers, and other companies write updates to their games and drivers on a regular basis. You should make a habit of checking those companies' sites every few weeks to see if there are any new updates for your game or hardware.
- Buying more RAM is an easy and relatively inexpensive way to improve your computer's performance dramatically.
- If your game runs slowly or the video or sound is choppy, you can change the game's frame rate, resolution, color depth, or use of shadows to improve its performance.
- The Ethernet port on the back of your Xbox is there for more than show—take advantage of the Xbox Live network!
- Newsgroups and chat rooms are great sources of information and entertainment, but you need to be sure the content and conversation are appropriate for you.

Chapter 11

Maintaining Your Home Network

By now I'm sure you've put a lot of work into getting your home network set up so it's perfect for your needs. You've got your hardware set up and working flawlessly, the cables are in the walls or hidden behind runners and don't get in anybody's way, and your router does a great job of keeping the bad guys out. The hard part is behind you, but you will need to pay attention to your network to keep it running smoothly. There's nothing so messy as changing the oil involved in regular home network maintenance, but by keeping up with developments in the operating systems you run, virus protection software, and the physical health of your computers, you can head off problems before they rear their ugly heads.

My job in this chapter is to show you how to maintain your network by backing up your important files—whether that means writing the files to a hard disk on a computer elsewhere on your network or storing your files on CD-ROMs—restoring files from your archives, setting system restore points to roll back your operating system in case you do something that makes it hiccup, updating your virus signatures so you don't get caught when the next big wave hits, and defragmenting your hard disks so you can bring up data quickly and reduce the wear and tear on your drives.

Backing Up Your Files with Microsoft Backup

I'm a pack rat. In fact, I was digging through a closet the other day and found some of my third grade homework. I won't tell you the grade, but I'm sure somewhere on a student evaluation form there's a note that says I need to prioritize what I keep and be willing to get rid of some of my practice spelling tests. I have gotten better over the years, though. I delete a lot of e-mail and have even been known to get rid of large files I downloaded off the Internet for reference but never ended up using. And yet, I keep a lot of items on hand, with the excuse that I never know when I might need them. Of course, not only do I keep the original files on hand, but I also keep a backup copy of everything.

Why is backing up your files important? Because there's nothing worse than having to do the same work twice, even if it's just visiting a Web site and downloading a file. Well, that's not entirely true. If one of your colleagues manages to delete the only copy of a presentation your boss is going to use to convince a client to fund the project that will justify everyone's existence at your company for the next calendar year, the consequences might be more severe than having to do the same work twice. If there's no project, you won't get to do the same work once!

Caution System Restore, a new functionality in Microsoft Windows XP, does back up your *system* before you make a major change, but it doesn't create backup copies of your *data files*. That means that if you lose your files because you inadvertently wrote over them during a program installation, you can't get them back through System Restore!

Using Backup in Windows 98 SE and Windows Me

I'm a big fan of programs that make important tasks easier. Sure, it's possible just to copy all the files you want to back up to a shared folder on another computer, or to write them onto a CD-ROM, but copying files in My Computer or Windows Explorer doesn't create a record of the files you backed up, so you'll have to decide which files to back up from scratch the next time you create an archive. Fortunately, the Windows operating system includes a tool you can use to back up your files: Microsoft Backup.

Note It's important to remember that Microsoft Backup, and most other backup programs, for that matter, can't create a copy of any files you are currently editing. Be sure all your files are closed before you start your backup!

Installing Backup

Microsoft Backup is available for your use in both Microsoft Windows 98 Second Edition (SE) and Microsoft Windows Millennium Edition (Me), but you'll need to dig into your Windows CD-ROM a bit to put the program onto your computer. There's no real voodoo you need to do to make it happen—it's just a matter of using the Add/Remove Programs tool to add Backup to your arsenal of system maintenance tools.

To install Backup in Windows 98 SE or Windows Me, follow these steps:

1. Insert your Windows installation CD-ROM into your computer's CD-ROM drive.
2. Click Start, choose Settings, and then choose Control Panel.
3. Double-click Add/Remove Programs and then click the Windows Setup tab.

4. In the Components list, click System Tools and then click Details.
5. Select the Backup check box and click OK twice.

Note If you didn't insert your Windows CD-ROM at the beginning of the process, you will be prompted to insert it now.

---

6. Remove your Windows installation CD-ROM from your computer's CD-ROM drive and restart your computer when prompted to do so.

Selecting Files to Back Up

Once you have Backup on your computer, you should take the time to back up the files you cherish. The dialog box you use to define the files and folders you want to back up gives you a lot of flexibility in picking what you want to include in the archives.

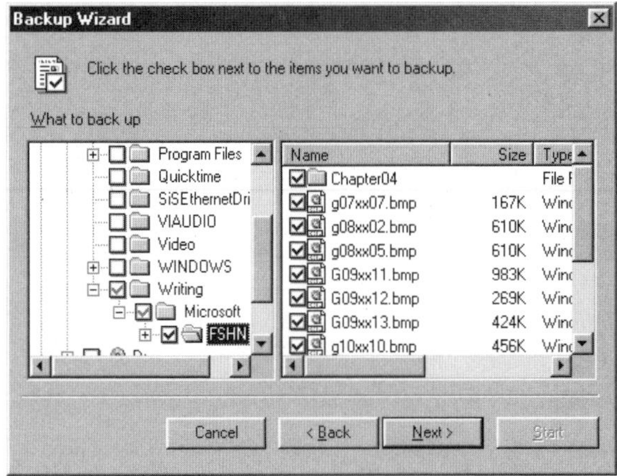

The dialog box indicates which files you've selected to back up using a series of symbols that appear in the check box next to a drive, folder, or file:

- If a drive or folder has a blue check in its check box, the entire contents of the drive or folder will be included in the backup operation.
- If a drive or folder has a gray check in its check box, at least one file in the drive or folder, or one of its subfolders, will be included in the backup.
- If the check box next to a drive or folder is clear, no files in the drive or folder will be included in the backup.

To back up your files using Microsoft Backup, follow these steps:

1. Click Start, choose Programs, choose Accessories, and then choose System Tools. Click Backup. If you don't have a backup device (such as a CD burner) connected to your computer, a message box will appear, asking if you want Windows to look for such a device. If you want to back up your files to a hard disk on your computer, or elsewhere on your network, click No. If you do have a new device you want to install, click Yes and follow the instructions that appear.

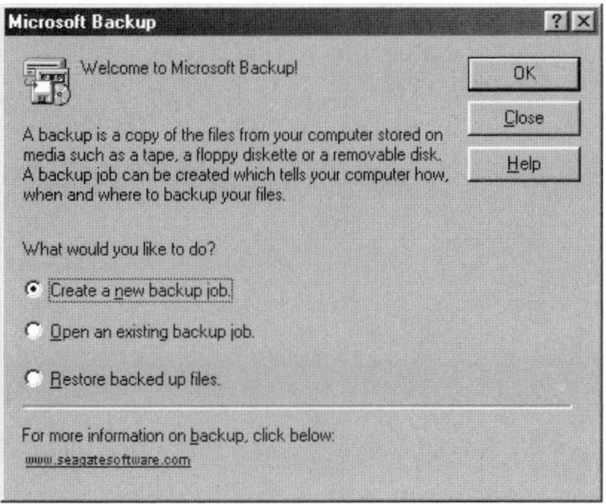

2. Select Create A New Backup Job and then click OK.
3. Select Back Up Selected Files, Folder, And Drives and then click Next.
4. In the left pane of the dialog box, use the controls to select the folders containing the files you want to back up.
   - Click an Expand control (it looks like a plus sign) to display the contents of a hard disk or in a folder.
   - Click a Contract control (it looks like a minus sign) to hide the contents of a hard disk or folder.
   - Click a folder icon to display the contents of the folder in the right pane.
5. Select the check box next to a folder to back up the contents of that folder (including all subfolders), or select the check box next to a file (in the right pane) to back up only those files you select within that subfolder. Click Next.

> **Note** If there are certain files within a folder you don't want to back up, you can select the check box next to the name of the folder, display the contents of the folder in the right pane, and clear the check box next to the name of any file you don't want to back up.

6. Select All Selected Files and then click Next.
7. Click the Folder icon next to the name of the file to which Backup will archive your files.

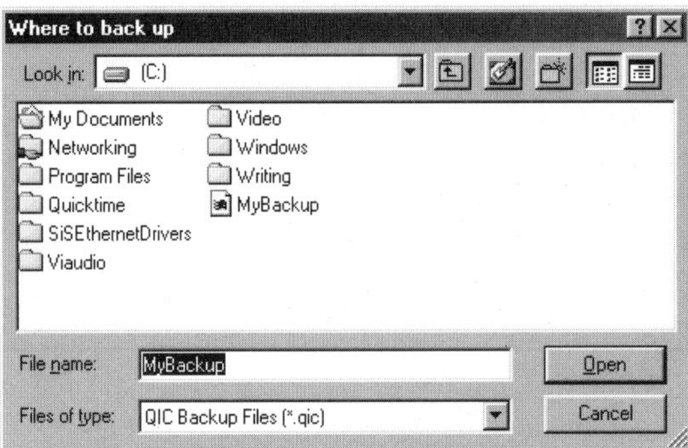

8 Use the controls in the Where To Back Up dialog box to pick the folder to which you want to write the backup file, type a name for the file in the File Name box, and then click Open. Click Next.

Note If you click the Look In down arrow, you'll see your entire computer as well as Network Neighborhood displayed in the list of drives. I often use the hard disks on other computers as a repository for important files. In fact, if a file's really important, I'll save it on two or three other computers and a CD-ROM.

---

9 Leave both check boxes selected so Backup will compress the files to save space, and verify that the files were backed up successfully. Click Next and then click Start.

10 If you are asked to save your backup job, type a name for the job and click OK.

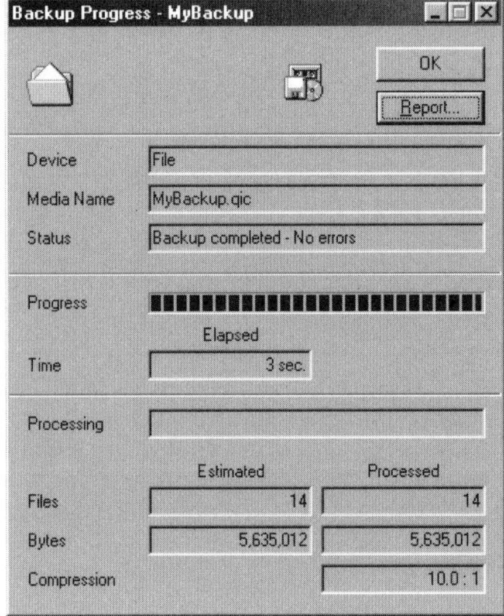

11 In the Backup Progress dialog box, click Report to view a report summarizing what went on during the backup, or click OK.

12 From the Job menu, choose Exit.

Changing Your Backup Type

When you think of backing up files, you probably have an image of simply copying files from one place to another. In some cases, that's exactly what you'll do. In fact, if you have only a few files (meaning fewer than one hundred or so) that you want to back up, and if the files are all in the same directory, you're very well served to use Backup to copy your files to another computer on your network or onto a floppy disk or CD-ROM. Be careful about putting your lone backup copy of anything on a floppy disk, though—the little guys fail at the worst times.

On the other hand, if you have a lot of files you want to back up and actually performing the backup takes away precious time you could use to play games or maybe even go outside and be active, you might want to back up just those files that have changed since the last time you made a backup. If so, you can choose to make a differential backup, where you back up only those files that have changed since you last made a complete ("all files") backup, or an incremental backup, where you back up only those files that have changed since the last "all files" backup or your last incremental backup.

How does Backup know if a file has been backed up? Easy. One of a file's properties notes whether the file has been archived, and another notes the time and date the archive was made. If you do a differential backup, the Backup program doesn't change the archived property to "true," so the file will be backed up every time. If you do an incremental backup, Backup does set the archived property to "true," so the file will be backed up in later jobs only if it has changed since the last incremental backup. In other words, modifying a file changes the archived property to "false."

Note If you do a differential or incremental backup, Backup doesn't archive all your files, so you may need to restore files from more than one archive to get everything back. Differential and incremental backups are faster to do and the archives take up less space, but if you compress your archive, the advantage of backing up all your files in every job will probably outweigh the space savings for partial backups.

To change the type of backup you perform with Backup, follow these steps:

1. Click Start, choose Programs, choose Accessories, and then choose System Tools. Click Backup.
2. Click the Backup Job down arrow, select the backup job you want to edit, click Options, and then click the Type tab.

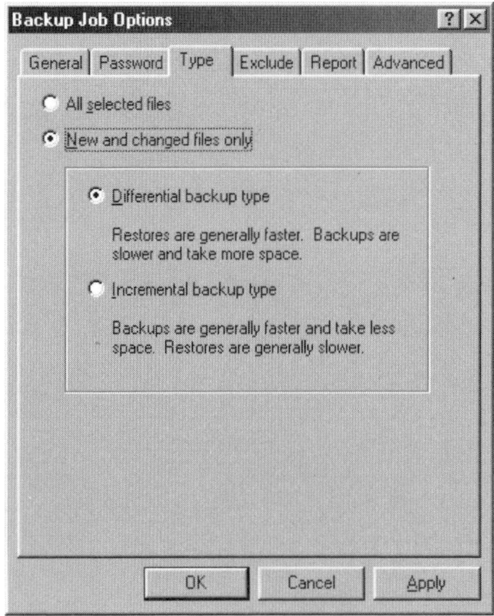

3. Select New And Changed Files Only and then either:
   - Select Differential Backup Type to back up only those files that have changed since the last All Selected Files backup.
   - Select Incremental Backup Type to back up only those files that have changed since the last All Selected Files backup or the last Incremental backup.

   Note You can revert to backing up every file you selected by selecting All Selected Files.

4. Click OK and then choose Save from the Jobs menu.

Changing Other Backup Options

I love it when a utility program gets out of your way and lets you get on with your life, so I was happy to see that in most cases the Backup program's default settings will be just what you need to archive your files. Of course, if you do want to change how Backup handles your archives, you can. I'd recommend reading through this section quickly to see if you get any ideas about how you could change your archives and then implement the changes you like.

Changing Compression and Overwriting Options One of the more useful inventions for storing digital data is the compression algorithm, which finds efficient ways to write the contents of a file. How does a compression algorithm work? Well, this is a vast oversimplification, but here goes. At its base, a computer file is a series of 1's and 0's, which are combined to make letters, numbers, symbols, formatting instructions, and so on. If that file contains a series of eight 1's in a row, you can write 8*1 instead of 11111111, saving five characters' worth of storage without losing any data. The popular compression algorithms can reduce certain types of files to as little as 1 percent of their original size without changing the file at all.

Because disk space is so cheap, particularly when you take compression technology into account, I would never overwrite an existing archive. Even if you get only some of your documents back if you restore your files from a relatively ancient archive, it's still better than overwriting a file, having a disk failure destroy it, and seeing your files disappear forever into the ether. If you need the disk space those archives are taking up, you should move your older disk archives onto a CD-ROM.

To change the compression and overwriting options for your Backup job, follow these steps:

1 In Backup, click the Backup Job down arrow, select the job you want to change, and click Options.

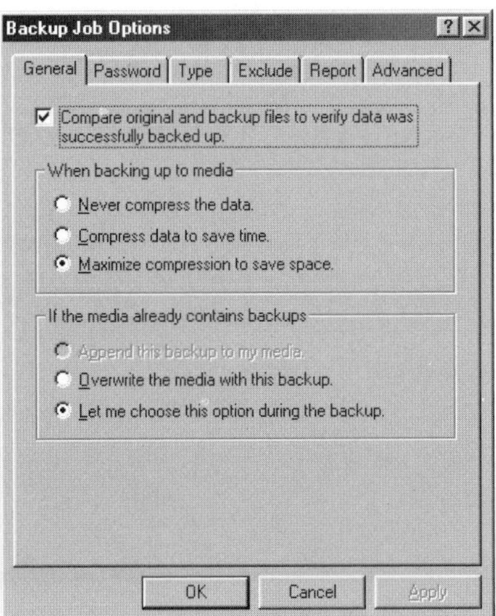

2. In the When Backing Up To Media section on the General tab, select Maximize Compression To Save Space. Pretty much the only time you should select Never Compress The Data is when the files are already compressed (in the case of MP3 sound files, for example).
3. In the If The Media Already Contains Backups section of the dialog box, do any of the following:
   - Select Append This Backup To My Media to write a new archive to the media.
   - Select Overwrite The Media With This Backup to replace the old archive with this file.
   - Select Let Me Choose This Option During The Backup to determine on a case-by-case basis whether to overwrite an existing archive.
4. Click OK.

Adding a Password When you work on a shared computer, you might be a bit concerned about whether anyone else can get to your files. If you want to protect your archives from prying eyes, you can require anyone who wants to restore files from the archive to enter a password.

To add a password to your Backup job, follow these steps:

1. In Backup, click the Backup Job down arrow, select the job you want to change, click Options, and then click the Password tab.
2. Select the Protect This Backup With A Password check box.
3. Type the password for your archive in the Password box and type it again in the Confirm Password box.
4. Click OK.

Excluding Specific Types of Files One of the fundamental lessons of archiving files is that you don't need to back everything up! Sure, you need to back up any documents you've created from scratch, but you don't need to put program executables in your archives. If you lose a program to a disk error, you should always restore the program from its original installation disks. Programs come with a lot of system files and other settings, which may not be carried over with a reinstallation.

To exclude specific types of files in your backup operation, follow these steps:

1 In Microsoft Backup, click the Backup Job down arrow, select the job you want to change, click Options, and then click the Exclude tab. Click Add.

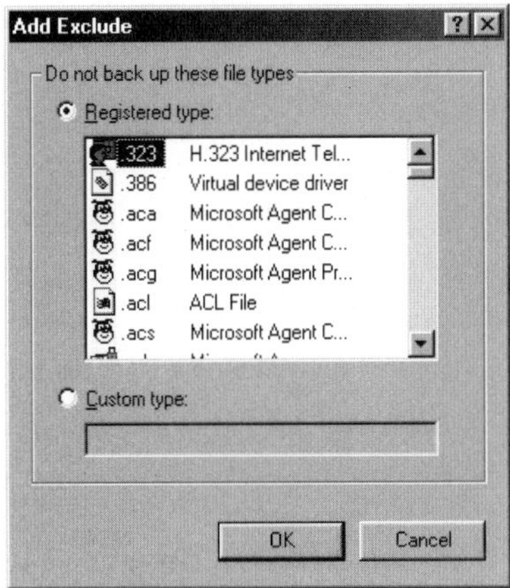

2 Click the file type you want to exclude from your backup and then click OK.

Note If you want to exclude more than one type of file from your backup, you will need to revisit this screen for each type you want to exclude.

---

3 If you want Backup to archive a file type you had previously excluded, click the Exclude tab of the Options dialog box, click the file type you excluded, and click Remove.

4 Click OK.

Customizing Your Backup Report When you archive your files using Backup, the program keeps a record of what it did as part of the operation. You can limit the entries in the report, but the information included in the report by default is useful. For example, you can see which files were skipped so you can figure out why they were skipped and back up the files separately.

To customize your Backup report, follow these steps:

1 In Backup, click the Backup Job down arrow, select the job you want to change, click Options, and click the Report tab.

2 Select the check box next to any report items you want included in your report and clear the check box next to any report items you don't want included in your report.

> **Note** The default listing, which includes everything except a list of all archived files (which would be quite long in many cases), is adequate in most every case.

3 Click OK.

Using Backup in Windows XP

Because Windows XP Home Edition uses system restore points (described in the later section entitled "Saving Your Bacon with System Restore Points") to back up your system, the program's designers didn't include Backup in the list of system utilities that you can add through the Add/Remove Programs tool. If you do want to use it, though, it's there for you.

Installing Backup

Even though Backup isn't part of Windows XP Home Edition, and you can't add it through the Add/Remove Programs tool, the programmers did recognize that many folks out there like to use Backup as their archiving method of choice, so they did make Backup available on your Windows XP CD-ROM. You just need to know where to look for it.

To install Backup in Windows XP Home Edition, follow these steps:

1 Put your Windows XP installation CD-ROM in your computer's CD-ROM drive and display the CD-ROM's contents in My Computer.

2 Double-click the Valueadd folder, double-click the Msft folder, and then double-click the Ntbackup folder.

3 Double-click Ntbackup.msi and, when the installation is complete, click Finish.

Backing Up Files in Windows XP

Just as in Windows 98 SE and Windows Me, Backup for Windows XP is set up to run a wizard that can step you through backing up or restoring your files. There are a few choices to make about what type of backup you want to run and where you want to store the files, but once you've made those decisions, the wizard does everything else for you.

> **Note** If the wizard doesn't run, you can choose Switch To Wizard Mode from the Tools menu to change from Advanced Mode to Wizard Mode.

To back up files in Windows XP, follow these steps:

1. Click Start, choose All Programs, choose Accessories, choose System Tools, and then choose Backup. If the wizard starts, click Next; if not, choose Switch To Wizard Mode from the Tools menu to run the wizard.

   Note If you don't want to use the wizard to step through setting up your backup job, clear the Always Start In Wizard Mode check box to bypass the wizard and display the Advanced Mode dialog box when you run Backup. You'll have access to all the same options you do when you go through the wizard, but the process won't be laid out in front of you as it is when you use the wizard.

   ---

2. Select Back Up Files And Settings and then click Next.
3. Select Let Me Choose What To Back Up and then click Next.

   Note Selecting any of the other option buttons (to back up just your personal files, to back up every user's files, or to back up all information on the computer) will move you to a page from which you choose the location and file name where you want the data to be archived.

   ---

4. In the left pane of the page, use the controls to select the folders containing the files you want to back up.
   - Click an Expand control (it looks like a plus sign) to display the contents of a hard disk or folder.
   - Click a Contract control (it looks like a minus sign) to hide the contents of a hard disk or folder.
   - Click a folder icon to display the contents of the folder in the right pane.
5. Select the check box next to a folder to back up the contents of that folder (including all subfolders), or select the check box next to a file (in the right pane) to back up only those files you select within that subfolder. Click Next when you're done identifying the files to back up.
6. Click Browse. In the Save As dialog box, select the directory in which you want to store the backup file, and click Save. Click Next and then click Finish.

Scheduling a Backup Job

One great feature of the version of Backup that comes with Windows XP is that you can have Windows run backup jobs on a regular schedule. For example, if you have a standing Friday night commitment and think (as you should) that doing a weekly backup of your important files is a good idea, you can schedule a backup job for every Friday night. What's more, you can schedule several types of backups so you don't have to wonder how long it's been since you did your last full backup. On my main computer, I back up the directory with the files from my active projects to another hard disk every night, archive my entire Writing directory (and all its subdirectories) to CD-ROM every Friday night, and back up all data files on all of my computers once a month.

Note Whenever I schedule a backup job for a time when I expect to be away from my computer, I always set up the job so it writes the archive file to a hard disk and not to a removable storage unit such as a CD or a floppy disk. If you're hurrying out the door to make your date, it's easy to forget to drop a writable CD or a floppy in the drive, which means the backup job won't run as scheduled.

To schedule a backup job in Windows XP, follow these steps:

1. Click Start, choose All Programs, choose Accessories, and then choose System Tools. Click Backup.
2. If the Backup Or Restore Wizard appears, click Advanced Mode.

3. Select the Schedule Jobs tab and click the day on which you want to schedule the backup. Click Add Job and then click Next.
4. Select the option button representing the files you want to back up and click Next. If you selected Back Up Selected Files, Drives, Or Network Data, a dialog box will appear that lets you specify the data you want to back up. Click Next.

5 Click Browse. In the Save As dialog box, select the directory in which you want to store the backup file, and click Save. Click Next and then click Finish.

6 Click the Select The Type Of Backup down arrow and select the type of backup you want to perform:

- Normal, which backs up all files and makes a note in each file's properties indicating the file has been archived.
- Copy, which backs up the files but doesn't mark them as archived.
- Incremental, which backs up any files that were modified or created since your last backup.
- Differential, which backs up any files that were modified or created since your last backup but doesn't mark them as archived.
- Daily, which backs up only those files that were created or modified on the day the job is run.

7 Click Next.

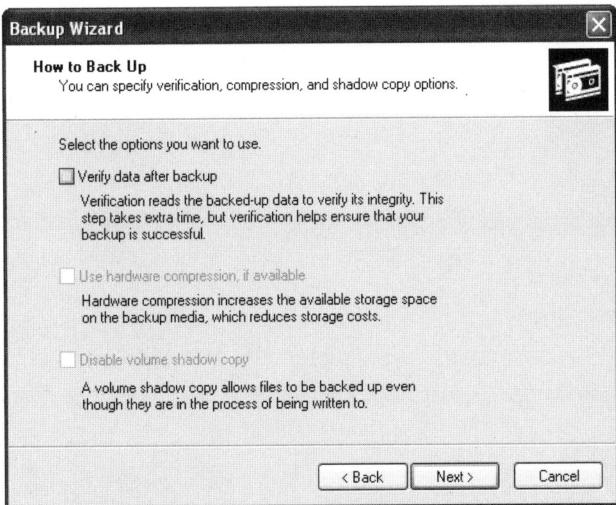

8 Select the Verify Data After Backup check box to have Backup check your archived data to be sure it can restore the files from the archive. If necessary, clear the Disable Volume Shadow Copy check box so Backup can back up any files you are editing when the job is run. Click Next.

Note You should always have Backup verify your archive to ensure the data can be restored. I've had times when I figured I was safe because I'd backed up my data, only to be horrified when my archives were corrupted and useless.

9 Select Append This Backup To The Existing Backups and then click Next.

Note Because disk space is so cheap these days, I always keep all my backups to guard against the possibility that one of the backup copies gets erased or becomes unusable. You can always transfer your older archives to another hard disk or a CD-ROM if you think they're taking up too much room.

10 Select Later to indicate you want the backup to run at a later time, type a name for the job in the Job Name box, and click Set Schedule.

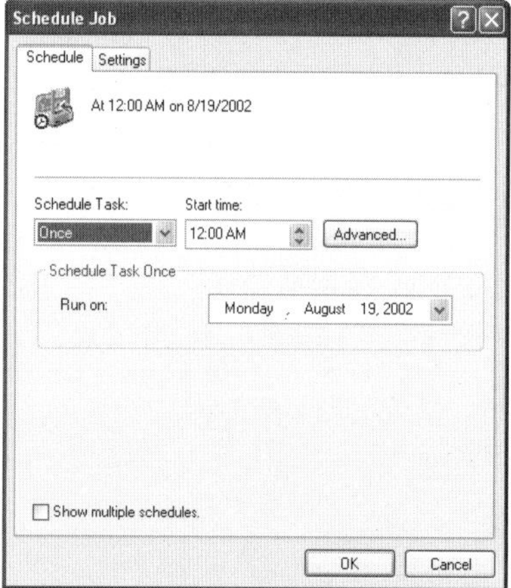

11 Click the Schedule Task down arrow and select the schedule on which you want the backup to be performed. Click OK.

Note Depending on the schedule you select, you'll be able to give Backup more details about when you want it to run the backup job. For example, selecting Daily lets you choose whether you want to run the job every day, every two days, and so on.

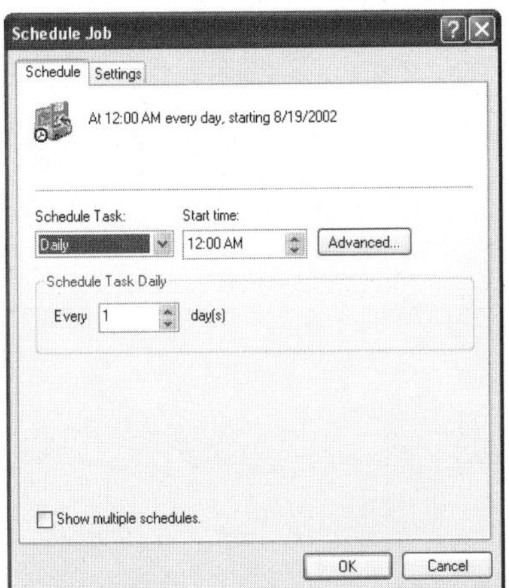

12 Type your password in the Password box and type it again in the Confirm Password box. Click Next and then click Finish.

Note The Automated System Recover element of the Backup program has been superceded by system restore points, which are discussed in the later section entitled "Saving Your Bacon with System Restore Points."

Restoring Files from a Backup

I hope you never have to use the instructions in this section of the book, but if worse comes to worse and your files are accidentally erased or become damaged after a power failure, you can bring them back by restoring saved versions of the files from your archives. You might be a bit chagrined that you have to resort to your backup copies because you lost the version of the file that contained your changes for the past week, but you'll be a lot happier than you would be if you had to create the entire file from memory.

Restoring Files from a Backup in Windows 98 SE or Windows Me

Just as you can use the Backup Or Restore Wizard to archive your files for safekeeping, you can use the wizard to put those files back into action on your computer if you need to. I always restore files to a new directory, both so I'm reminded that the files are archived copies and so I don't accidentally overwrite any other versions of the files I may have overlooked on my hard disk.

To restore files from an archive created with the Backup program in Windows 98 SE or Windows Me, follow these steps:

1 Click Start, choose Programs, choose Accessories, and then choose System Tools. Click Backup.

2. Select Restore Backed Up Files and then click OK.
3. If necessary, click the folder icon to display the Restore From dialog box, and select the archive from which you want to restore your files. Click Open.

4. Navigate to the folder or individual file you want to restore, select the check box next to the file set you want to restore, and click OK.
5. Select the check box next to any files or directories you want to restore and click Next.
6. Click the Where To Restore down arrow and select Alternate Location.
7. Click the Open folder icon, select the directory in which you want to restore the files, click OK, and then click Next.
8. Select Do Not Replace The File On My Computer and then click Start.
9. Click OK. In the Restore Progress dialog box, click Report to see a summary of what went on in the restore operation or click OK.

Restoring Files from a Backup in Windows XP

If you've used Backup to restore files in Windows 98 SE or Windows Me, the Restore feature in the Windows XP version of the program will be very familiar. Once again, you can move through the Backup Or Restore Wizard to select from which archive you want to restore your files, where you want them to go, and whether the program should overwrite any existing files with the same name as an archived file.

To restore files from an archive created with the Backup program in Windows XP, follow these steps:

1. Click Start, choose All Programs, choose Accessories, and then choose System Tools. Click Backup.

2 Click Next, select Restore Files And Settings, and click Next.

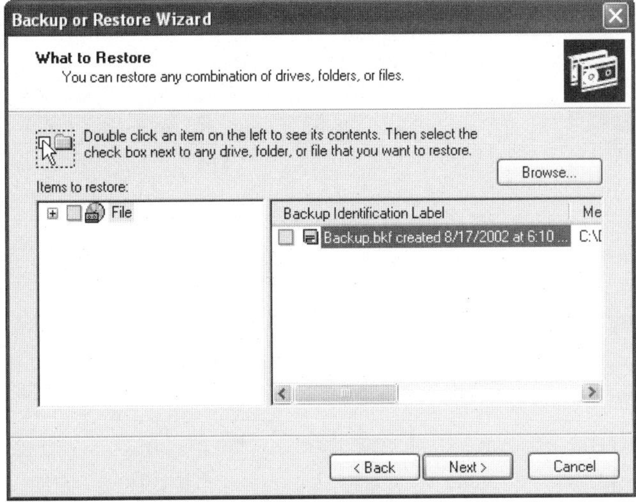

3 Double-click the archive from which you want to restore your files, select the check box next to any files or directories you want to restore, and click Next.

Note If the archive you want isn't displayed in the Items To Restore pane of the wizard screen, click Browse to search your network for the backup file you want.

---

4 Click Advanced, select Alternate Location, and click Browse. In the Restore Path dialog box, select the directory in which you want to copy the files from your archive, and click OK.

5 Click Next and then, if necessary, select Leave Existing Files.

6 Click Next twice and then click Finish.

7 Click Report to view a report of the restore operation or click Close.

Backing Up to a CD-ROM

Backup is a great program, but it isn't your only option when it comes to archiving your files. If you bought a computer with a drive that lets you create your own CD-ROMs (or if you bought a drive of your own later) you can write your files to a CD, put the CD somewhere out of the sun, and be assured that your files will be there when you need them. CD recorders are relatively inexpensive, with some very good universal serial bus (USB) 2.0 models costing about as much as a large hard disk. The CD recorder I bought even came with a USB 2.0 expansion card, so I popped it into my main computer, plugged in the CD recorder, and was busy backing up my files in a matter of minutes.

Note A standard CD-ROM can hold about 700 MB of data, which should be plenty of room for most of your files. If not, you can either compress some or all of your files, or find a convenient breaking point and spread your files out over two CDs. You could also purchase a writable DVD drive. DVDs can hold more than 4 GB of data, and prices of those drives are dropping quickly as they become more common.

To back your files up to a CD, follow these steps:

1. Insert a blank recordable CD into your CD recorder.
2. Start your CD recording program, either one that was included with your CD recorder or one you purchased separately.
3. Use the controls in the program to define the files you want to write to your recordable CD. In the program I use, I just copy the files to the window assigned to the CD.

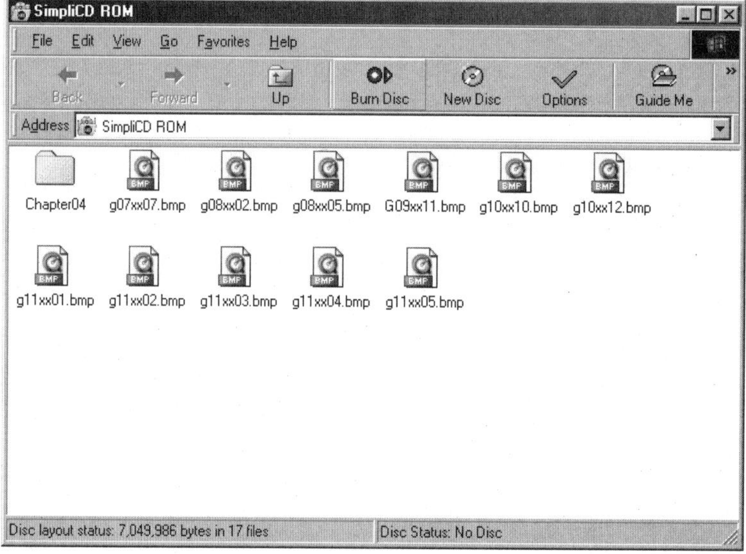

4. Start the copy process, usually by clicking OK or a similar button in your program. In the program I use, I click Burn Disc.
5. Follow the directions in your program to name the CD and then click OK.

Reducing the Size of Your Files

Even though the hard disks on my computers are ridiculously large for what I use them for, I still have Backup compress my files so I don't waste disk space. You never know—I may go on a digital video or electronic composing kick and start writing massive multimedia files to my hard disks. If that were the case for me, or if it's the case for you, it would be best to compress any large data files not used on a regular basis but wanted handy. In Windows XP, you can create a compressed folder in which any files put into it are compressed using the popular Zip compression algorithm. Windows 98 SE and Windows Me don't come with a built-in Zip utility, but there are plenty of inexpensive archival programs available from download sites around the world. I recommend you look in the Windows section of Tucows, which you can visit on the Web at *http://www.tucows.com/*. WinZip, a popular, reasonably priced, and easy-to-use program, is almost always one of the top ten downloads on the Tucows network.

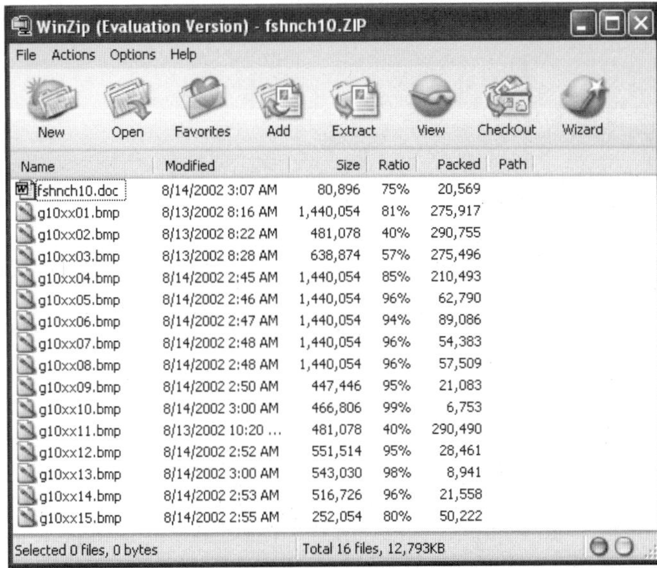

Note If Compressed (Zipped) Folder isn't associated with Zip files on your Windows XP computer, meaning that you have another program that will zip your files, a message box will appear, asking if you want to associate zip files with Compressed (Zipped) Folder. Click Yes to do so.

To compress a file or folder using the Zip utility in Windows XP, follow these steps:

1. Right-click the files or folders you want to compress, choose Send To, and choose Compressed (Zipped) Folder.
2. Windows XP will create a new folder with an icon representing the file you used to create the archive, indicating the files in the folder are compressed. You can add new files to the archive by dragging them into the zipped folder.

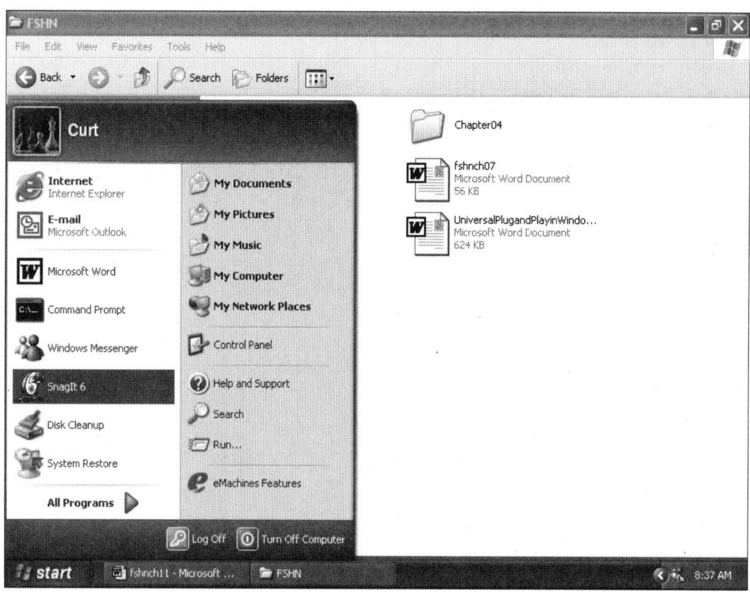

Saving Your Bacon with System Restore Points

I'm not exaggerating too much when I say that system restore points, which remember your computer's configuration in Windows XP, make it easier to wipe out problems if they occur in your system. You can use the System Restore feature to remove any system changes that were made since the last time you remember your computer working correctly. System Restore does not affect your personal data files (such as Microsoft Word documents, browsing history, drawings, favorites, or e-mail), so you won't lose changes made to these files. Windows XP creates restore points every day and also at the time of significant system events (such as when an application or driver is installed). You can also create and name your own restore points at any time. If something goes wrong, you select a restore point and Windows XP undoes any system changes made since that time.

Note The analogy I like to use for creating restore points is that, in a way, it's the opposite of saving a file after you've made changes you'd hate to have to make again. In the case of a system restore point, however, it's a matter of putting your system back in good working order after installing new software or hardware makes your computer unstable. If you're a gamer, you probably know to save your game just before you get into a big battle or other important encounter. When you do that, you ensure you come right back out at the spot you want and can get down to business.

When you run System Restore, a calendar is displayed to help you find restore points. If you don't use your computer every day, some days might not have any restore points. If you use your computer frequently, you might have restore points almost every day, and some days might have several restore points.

Creating a System Restore Point

Windows XP creates a restore point after every significant change to your system, but if you've got your system running just right and want to be sure you can reset the system to its current state if something goes wrong, you can create a restore point of your own. The process takes all of about 30 seconds, and it's a great way to ensure the continued health of your computer.

To create a system restore point, follow these steps:

1 Click Start. Choose All Programs, choose Accessories, choose System Tools, and choose System Restore. Select Create A Restore Point and click Next.

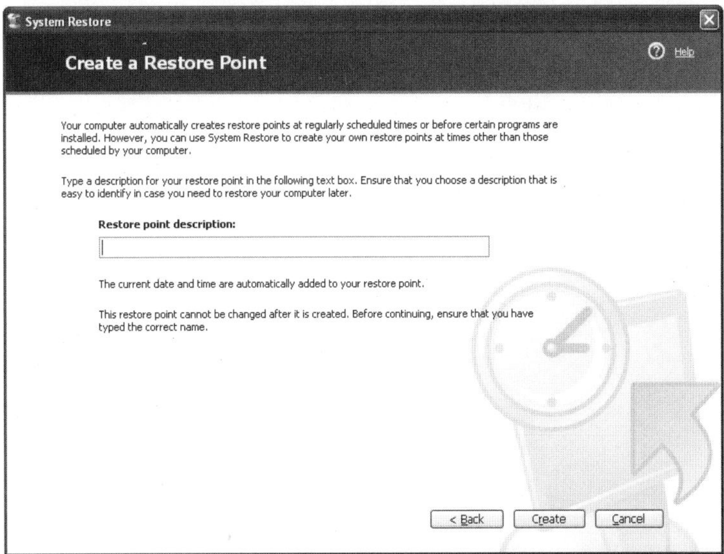

2 In the Restore Point Description box, type a name to identify this restore point. System Restore automatically adds the date and time you make the restore point to the point's name, so you don't have to add it yourself.

3 Click Create.

Restoring Your System Using a System Restore Point

If you're running Windows XP, it's important to remember that not all hardware and software will work correctly, even if that hardware or software works with another version of Windows you run on another computer. I'm sure that won't stop you from trying to make your hardware work on a Windows XP computer, but installing hardware that hasn't been tested with Windows XP makes your system unusable. If the unfortunate happens and you need to reset your computer using a system restore point, you can do so from within the Windows Help system. Once you restart your computer, you'll be able to take a closer look at whatever it was that happened to make your computer unstable.

Restoring a computer doesn't "use up" the system restore point, so you can try different things, secure in the knowledge that you can put your computer back in working order. Even so, it's not something you want to do casually—restoring your computer from a system restore point is serious business and should be used only when removing the hardware and all its drivers and supporting software doesn't make your computer stable again.

To start the computer using a system restore point, follow these steps:

1 Click Start. Choose All Programs, choose Accessories, choose System Tools, and choose System Restore. Select Restore My Computer To An Earlier Time, and click Next.

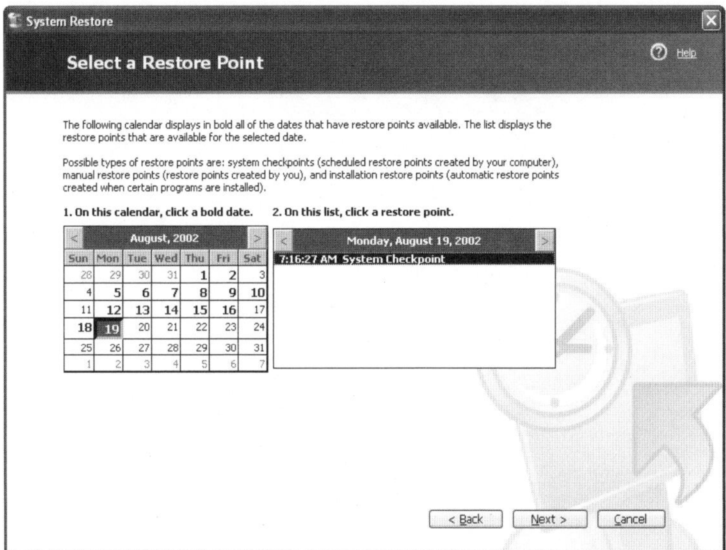

2 Click the calendar to display the system restore points available on the date with the system restore point you want to use. Select the restore point from the list that appears, and click Finish.

Uninstalling a Device Driver in Windows XP

Another variation on the problem of installing new hardware is when you have a device, such as a CD recorder or scanner, that works just fine, but something goes wrong when you follow my advice and install the latest and greatest driver that you found while searching the manufacturer's Web site. It doesn't happen often, but from time to time your computer just won't react well to the new driver. It could be a bad interaction with another driver on your system, it could be that the driver wasn't tested on a computer matching your configuration, or someone may have accidentally posted the wrong version of the driver to the Web site. In any case, because Windows doesn't erase an old driver when you update it, you can go back to the previous version of the driver and restore your system (and yourself) to blissful stability.

To roll back to the previous version of a driver in Windows XP, follow these steps:

1 Click Start and then choose Control Panel. Click Performance And Maintenance and then click System. Click the Hardware tab and then click Device Manager.

2 In the Device Manager dialog box, right-click the device for which you want to reinstall the previous version of the driver, and choose Properties.

3 Click the Drivers tab and then click Roll Back Driver.

4 Click OK and, when prompted to do so, restart your computer.

Updating Virus Signature Files

The Internet is always changing, with new Web sites being added every day, new folks signing on for the first time, and new viruses, worms, and Trojan horses trying to get into your computer and make mischief.

See Also *For a more complete description of the threats to your computer, see Chapter 5, "Making Your Network More Secure."*

Because the dangers posed to your computers are always changing, it's important that you purchase one or more virus-protection programs and update the virus signature files the programs use to scan files that you copy onto your computer, that reside on the Web sites you visit, and that are attached to the e-mail messages you receive. The craftier virus writers own copies of the popular virus-scanning software, and they take great pains to ensure their creations will get past the current generation of protection programs. The programmers on the side of all that is good work hard to have answers for the threats to your computing safety, but if you don't add the new detection patterns to your virus scanner's arsenal, you're a sitting duck.

Many virus-scanning programs let you schedule visits to the vendor's site so you can download the latest and greatest updates and be protected against new viruses. No updates can save you from a virus that hasn't been analyzed by the scanner manufacturers, but updating your virus signatures frequently (I recommend at least once a week, and preferably every day if you have an "always on" Internet connection) will save you a lot of grief.

There are a lot of virus-scanning programs out there, but one common program is Norton AntiVirus. I've spelled out the steps I would take within that program to schedule regular updates to my virus signature files. If you use another program, be sure to follow the directions that came with your program, though that will usually mean going to the company's Web site and downloading the new signature file.

To schedule regular updates to your virus signature files, follow these steps:

1 Run your virus-scanning program and choose Schedule Updates from the File menu.

2 Select the Enable Scheduled Automatic Updates check box and click Schedule.

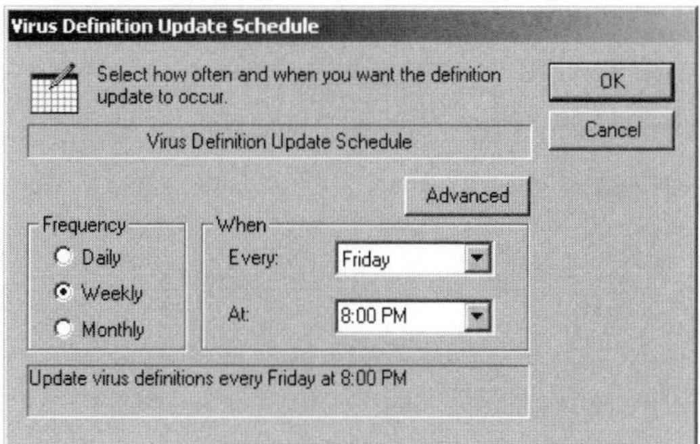

3 In the Frequency section of the dialog box, select the option button representing the frequency with which you want to check for updates,

and use the controls in the When section of the dialog box to specify the time the update is to take place. Click OK twice and then click Exit.

Note If the program puts an icon in the taskbar when virus checking is turned on, be sure the icon is still there!

Installing Security Updates from Microsoft Sites

Just as there are virus writers out there searching for new and interesting ways to get into your files and make your life miserable, there are folks who study operating systems with the goal of finding security problems that could be exploited. Some of these analysts have your best interests at heart, but many do not. And, just as you can update your virus scanners to catch new viruses that come along, you can update your copy of Windows to guard against any problems the development team has found.

To install a Windows security update from a Microsoft site, follow these steps:

1. Visit *http://windowsupdate.microsoft.com/*. After the Microsoft site detects your computer's operating system and asks to install software that will scan your computer and determine which updates you need, click Yes.
2. Click Download.
3. Click Start Download, and click Yes. When the installation is complete, click Yes to restart your computer.

Note While you're at the Windows Update site, you should look around to see if there are any updates available for other programs, such as Microsoft Internet Explorer.

How to Recognize a Valid Update File

I'll start with the obvious and state that one way you'll know an update file isn't valid is if it's sent to you as an e-mail attachment, particularly if that attachment comes from someone you don't know. As is the case with every e-mail attachment from a stranger, don't trust it! Strangers don't have your best interests at heart!

It's a bit trickier if you receive an e-mail message and are told to visit a Web site with what promises to be an important security update. For example, you might receive a message telling you to visit *http://www.microsoft.com@127.265.0.1/update.htm*. If you do, watch out! The address isn't actually a Microsoft address.

How can you tell? The "at" sign (@) gives it away. The @ is used for pages that require a user name and password to gain access. For example, on a page that requires you to log on with a name and password, the actual Uniform Resource Locator (URL) your browser would transfer after you fill in the log-on form would look something like *http://user:pa55w0rd@www.microsoft.com/*.

Note The @ can also be written as %40, which means the URL *http://www.microsoft.com%40127.265.0.1/update.htm* would take you to the same bad place as the URL with the @.

If the page you request in your browser doesn't require a user name and password, it just ignores everything to the left of the @ and reads the rest of it. To the human eye, however, the deception is almost perfect. First, the @ is perfectly legitimate in e-mail messages. Plus, as a user of the Web, you're trained to look at the first bit of a URL and ignore the stuff after you see .com, .org, or something similar. Remember what I said about social engineering in Chapter 5, "Making Your Network More Secure"? This is a prime example of how effective it can be. So, be on the lookout for this type of URL, particularly in e-mail messages in which a stranger, or someone you know who doesn't usually send you Windows security update mailings, tells you to go somewhere and install a file that will solve your security problems. Chances are you'll end up with more problems than you started with.

See Also *For an in-depth discussion of fake URLs and how to spot them, visit* http://curtis.frye.rules@www.pc-help.org/obscure.htm.

Automate with Windows Update

One very safe way you can search for updates to your computer is to use the Windows Update site. When you visit the Windows Update site, a program on that site installs a software program on your computer and uses that program to scan your system to see what hardware and software you have installed.

Windows Update and Your Privacy I wouldn't be surprised if you were concerned about sending your computer's information over the Internet as part of Windows Update, but none of your information is retained or used for any other purpose than making your computer more secure. Here's an excerpt from the Windows Update privacy statement, which tells you what information the program collects and how it's used:

> To provide you with the appropriate list of updates, Windows Update must collect a certain amount of configuration information from your computer. This information includes your operating system version number and Product Identification number, your Internet Explorer version number, version numbers of other software installed on your computer, and Plug and Play ID numbers of hardware devices on your computer.
>
> The Product Identification number is collected to confirm that you are running a validly licensed copy of Windows. A validly licensed copy of Windows ensures that you will receive ongoing updates from Windows Update. Windows Update does not collect your name, address, e-mail address, or any other form of personally identifiable information. The configuration information collected is used only for the period of time that you are visiting the site, and is not saved.
>
> Windows Update also tracks and records how many unique machines visit its site and whether the download and installation of specific updates succeeded or failed. In order to do this, Windows generates a Globally Unique Identifier (GUID) that is stored on your computer to uniquely identify it. Windows Update records the GUID of the computer that attempted the download, the ID of the item that you attempted to download and install, and information about your operating system version and Internet Explorer version. Because Windows Update does not collect personally identifiable information, the configuration information and GUID cannot be used to identify you.

To use Windows Update to find drivers for hardware on your computer, follow these steps:

1. Save your work and close any open programs. Run your Web browser, type **http://windowsupdate.microsoft.com/** in the Address box, and press Enter. If the site asks to install some software on your computer, verify that the dialog box that appears indicates that Microsoft has authorized the software, and click Yes.

   Note You may need to click Yes more than once during this process.

2. Click Scan For Updates and then click Review And Install Updates to display a list of the updates available for your computer.

3 Remove any updates from the list by clicking the Remove button next to the update and then click Install Now.

Note Updates marked Critical should always be installed.

---

4 Close your Web browser and restart your computer to complete the installation.

Monitoring Your Security Logs

If your Windows XP computer is connected directly to the Internet through a hub, you should definitely turn on the Internet Connection Firewall (ICF). But turning on the firewall isn't enough to ensure your computer is secure. One important aspect of running a firewall, which many folks overlook, is that you need to see what the firewall has been up to in terms of protecting your system against attack. It's true that you can't reprogram ICF from scratch, but you can get a better feel for what it's doing and see if you need to augment your protection in other ways.

To view your ICF security log, follow these steps:

1 Click Start and choose Control Panel. Click Network And Internet Connections and then click Network Connections.

2 Click the connection for which ICF is enabled and then, under Network Tasks, click Change Settings Of This Connection.

3 On the Advanced tab, click Settings.

4 In the Log File Options section of the Security Logging tab, under Name, click Browse.

5 Scroll to Pfirewall.log, right-click Pfirewall.log, and choose Open.

6 Double-click the log file to open it and view the contents.

Running ScanDisk

One of the weak links in the computer world is the floppy disk and its cousin the hard disk. Both types of disks fall in the general category of *magnetic media*, which means that computers use magnetism to record data on the disk and to read data from it. It also means that, while disks are extremely reliable, they are prone to failure at the worst possible times. If you've ever put a floppy disk behind a stereo speaker and seen your files turn to gibberish, you know what I'm talking about. Of course, the disks spin very, very quickly inside a drive, so there's physical wear and tear as well.

In Windows 98 SE and Windows Me (not Windows XP), you can use the ScanDisk system utility to take a look at your disks to see if there are any areas on the disk that aren't physically able to retain data. If there are only a few blocks on your disk that ScanDisk marks as not working, you're probably fine. If, on the other hand, the number of blocks that won't hold data increases quickly, you should back up all your data immediately and replace the hard disk as soon as possible.

To run ScanDisk in Windows 98 SE or Windows Me, follow these steps:

1 Click Start, choose Programs, choose Accessories, and then choose System Tools. Click ScanDisk.

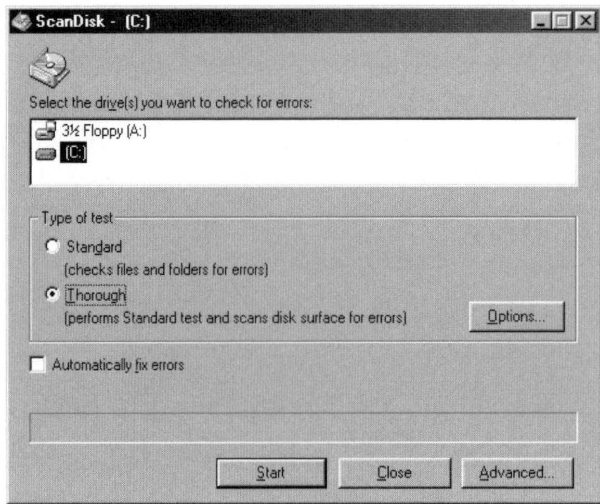

2 Select the drive you want to scan.

Note If you want to scan more than one drive on your computer, Ctrl-click any additional drives you want to scan.

3 Choose the type of scan you want to perform by following either of these steps:

- Select Standard to check files and folders on your drives for errors.
- Select Thorough to check your files and folders for errors and check the physical surface of your hard disks for errors. This type of scan can take a long time for large drives.

4 Click Start.

When the scan is done, you'll see a report indicating what errors, if any, were found, and you'll be given the opportunity to fix any errors in files or folders.

Note You did make a backup copy of your important files, right?

Defragmenting Your Drives

After you've used a computer for a while, you might come to the point where you need to erase or archive some files so you'll have enough room for that hour-long video you took when your sister tried to ride her mountain bike over your car. When you erase a file, you don't really get rid of it forever, at least not at first. Instead, what you do is delete the record of the file in your disk's *file allocation table* (FAT) and free up the disk space to be used to store another file.

Lingo A file allocation table is a record of the location of the files on a disk.

After a while, Windows will run out of new places to put files on your computer and will begin overwriting old data with new data. When it does, it will try to store the file in one uninterrupted segment of your disk, but it may need to break the file up among several different areas to fit it all in. When that starts to happen a lot, your disk is said to be fragmented because there are fragments of files spread throughout your disk. The Disk Defragmenter uses the information in the FAT to determine which file fragments belong together and to rewrite the data on your disk so the files are once again written in solid blocks. That makes file access a lot faster and more reliable because Windows doesn't need to hunt all over the disk for the next page of your letter home from school.

To defragment your drives in Windows 98 SE or Windows Me, follow these steps:

1. Click Start, choose Programs, choose Accessories, and then choose System Tools. Click Disk Defragmenter.
2. Click Start.

To defragment your drives in Windows XP, follow these steps:

1. Click Start, choose All Programs, choose Accessories, and then choose System Tools. Click Disk Defragmenter.

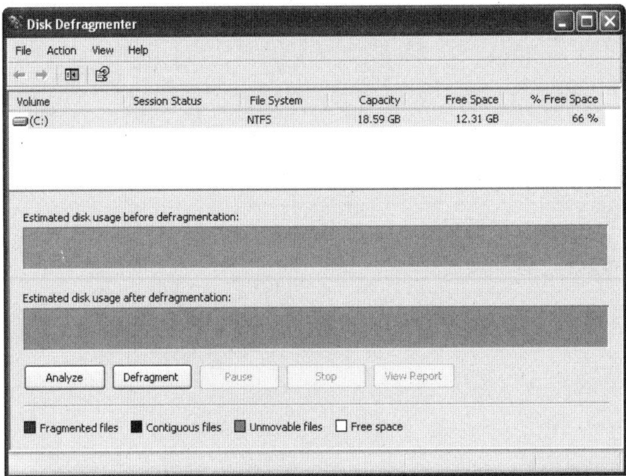

2 Click the drives you want to defragment and, if you want, click Analyze to have Disk Defragmenter analyze your drives to determine how much space would be saved and how much your files would be clustered after defragmentation. If the analysis shows little improvement, you can click Cancel to bypass the operation for the time being.

3 Click Defragment.

When the operation is done, you can click View Report to see a synopsis of what went on during the defragmentation.

Key Points

- You should back up important files regularly. Remember, a minute or two spent ensuring you have your data may save the days it would take to re-create it.
- You don't always need to back up all your files. If you're short on space or have a reliable backup of files that haven't changed, you can perform a differential or incremental backup.
- You'll need your Windows CD to install Microsoft Backup on your computer. It's on the Windows XP Home Edition CD, but you'll need to dig for it a bit.
- When I back up files, I don't use compression unless I'm trying to fit ten pounds of files into a five-pound bag. Even though the compression algorithms Backup uses are battle-tested and reliable, it's just one more thing that could potentially go wrong.

- It's a good idea to schedule regular file and virus signature updates. Remember, though, that if you're backing up files to a CD, it's better to be there so you won't forget to put a CD in the drive.
- Make it a habit to read your ICF logs every now and then to see what's being thrown at your computers. If you see something that you'd like to know more about, look up key terms from the entries on the Web.
- Floppy disks and hard disks can (and do) fail at the most inopportune times, so it's a good idea to run ScanDisk and Disk Defragmenter every now and then to see if anything is amiss. You can also use Disk Defragmenter to speed up access to your files.

Chapter 12

Troubleshooting Your Home Network

Throughout this book I've done my best to give you solid advice on how to set up your home network so you can share files, printers, and even Internet access. While I hope everything goes smoothly, I do understand that things can go wrong and that you might need to "look under the hood" to fix a problem. Not to worry! Fixing your network isn't as hard as you might think, and the knowledge you gain while installing your network will serve you in good stead.

My job in this chapter is to reiterate some background information on home networks and then walk you through specific scenarios that reflect problems you might have with your home network.

Remembering How Your Garden Grew

Before you troubleshoot home networking issues, it is important to remember how your network is structured. There are several common home network topologies:

- The computers are connected to a hub, and there is no Internet connection. In this configuration, the computers are typically assigned Internet Protocol (IP) addresses in the range of 169.254.*x*.*y* (where *x* and *y* are numbers between 1 and 254).

- The computers are connected to a hub. One computer has a connection to the Internet that is shared by using Internet Connection Sharing (ICS). This connection could be a dial-up connection or a broadband connection, typically a Digital Subscriber Line (DSL) or a cable modem. In this configuration, the computer that shares the connection typically assigns IP addresses to other computers on the home network. The computer sharing the connection will probably have the IP address 192.168.0.1 configured for the NIC that is connected to the home network. Other computers on the network should have addresses in the range 192.168.0.*x* (where *x* is an unused number between 1 and 254).
- The computers are connected to a hardware network address translation (NAT) device that provides a connection to the Internet. In this configuration, the computers typically receive an IP address from the NAT device. The NAT device typically uses the address 192.168.0.1 and assigns addresses to other computers in the range 192.168.0.*x* (where *x* is a number between 2 and 254).
- The computers are connected to a hub, and the hub is connected to the Internet via a broadband connection. This configuration is also known as an edgeless network. In this configuration, the computers on the home network each have an IP address that is provided by the Internet service provider (ISP). The addresses that are used vary depending on the ISP.
- The computers are connected to a hub, and each computer has a separate connection to the Internet (either dial-up or broadband). In this configuration, the computers typically use automatically assigned IP addresses for their home network adapters (169.254.*x*.*y*—where *x* and *y* are numbers from 1 to 254) and use ISP-provided addresses for their Internet connection.

My Computer Doesn't Recognize My Installed Network Hardware or My Connection

There are a few things you can do if your computer doesn't recognize your hardware or if you're not getting a network connection.

- Restart your computer. Yes, it's cliché, but you might have made a change since the last time you fired up your machine and forgot to restart it afterwards so the change could take effect.

- If possible, be sure to use the cables that came with the unit. If you bought cables on your own, be sure that you purchased the proper kind of cable for use with the hardware. For example, an Ethernet cable can look similar to a standard residential telephone cable. However, Ethernet cables have a wider and thicker connector on the end than residential telephone connectors. What makes the two cables easy to confuse is that a telephone connector will fit into an Ethernet port, but the cable could actually damage your Ethernet adapter.
- If you're using a Cat-5 cable to connect two pieces of hardware and the connection isn't working, you might have a faulty cable. If the connection works after replacing the cable, you've found the culprit. If not, you should check the cable to ensure it's the correct kind of cable for the connection you're making. Remember that when you connect a NIC to an Ethernet port on a hub, you use a patch cable, but when you extend a network by connecting a router to a hub, or a hub to another hub, you need to use a crossover cable. You can distinguish a patch cable from a crossover cable by checking the order of the wires in the connector. (That's why the strands have different-colored insulation and the connectors are made from clear, or at least translucent, plastic.) If the colors are in the same order in the connectors, you have a patch cable. If the colors are in a different order, you are the proud owner of a crossover cable.
- Check the physical connection between computers. The back of each NIC in a desktop computer will probably have visible lights to indicate a good connection. If you're using a hub or switch to connect the computers, check to ensure that the hub or switch is turned on and that the lights are on for each client connection, indicating a good link.
- Ensure you've plugged your cables into the proper ports on all your equipment. For example, your router might have a port labeled Modem or WAN (wide area network), which is where you absolutely must plug in the patch cable from your modem. You should also be sure that you're not trying to use the same port twice. On most routers and hubs, there is an Uplink port you can use to extend your network. The trick is that the Uplink port usually shares writing with a regular port, so if you're using the Uplink port, you can't use one of the Ethernet ports. For example, if your router has five ports, one of which is an Uplink port, you'll be able to plug three devices into your router and *either* plug a fourth device into the port next to the Uplink port or run a crossover cable from your Uplink port to a hub.

My Wireless Network Is Sick, Ailing, or Dead

If your wireless network doesn't seem to be well, the first two things you should do are ensure that your router has power and check that it is connected to your modem. You should also look at the lights on your router to be sure data is flowing normally. If the router indicates data is flowing, try pressing the router's Reset button, if it has one. Many routers can be reset by using a pen or stylus to press a button on the face of the router. If not, you can reset the router by turning it off and on, or unplugging it for ten seconds and then plugging it back in. If resetting the router doesn't fix the problem, investigate each of the following scenarios.

My Connection Works Fine...Sometimes

When you use a wireless network, you're asking your computers and router to share the airwaves with other devices. While it isn't common for items such as microwaves or the neighbor's wireless network to interfere with your network, it is possible. You may also get some interference if you have a cordless phone that operates at 2.4 gigahertz (GHz) (it'll say so on the box), but what usually happens then is that calls get dropped, not your network.

My Wireless Network Sends Data Very Slowly

If your network transmits data at well below the speeds you would expect, remove computers from your network. Your modem and router are like highways—there's only so much data you can fit through them at one time until things start to slow down. If your network has a lot of computers on it, you are splitting your network's bandwidth among each of them and hurting your overall transmission rates.

My Computer Is Close to My Wireless Router, but It Doesn't See the Network

If your computer is close to your wireless router but can't find it when it scans for available networks, there is probably some sort of interference preventing the signal from reaching your computer. There could be power lines in the wall or a nearby microwave oven, cordless phone, or other wireless device that's interfering with your network traffic. If you think that might be the problem, try moving your network hardware so the obstruction is no longer in the way.

My Computer Still Can't Find My Wireless Router

When your computer is close to your router but it still can't find the network when it scans the airwaves, you might have set your computer to look for a network with the wrong name or to look for a peer-to-peer network when your network is actually an infrastructure network. Your computer's wireless NIC might also be looking for a network on the wrong channel. You should configure your NIC so it scans every channel available, not just one or two, so it has a fair shot at finding your network when it looks.

My Computer Can't Find My Workgroup

This problem usually surfaces when you reinstall a network after you've had problems or when you add a computer to a network. In most cases, you will have entered the wrong workgroup name when you configured your computer for home networking. It's no big deal to fix—just verify your workgroup's name on a computer that is on the network and run the Home Networking Wizard on the computer you're having trouble with.

To find a computer's workgroup name in Microsoft Windows XP, follow these steps:

1. Click Start, right-click My Computer, and choose Properties.
2. Click the Computer Name tab.

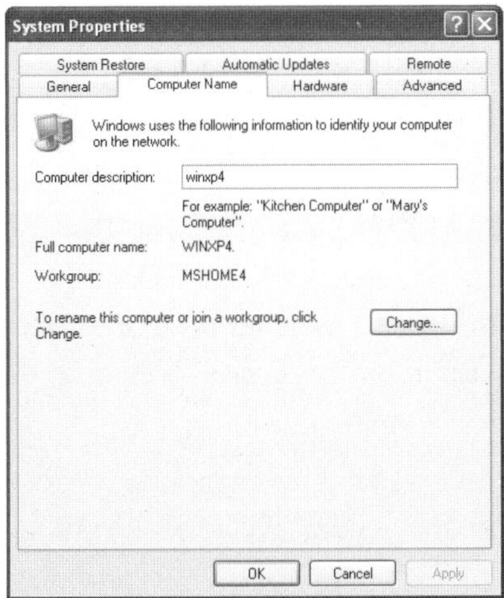

3. If the workgroup name is incorrect, select Change.
4. Type the correct name in the Workgroup box and click OK twice.
5. Restart your computer when prompted to do so.

To find a computer's workgroup name in Microsoft Windows 98 Second Edition (SE) or Microsoft Windows Millennium Edition (Me), follow these steps:

1. Click Start, choose Settings, and then choose Control Panel.
2. Double-click the Network icon.
3. Select the Identification tab.
4. If the workgroup name is different from that of the other computers on your network, type the correct name in the Workgroup box and click OK twice.
5. Restart your computer when prompted to do so.

I Need to Troubleshoot My Broadband Modem Connection

If your broadband modem connection is causing you problems, you should check the modem's lights. Most modems have four or five lights, and their names (and functions) will be something like this:

- Power, which indicates whether the router is on. It doesn't do too much if it isn't plugged in, or if the adapter is plugged into an outlet but the other end of the power cord isn't plugged into the back of the modem.
- Cable, which tells you whether the router is getting a signal from the cable network. This light might be named Line, or WAN if you have a DSL connection, and shouldn't flicker at all. If it does, either your modem uses this light instead of a Data light to indicate network activity, or your connection isn't stable, which might indicate a cable or connector problem.
- PC, which tells you whether the modem knows your computer, or the router you use to connect other computers to your network, is on the network. This light shouldn't flicker at all, either. If it does, your connection isn't stable, which might indicate a cable or connector problem.
- Data, which tells you whether there is data moving through the modem. This light will usually flash off and on when everything's in good shape, or it might stay solid if it's used to indicate a solid connection. If the light stays a solid green, you might have a malicious program on your computer that's sending out data, either in an attempt to infect other computers or as part of a distributed denial of service

attack intended to disable other computers by bombarding them with transmissions.

- Test, which indicates your modem is going through self-diagnostics. You'll usually see this light on only after you power up the modem. If you see it at other times, it could indicate problems with the modem.

My Printer Presents Pesky Problems

Printers are just like computers in that you might run into difficulties reaching them over a network. If you do have trouble with your printer, don't despair! I've listed some of the common printer problems and their solutions.

My Printer Doesn't Appear in the Printers Section of Control Panel or the Print Dialog Box of Any Program

The first thing you should do is ensure your printer is connected to a computer on your network. Verify that the universal serial bus (USB) or parallel cable connecting your printer is seated firmly in both the printer and your computer (or a USB hub if your printer is one of many USB devices connected to your computer). Once the printer is connected securely, be sure it is turned on. If your computer is turned on and it has a Reset or Online/Offline button, you should press it to see if the printer responds.

My Printer Appears on My Network but I Still Can't Print

If I had a nickel for every time I said to myself, "Everything looks right...why won't the darn thing print?" I'd have about a dollar. Even so, it's frustrating when it happens. Here are some things you can do to figure out why your printer won't respond, even when it looks like it's available on the network.

- Make sure your printer is still plugged in and turned on. Sometimes when you remove a printer, a "ghost" will remain on the system, and you'll need to delete the printer and reinstall it to get it to work again.
- Make sure the computer to which your printer is connected is turned on and connected to the network.
- Check the printer front to see if the Alarm or Error light is illuminated. If so, there's a problem you'll need to correct, even if it's just by pressing the Reset or Online/Offline button or turning the printer off and back on.
- Check the printer's paper tray to ensure that it has paper and that the tray is pushed all the way in.

- Try to print a document, and see if the Manual Feed option is selected in the Print dialog box. If so, change it to Paper Cassette or Paper Tray, depending on your printer's options.

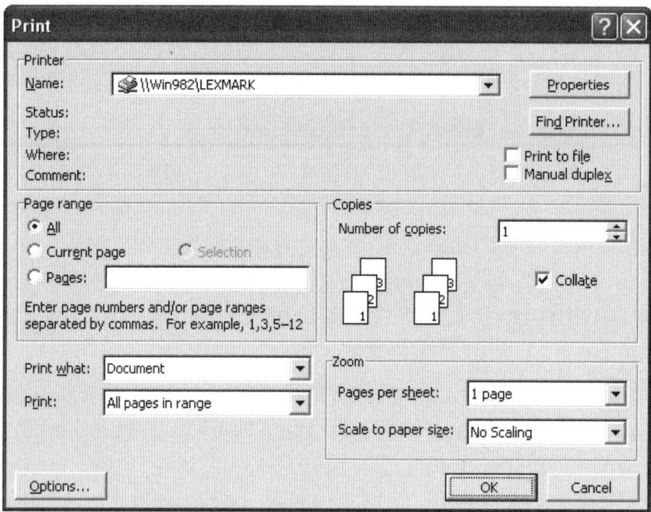

- Make sure you don't need to enter a password to gain access to the printer.
- Make sure the printer is shared.
- I don't know how many times I've made this mistake, but I'd enjoy knowing that I spared you a similar fate: Make sure you've selected the correct printer in the Print dialog box! I cost myself U.S.$20 at a copy shop one time because I selected the high-end color printer instead of the cheap black-and-white printer. I received a beautiful rendering of my all-text report for my trouble, but I'd hoped to spend the money on something else.

A Computer Has Vanished! (from Network Places)

You might run into a situation in which you can browse the Web just fine from every computer on your network, but you can't see one or more of your Windows 98 computers in My Network Places on a Windows XP computer. That's because there's a difference in the ways that Windows 98 Second Edition (SE) and Windows XP computers deal with network connections. The difficulty lies in differing interpretations of the network basic input/output system (NetBIOS) standard, and it's well beyond the scope of this book to describe that protocol and what you'd need to do to fix your network.

The good news is that your home network does recognize that your Windows 98 SE computer is on the network—if that were not the case, you wouldn't be able to surf the Web from your Windows 98 computer. Fortunately, there is a way to establish a connection to the shared folders on your Windows 98 computer, though you'll need to do it from each of your Windows XP computers. The process is very similar to mapping a network drive, which I discussed in Chapter 7, "Getting Your Network to Work for You." The difference, though, is that you need to find the network address of the computer that's dropped out of sight in My Network Places.

To connect to a computer that is on your network but is not visible in My Network Places, follow these steps:

1. On the computer that isn't visible in My Network Places, click Start and then choose Run.
2. In the Run dialog box, follow either of these steps:
   - If the computer is running Windows XP, type **cmd**.
   - If the computer is running Windows 98 SE or Windows Me, type **command**.
3. In the command window, type **ipconfig** and then press Enter.

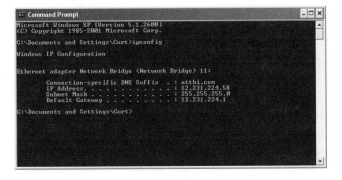

```
Command Prompt
Microsoft Windows XP [Version 5.1.2600]
(C) Copyright 1985-2001 Microsoft Corp.

C:\Documents and Settings\Curt>ipconfig

Windows IP Configuration

Ethernet adapter Network Bridge (Network Bridge) 11:

        Connection-specific DNS Suffix  . : attbi.com
        IP Address. . . . . . . . . . . . : 12.231.224.58
        Subnet Mask . . . . . . . . . . . : 255.255.255.0
        Default Gateway . . . . . . . . . : 12.231.224.1

C:\Documents and Settings\Curt>
```

4. Open My Computer, click Tools, and then click Map Network Drive.
5. In the Drive list, select a drive letter that is not already in use on your computer.
6. In the Folder box for Windows XP (it's called Path in Windows 98 SE and Windows Me), type the IP address of the computer you're connecting to with a leading \\, and add the shared folder name.

Note If you want your computer to always try to connect to this drive whenever you log on, select the Reconnect At Logon check box.

7. Click Finish to add the shared folder to My Computer on your computer as a drive. If your computer has Windows XP installed and you want the shared volume to appear in My Network Places, you'll need to run the Add A Network Place Wizard.
8. Click Start and choose My Network Places. In the Network Tasks panel, click Add A Network Place.
9. Click Next and then select Choose Another Network Location. Click Next.
10. Click Browse, click the drive letter representing the shared folder you mapped, and then click OK.
11. Click Next, type a name for the network location in the Type A Name For This Network Place box, and click Next.
12. Click Finish.

Note In Windows XP, if you want to display the contents of the new network place when you close the wizard, select the Open This Network Place When I Click Finish check box.

File and Printer Sharing in Windows XP Doesn't Work

One of the best parts of creating a home network is that you're able to share files and printers between computers, so it's especially frustrating if your file and printer sharing just isn't happening. The first thing to keep in mind is that if you're using Internet Connection Sharing (ICS) to share an Internet connection, Internet Connection Firewall (ICF) must be disabled on every computer on your home network. If not, ICF will block the data before it reaches the target computer on your network. If your computers share your Internet connection through a hub, and are therefore connected directly to the Internet, you should use ICF on every Windows XP computer and one of the firewalls mentioned in Chapter 5 for computers running Windows Me or Windows 98 SE. And, of course, if you have a router that acts as a firewall, you don't need a software firewall on any computer on your network.

Another aspect of home network sharing is that all network access to a Windows XP Home Edition computer, or to a Windows XP Professional computer in a workgroup, uses the Guest account. Before you continue troubleshooting, make sure that the Guest account is set up for network access. But, because allowing the Guest account to have network access opens yourself up to outsiders trying to get in, you should turn off the Guest account's network access as soon as you're done troubleshooting.

To set up the Guest account for network access, follow these steps:

1. Click Start, choose Run, type **cmd** in the Open box, and click OK.
2. Type **net user guest** and press Enter.
3. If the account is active, you'll see Account Active Yes or something similar.
4. If the account is not active, type **net user guest /active:yes** to give the Guest account network access.
5. If you see any response other than The Command Completed Successfully, make sure that you are logged on as an Administrator and then confirm that you typed the command properly before you press Enter again.

Once you're certain the computers are set up for sharing, locate the computer name for each computer and make sure that the folder you're trying to reach is shared. You can see all the shared folders on a computer by running the File Sharing Management Console program.

To see a list of shared folders on your network, follow these steps:

1. Click Start, click Run, type **fsmgmt.msc** in the Open box, and click OK.
2. In the left pane, click Shares to display a list of shared folders on your network in the right pane. Write down the name of the one shared folder from each computer so you can try to open the share later in the procedure.
3. Click Start, choose Run, type ***computername*** (where *computername* is the name of another computer on the network), and press Enter. Click one of the shared folder's icons to confirm that the connection is functioning.

If you cannot open a shared folder, test in the opposite direction between the computers or test between other computers to ensure that the problem is not with a particular computer on the network.

If you still cannot connect to the other computer by using the previous steps, test again, but replace *computername* with the name of the computer you're using. This tests the connection locally, and unless something's seriously wrong, you'll see a window that displays an icon for each shared folder on the computer. Try opening one of the shares; if you don't see a window with the shares on the computer, or if you receive an error message, search the Microsoft

Knowledge Base for additional information about the specific error message that you received. To search the Microsoft Knowledge Base, visit *http://www.microsoft.com* and click Support.

If you do not receive any error messages, or if you do not find related information in the Microsoft Knowledge Base, check the Network Setup Wizard log file for errors in any steps that are not followed by successes.

To open the Network Setup Wizard log file, follow these steps:

1. Click Start and choose Run.
2. Type **%SystemRoot%\nsw.log** in the Open box and press Enter.

If you find errors in the log (such as with setting the computer name or installing Client for Microsoft Networks), search the Microsoft Knowledge Base for additional information about manually configuring the computer with proper settings.

When Network Internet Connectivity Falters: Using Windows XP

In Windows XP, for most issues that involve Internet connectivity, start by using the Network Diagnostics tool to gather configuration information, identify the source of the issue, and perform automated troubleshooting of the network connection. (If you're not using Windows XP, you can address Internet connectivity by following the procedures in the next section.)

To use the Network Diagnostics tool, follow these steps:

1. Click Start and choose Help And Support.
2. Click Use Tools To View Your Computer Information And Diagnose Problems and then click Network Diagnostics in the list on the left.
3. Click Scan Your System. When the process is finished, check for any items marked Failed in red, click the Expand control next to those categories, and view the additional details about what the testing showed.

I Can Log On to the Internet but Can't Reach Other Computers

Once you step away from your home network and try to interact with computers elsewhere on the Internet, you need to be prepared to accept that the problem might not be on your end. Any of the following issues can cause problems when you try to communicate with a server on the Internet:

- The computer hosting the Web site you're trying to view is not functioning properly or has been temporarily removed from the Internet.

- Your Internet browser is not configured properly.
- The Transmission Control Protocol/Internet Protocol (TCP/IP) configuration for your dial-up connection to your ISP is incorrect.
- Your ISP's Domain Name Service (DNS) server is not working properly.

To determine the cause and resolution of the problem that you are experiencing, use the following procedures in the order in which they are presented. After you complete a procedure, try again to see whether you can successfully communicate with servers on the Internet.

Try a Known Good Server

If you cannot communicate with a specific server on the Internet, try to connect to the Microsoft Web site by using its fully qualified domain name (FQDN), such as *http://www.microsoft.com*. If you can connect to the Microsoft Web site by using its FQDN, the TCP/IP configuration on your computer is correct. And so, for that matter, is everything else.

If you can connect to the Microsoft Web site but you cannot connect to another specific Internet site after several tries, the other site might not be functioning properly or might be temporarily removed from the Internet. Try to connect to some different Web sites. If you can connect to some Web sites but not to other Web sites, it's possible that your ISP's domain name services aren't working properly. It might also be true that the computers your ISP's computers contact to locate unknown IP addresses aren't working. In short, the problem could be just about anywhere on the Internet.

If you cannot connect to any Web sites, there might be a problem with your Internet browser configuration or with the TCP/IP configuration for your dial-up connection to your ISP. You can test your local connections by trying to connect to a computer or router on your home network. For example, if your router's IP address is 192.168.0.1, type **http://192.168.0.1/** in your Web browser's Address box and see if the router's configuration page comes up. If it does, the problem isn't on your end.

Make Sure That Your Browser Configuration Is Correct

Make sure that your Web browser (for example, Microsoft Internet Explorer) is correctly configured to connect to the Internet through the dial-up connection to your ISP, and make sure that your Internet browser is not configured to connect through a *proxy server* unless your ISP or business tells you to do so.

Lingo A proxy server is a computer or a program that acts as a "go-between" barrier between a local area network (LAN) and the Internet.

To verify your proxy server settings, follow these steps:

1. Start Internet Explorer and then choose Internet Options from the Tools menu.
2. Click the Connections tab and then look at the settings that relate to your ISP. You can see whether your browser is using a proxy server from within the same dialog box by clicking LAN Settings.

Confirm Your IP Address

If your ISP has given you a static (permanent) IP address, make sure that the TCP/IP configuration for your ISP connection contains the correct information. Follow these steps:

1. Connect to your ISP.
2. Click Start, choose Run, type **ipconfig /all** in the Open box, and press Enter.

The IPCONFIG/ALL command displays Windows TCP/IP settings for all your NICs and modem connections. The address for a modem connection is displayed as NDISWAN *x* adapter, where *x* is a number. The default gateway for the NDISWAN *x* adapter is the same as the IP address; this is normal and by design. More than one NDISWAN *x* adapter might be displayed. Any NDISWAN *x* adapters that are not currently in use display zeros for the IP address.

If the IP address that is displayed for your dial-up connection to your ISP does not match the IP address that your ISP gave you, change the IP address that is displayed so that it matches the address that your ISP gave you.

To change a static IP address on your computer, follow these steps:

1. Click Start, choose Settings, choose Control Panel (or, in Windows XP, click Start and choose Control Panel), and then click Network Connections.
2. Right-click your Internet connection, choose Properties, and click the Networking tab.
3. Click the Internet Protocol adapter, and then click Properties.
4. If necessary, change the TCP/IP settings to match the settings provided by your ISP, click OK, and then click OK again.

When Routing Conflicts Need Resolution

If you simultaneously connect to a local network by using a NIC and to your ISP by using a modem, configure your dial-up connection so that any routing conflicts are resolved in favor of your dial-up connection to your ISP.

To resolve routing conflicts in favor of your connection to your ISP in Windows XP, follow these steps:

1. Click Start, click Control Panel, click Network And Internet Connections, and then click Internet Connections.
2. Right-click your Internet connection, click Properties, and click the Networking tab.
3. Click the Internet Protocol adapter, click Properties, and then click Advanced.
4. Select the Use Default Gateway On Remote Network check box and then click OK twice.

Conflict Resolution: Check the Transfer and Receive Lights

If you simultaneously connect to a local network by using a NIC and connect to your ISP by using a modem, a conflict between your NIC and your modem can prevent your modem from sending information to servers on the Internet.

To verify that TCP/IP packets are being routed through your modem to your ISP, follow these steps:

1. Connect to and log on to your ISP.
2. Click Start, choose Run, type **ping *IP address*** in the Open box, andclick OK.

Note In the command in step 2, *IP address* is the IP address of a known good server on the Internet. If you do not know the IP address of a server on the Internet, use the IP address for *ftp.microsoft.com*, 207.46.133.140.

---

3. If the transfer (Tx) light in Dial-Up Networking Monitor flashes when you ping a server on the Internet, TCP/IP information is being routed through your modem to your ISP.
4. If the transfer (Tx) light in Dial-Up Networking Monitor does not flash when you ping a server on the Internet, packets are not being routed through your modem.
5. If the receive (Rx) light in Dial-Up Networking Monitor does not flash when you ping a server on the Internet, packets are not being received from your ISP. Contact your ISP for assistance.
6. If the receive (Rx) light in Dial-Up Networking Monitor flashes a lot when you ping a server on the Internet but you still cannot connect to the server by using its FQDN, there might be a name resolution issue.

When the lights flash for a while, it means your computer located the computer's address and is trying to contact it. If the lights flash briefly and then stop, it means your computer tried to find the address of the computer you want to ping and couldn't do so. (I am assuming that your home network's configuration is correct and that you can connect to computers on your home network.)

Test the Name Resolution

A DNS translates the names of computers on the Internet to their corresponding IP address and vice versa. The technical name for the process is *host name resolution*. If you cannot connect to a server on the Internet by using its FQDN, there might be a problem with the DNS configuration of your dial-up connection to your ISP or with your ISP's DNS server.

To determine whether there is a problem with the DNS configuration of your dial-up connection to your ISP, follow these steps:

1 Click Start, click Run, type **ipconfig /all** in the Open box, and press Enter.

> **Note** If the IP address for your DNS server does not appear, contact your ISP to obtain the IP address for your DNS server.

2 To verify that your computer can communicate with your DNS server, type **ping** followed by your DNS server's IP address. The reply looks something like this:

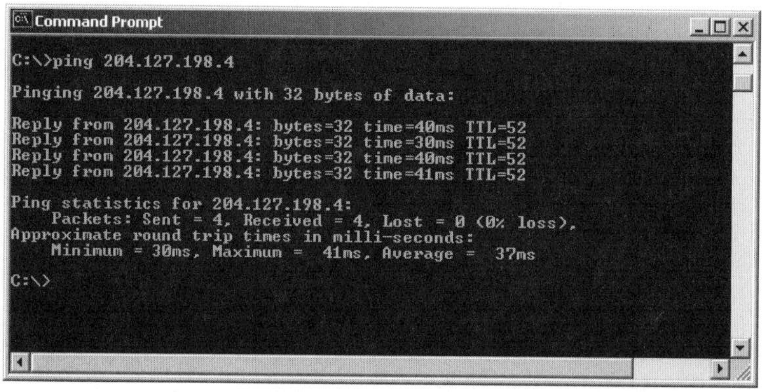

```
Command Prompt
C:\>ping 204.127.198.4

Pinging 204.127.198.4 with 32 bytes of data:

Reply from 204.127.198.4: bytes=32 time=40ms TTL=52
Reply from 204.127.198.4: bytes=32 time=30ms TTL=52
Reply from 204.127.198.4: bytes=32 time=40ms TTL=52
Reply from 204.127.198.4: bytes=32 time=41ms TTL=52

Ping statistics for 204.127.198.4:
    Packets: Sent = 4, Received = 4, Lost = 0 (0% loss),
Approximate round trip times in milli-seconds:
    Minimum = 30ms, Maximum =  41ms, Average =  37ms

C:\>
```

3 If you cannot successfully ping the IP address of the DNS server, you can try to use the Tracert tool to see where the problem lies. Click Start,

choose Programs, choose Accessories, and then click Command Window. In the Command Window, type **tracert *IPAddress***, where *IPAddress* is the IP address of the DNS server.

```
Command Prompt
C:\>tracert www.techsoc.com

Tracing route to www.techsoc.com [216.15.139.248]
over a maximum of 30 hops:

  1    10 ms    10 ms    30 ms  10.142.0.1
  2    10 ms    20 ms    20 ms  12.244.84.65
  3    20 ms    10 ms    30 ms  12.244.64.129
  4    10 ms    20 ms    20 ms  12.244.72.34
  5    10 ms    20 ms    30 ms  gbr1-p70.st6wa.ip.att.net [12.123.44.57]
  6    10 ms    60 ms    10 ms  gbr4-p70.st6wa.ip.att.net [12.122.5.161]
  7    60 ms    60 ms    60 ms  tbr2-p012402.cgcil.ip.att.net [12.122.10.61]
  8     *        *        *     Request timed out.
  9    80 ms    80 ms    60 ms  gbr5-p20.sl9mo.ip.att.net [12.122.11.122]
 10    60 ms    60 ms    90 ms  ar6-p310.sl9mo.ip.att.net [12.123.24.121]
 11    71 ms    60 ms    80 ms  att.cybercon.com [12.125.64.6]
 12    60 ms    70 ms    81 ms  gig12.sw2.cybercon.com [216.15.195.62]
 13    80 ms    60 ms    91 ms  techsoc.com [216.15.139.248]

Trace complete.

C:\>_
```

If the trace doesn't go beyond your ISP's network, contact your ISP to verify that you are using the correct IP address and that the DNS server is working properly.

4 If you can ping the IP address of your DNS server but cannot connect to a server on the Internet by using its FQDN, your DNS server might not be resolving host names properly. If more than one DNS server is available for your ISP, configure your computer to use a different DNS server. If using another DNS server resolves the issue, contact your ISP to correct the issue with the original DNS server.

5 When you have verified the correct IP address for your DNS server, update the TCP/IP settings for your dial-up connection to your ISP.

To change or add a valid IP address for your DNS server for a Dial-Up Networking phonebook entry in Windows XP, follow these steps:

1 Click Start, choose Control Panel, and click Network Connections.

2 Right-click your Internet connection, choose Properties, and then click the Networking tab.

3 Click the Internet Protocol adapter and click Properties.

4 Click Use The Following DNS Server Addresses and type the correct IP address in the Preferred DNS Server text box.

5 Click OK twice and restart your computer if prompted to do so.

Appendix

Which Windows Should You Do?

One of the most basic decisions you need to make when you want to create a home network is whether you need to upgrade your operating system. There's no doubt that Microsoft Windows XP is the best operating system discussed in this book for creating a home network, and you should strongly consider upgrading to Windows XP on at least the computer with which you connect directly to the Internet. The following tables provide all the detail you need to weigh the capabilities of Windows 98 Second Edition (SE), Windows Millennium Edition (Me), and Windows XP Home Edition. The first six tables compare the general features of the three major editions of the Windows operating system; tables seven through nine compare features specific to home networking, game playing, and multimedia applications; and the last table compares the features of Windows XP Home Edition and Windows XP Professional.

Note If you're just interested in setting up a home network, you can use Windows XP Home Edition with confidence that you'll get everything you need in your operating system. If you're a business user or want to set up security on a file-by-file basis, you should certainly go for Windows XP Professional.

Table A-1 Reliability: Windows 98 SE, Windows Me, and Windows XP Home Edition
(0 = Not Implemented, / = Partially Implemented, X = Fully Implemented)

Feature	Feature Description	Windows 98 SE	Windows Me	Windows XP Home Edition
Built on New Windows Engine	With Windows XP Home Edition, Microsoft merged features of its consumer operating systems with the power, security, and reliability of the Windows 2000 engine to create an easier-to-use, more dependable operating system.	0	0	X
Windows File Protection	Prevents you or your applications from accidentally changing the core operating system files, protecting your system.	/ Windows 98 includes a system file, which helps protect against some types of crashes.	X	X
Protected Kernel Mode Architecture	Your applications do not have access to the software code kernel upon which your operating system is based. This greatly improves the reliability of your system.	0	0	X
Process Separation	Errant applications will not cause your computer to crash. Each application is in a completely separate, protected memory space.	/	/	X
Side-by-Side DLLs	These provide you with a mechanism for multiple versions of individual Windows components to run "side by side." Now you won't have to worry that your applications will conflict with each other and cause application instability.	0	0	X

Table A-2 Performance Monitoring: Windows 98 SE, Windows Me, and Windows XP Home Edition
(0 = Not Implemented, / = Partially Implemented, X = Fully Implemented)

Feature	Feature Description	Windows 98 SE	Windows Me	Windows XP Home Edition
System Monitor	Analyzes hundreds of different system metrics, including memory, disk, and network throughput.	0	X	X
Task Manager	Provides you with useful computer performance information and allows you to terminate inactive programs. You can also opt for a reporting mechanism that suits your specific requirements.	0	0	X
Enhanced Battery Life	Enables you to improve the battery life of your mobile computer by conserving display power in two ways: Lid Power: When the lid of a mobile computer is closed, the display is powered off. LCD Dimming: When a mobile computer is running on battery power, the display is dimmed. Upon reconnection to AC power, the original brightness is restored.	0	0	X

Table A-3 Security and Privacy Protection: Windows 98 SE, Windows Me, and Windows XP Home Edition
(0 = Not Implemented, / = Partially Implemented, X = Fully Implemented)

Feature	Feature Description	Windows 98 SE	Windows Me	Windows XP Home Edition
Internet Connection Firewall	The Internet Connection Firewall protects your computer from intrusion when you are connected to the Internet.	0	0	X
Credential Manager	Credential Manager is a secured store for password information. This feature allows you to input user names and passwords for various network resources and applications (such as e-mail) once, and then have the system automatically supply that information for subsequent visits to those resources without your intervention.	0	0	X

Table A-4 Ease of Use: Windows 98 SE, Windows Me, and Windows XP Home Edition
(0 = Not Implemented, / = Partially Implemented, X = Fully Implemented)

Feature	Feature Description	Windows 98 SE	Windows Me	Windows XP Home Edition
Easy Set-Up Wizard	An easy-to-understand tutorial walks you through the installation process for the operating system, prompting you, when necessary, to enter information that will customize your PC.	0	X	X
Dynamic Update	Provides different application and device compatibility updates, some driver updates, and emergency fixes for setup or security issues at operating system setup to help you keep your operating system current and functioning smoothly.	0	0	X
Personalized Welcome Screen	The welcome screen can be personalized to allow you to share the same computer with your friends and family. Each individual can create his or her own unique account. These accounts are easily created during setup or from Control Panel. By default the accounts are not password-protected, but you can set a password on your specific account.	0	0	X
Fast User Switching	This gives you and your family or friends the ability to share a single computer without having to close each other's applications each time you need to access your own account.	0	0	X
Start Menu	Organizes your programs. It is the primary way to access files, folders, and programs on your computer. Windows XP Home Edition offers an enhanced Start menu. Access to important and frequently used tasks and applications is made easier with a Frequently Used Programs list and prominent positioning of your most critical folders.	/	/	X
Task-focused Design	Allows you to view the Windows options associated with your current task. For example, if you are creating a Word document, a dynamic menu appears that lists appropriate tasks such as cut, paste, and copy.	0	0	X
Taskbar Grouping	Open files are grouped according to the type of application they are, keeping your taskbar clean and organized.	0	0	X
Desktop Clean Up Wizard	The Desktop Clean Up Wizard periodically checks your desktop and gives you the opportunity to move unused shortcuts.	0	0	X

Table A-5 File Management and Searching: Windows 98 SE, Windows Me, and Windows XP Home Edition

(0 = Not Implemented, / = Partially Implemented, X = Fully Implemented)

Feature	Feature Description	Windows 98 SE	Windows Me	Windows XP Home Edition
Search Companion	A search companion identifies what kind of help you need and retrieves search information relevant to your task at hand.	0	0	X
File Management	You can quickly find what you need by grouping files and folders and using thumbnail views and organization that makes sense to you.	0	0	X
Indexed File System	Provides you with the capability of indexing the contents of the file system; this allows you to locate files based on a file name or search string.	0	0	X
Files and Settings Transfer Wizard	Enables the transfer of files, documents, and settings from one computer to another. The wizard walks you through migrating files, documents, or settings from an old computer to a new one.	0	0	X

Table A-6 System Maintenance and Help Systems: Windows 98 SE, Windows Me, and Windows XP Home Edition.

0 = Not Implemented, / = Partially Implemented, X = Fully Implemented)

Feature	Feature Description	Windows 98 SE	Windows Me	Windows XP Home Edition
System Restore	The System Restore feature of Windows XP Home Edition enables you to restore a PC, in the event of a problem, to a previous state without losing personal data files. System Restore actively monitors system file changes to record or store previous versions before the changes occurred. System Restore automatically creates easily identifiable restore points, which allow you to restore the system to a previous point in time.	0	X	X
Compatibility Mode	You can enable an application to run within a compatibility mode that helps mimic older versions of Windows using the built-in compatibility technology.	0	0	X
DualView	DualView allows two monitors to host the Windows desktop, while being driven off of a single display adapter. In the case of laptop computers, this could be the internal LCD display as well as an external monitor. For desktops there are a variety of high-end display adapters that will support this functionality.	0	0	X
ClearType	Supports Microsoft ClearType, a text display technology with enhanced screen resolution, making it easier to read text on your computer screen.	0	0	X

Table A-6 System Maintenance and Help Systems: Windows 98 SE, Windows Me, and Windows XP Home Edition. *(continued)*
0 = Not Implemented, / = Partially Implemented, X = Fully Implemented)

Feature	Feature Description	Windows 98 SE	Windows Me	Windows XP Home Edition
Uninstall	Uninstall provides the ability to restore an upgrade to the previous Windows operating system you were using. This feature applies only if you are upgrading your computer from Windows 98 and Windows Me. It provides the ability to uninstall at any point during setup.	0	0	X
Help and Support Center	Help has been enhanced for Windows XP Home Edition. Help now features the ability to search across multiple information sources, such as your computer manufacturer's home page, Microsoft Knowledge Base, and so on. In addition, you can now print a chapter from the online documentation. Windows XP Home Edition has also integrated the concept of Favorites into the Help subsystem.	/ Windows 98 includes an HTML-based online help system.	X	X
Remote Assistance	Provides the ability to invite a trusted friend or support professional who also runs Windows XP to be a remote assistant. Through an Internet connection, your assistant can chat with you, observe your working screen, and, with permission, remotely control your computer.	0	0	X
Extensible Search	Lets you search across multiple remote and online providers to get the most information for the topic you're investigating.	0	0	X
Get Help over the Web	Provides a mechanism to easily view server Help content from a desktop computer.	0	0	X
Windows Update	Windows Update can provide new device drivers in addition to application compatibility fixes so you'll have more support for your devices and applications. Updates downloaded from Windows Update can also be applied to all users on a computer at one time. Windows Update is now integrated with the Help and Support Center in Windows XP Home Edition. The Device Manager will also search Windows Update for new drivers when you insert a new device.	/	/	X
Device Driver Rollback	Provides the capability of replacing an unstable device driver (does not include printer drivers) with a previously installed version that worked. This helps you focus on a particular device that is causing problems instead of the entire system.	0	0	X
Microsoft Incident Submission	You can automatically submit an electronic support incident to Microsoft, collaborate with support engineers, and manage your submitted incidents.	0	0	X

Table A-7 Networking Capabilities: Windows 98 SE, Windows Me, and Windows XP Home Edition
(0 = Not Implemented, / = Partially Implemented, X = Fully Implemented)

Feature	Feature Description	Windows 98 SE	Windows ME	Windows XP Home Edition
Windows Messenger	Communicate with friends, family, and colleagues in real time. Choose text, voice, or video. Collaborate with buddies, transfer files, and share applications and whiteboard drawings.	/ You can download MSN Messenger, which lets you have text and voice conversations.	X	X
Home Networking	Allows you: To set up a home network, including physical connections such as for printers or faxes, installing protocols and bridging. To share an Internet connection with all computers on a network. To share resources on a computer. Home networking is enhanced with the Internet Connection Firewall to help protect your home network from unauthorized access while you're connected to the Internet.	/ You need to add Internet connectivity tools from your Windows CD-ROM.	/ Wizards and network connections aren't as advanced as in Windows XP.	X
Network Bridge	Simplifies the configuration and setup of home networks that use mixed connections by linking the different types of networks.	0	/ Can bridge only 2 segments.	X
Internet Connection Sharing	Allows multiple computers in your home to access the Internet at the same time via the same broadband or dial-up connection. Windows XP Home Edition is now available with the option to remotely disconnect your dial-up connection to use your phone line and resume the connection again.	X	X	X Windows XP Home Edition provides more built-in support for cameras and scanners.
Internet Explorer	Internet Explorer 6 is the latest major update to Internet Explorer technologies and provides a private, reliable, and flexible Internet browsing experience. Internet Explorer 6 includes many new and enhanced features that can simplify the daily tasks that you perform while helping you to maintain the privacy of your personal information on the Web. The latest version of Internet Explorer has also taken steps to improve Web browser reliability with the option of fault collection services. With the new browser capabilities, including media playback and automatic picture resizing, you can customize your Web experience.	/ Can be downloaded from the Internet.	X Windows Me includes Internet Explorer 5.5.	X

Table A-8 Built-In Game and Music Support: Windows 98 SE, Windows Me, and Windows XP Home Edition.
(0 = Not Implemented, / = Partially Implemented, X = Fully Implemented)

Feature	Feature Description	Windows 98 SE	Windows ME	Windows XP Home Edition
Internet-enabled games	Using the Internet, you can be matched with players from around the world on games like Internet Backgammon, Internet Checkers, Internet Reversi, and Internet Spades, or you can invite your friends to play against you in other Internet-based games.	0	0	X
Windows Media Player for Windows XP	Windows Media Player for Windows XP brings together the most common digital media activities in one place. Windows Media Player for Windows XP provides new features such as DVD playback, native CD burning, and the ability to export video to portable devices. Also included are new and improved video controls, offline metadata support (for enhanced DVD viewing), and a more streamlined and flexible user interface.	0 Download MP7	/	X
My Music	Enables you to quickly view a list of music files in a folder and perform basic management tasks such as retrieving, adding, sorting, and deleting. It is now task-based to help you work more efficiently.	0	/	X
Auto-Recognition	If you insert a CD, ZIP, or JAZ disk, or compact flash card, Windows will automatically recognize it and launch the corresponding application. For example, your CDs will begin playing on Windows Media Player for Windows XP.	0	0	X
CD Burning	Saving critical information to a CD is as easy as saving to a floppy disk or hard disk. By selecting a folder of software, photos, or even your music, and dragging it to the CD-R device icon, you can create your own CDs.	0	0	X
Portable Music Devices	Windows Media Player for Windows XP provides you with the ability to connect to your music and devices in a way that best suits your needs.	0	X With Windows Media Player 7	X With Windows Media Player for Windows XP

Table A-9 Managing Pictures and Video: Windows 98 SE, Windows Me, and Windows XP Home Edition
(0 = Not Implemented, / = Partially Implemented, X = Fully Implemented)

Feature	Feature Description	Windows 98 SE	Windows ME	Windows XP Home Edition
My Pictures	Enables you to quickly view a list of photos in a folder and perform basic management tasks like adding, sorting, and deleting picture files. You can also: Order prints directly from the Internet. Link to the Camera And Scanner Wizard for fast access. View images in a slideshow. Publish pictures to the Internet. Compress pictures for easier e-mail distribution. Optimize printing your pictures to make the best use of high-quality photo paper.	0	/	X
Scanner and Camera Wizard	Provides you with the ability: To scan a single image from a flatbed scanner. To scan images from a scanner based on a scanner event. To scan a collection of images. To scan multipage documents or images from a scanner into a single image file. To scan multipage documents or images from a scanner into separate image files.	0	/	X
Web Publishing Wizard	The Web Publishing Wizard walks you through publishing your pictures to the Web quickly and easily so you can share them with others.	0	0	X
Order Photo Prints from the Internet	With My Pictures, you can order your digital pictures directly over the Internet and have them delivered to you. This feature is subject to local vendor availability.	0	0	X
Windows Movie Maker	Provides the ability to easily capture, edit, organize, and share home movies.	0	X	X

Table A-10 Capabilities: Windows XP Home Edition and Windows XP Professional
(0 = Not Implemented, X = Fully Implemented)

Features	Windows XP Home Edition	Windows XP Professional
All Features of Windows XP Home Edition		
New user interface—makes it easy to find what you need when you need it.	X	X
A reliable foundation you can count on—keeps your computer up and running.		
Windows Media Player for Windows XP—a single place for finding, playing, organizing, and storing digital media.		
Network Setup Wizard—connect and share the computers and devices in your home.		

Table A-10 Capabilities: Windows XP Home Edition and Windows XP Professional *(0 = Not Implemented, X = Fully Implemented) (continued)*

Features	Windows XP Home Edition	Windows XP Professional
Windows Messenger–a communications and collaboration tool with instant messaging, voice and video conferencing, and application sharing.	X	X
Help and Support Center–a resource that helps you recover from problems and get help and support.		
Mobile Support		
Advanced laptop support (including ClearType support, DualView, and power management improvements).	X	X
Wireless connections–automatic 802.1x wireless network configuration.	X	X
Remote Desktop–remotely access your Windows XP Professional PC from another Windows PC so you can work with all your data and applications while you're away from your office.	0	X
Offline Files and Folders – access to files and folders on a network share when disconnected from the server.	0	X
Multitasking Capability		
Fast start-up and power management improvements–faster boot and resume times.	X	X
Multitasking–allow multiple applications to run simultaneously.	X	X
Scalable processor support–up to two-way multiprocessor support.	0	X
Security and Privacy		
Internet Connection Firewall–automatically shields your PC from unauthorized access when you're on the Internet.	X	X
Internet Explorer 6 privacy support–maintain control over your personal information when visiting Web sites.	X	X
Encrypting File System–protects sensitive data in files that are stored on disk using the NTFS file system.	0	X
Access Control–restrict access to selected files, applications, and other resources.	0	X
Compatibility with Microsoft Windows Servers		
Centralized administration–join Windows XP Professional systems to a Windows Server domain to take advantage of the full range of management and security tools.	0	X
Group Policy–simplifies the administration of groups of users or computers.	0	X
Software Installation and Maintenance–automatically install, configure, repair, or remove software applications.	0	X
Roaming User Profiles–access to all your documents and settings no matter where you log on.	0	X

Table A-10 Capabilities: Windows XP Home Edition and Windows XP Professional *(0 = Not Implemented, X = Fully Implemented) (continued)*

Features	Windows XP Home Edition	Windows XP Professional
Remote Installation Service (RIS)—support for remote operating system installations where desktops can be installed across the network.	0	X
Global Communications and Accessibility		
Single Worldwide Binary—enter text in any language and run any language version of Win32 applications on any language version of Windows XP.	X	X
Multilingual User Interface (MUI) add-on—change the user interface language to get localized dialog boxes, menus, help files, dictionaries, and proofing tools, and so on.	0	X

Glossary

10Base-T The Ethernet standard for baseband LANs (local area networks) using twisted-pair cable carrying 10 Mbps (megabits per second) in a star topology. All nodes are connected to a central hub known as a multiport repeater.

100Base-T An Ethernet standard for baseband LANs (local area networks) using twisted-pair cable carrying 100 Mbps (megabits per second). The 100Base-T standard is comprised of 100Base-T4 (four pairs of medium-grade to high-grade twisted-pair cable) and 100Base-TX (two pairs of high-grade twisted-pair cable). *Also called:* Fast Ethernet

Active Directory A Microsoft technology, part of the Active Platform, that is designed to enable applications to find, use, and manage directory resources (for example, user names, network printers, and permissions) in a distributed computing environment. Distributed environments are usually heterogeneous collections of networks that often run proprietary directory services from different providers. To simplify directory-related activities associated with locating and administering network users and resources, Active Directory presents applications with a single set of interfaces that eliminates the need to deal with differences between and among these proprietary services. Active Directory is a component of the Windows Open Services Architecture (WOSA).

add-on 1. A hardware device, such as an expansion board or chip, that can be added to a computer to expand its capabilities. *Also called:* add-in. 2. A supplemental program that can extend the capabilities of an application program.

Address Resolution Protocol (ARP) The identification of a computer's IP (Internet Protocol) address by finding the corresponding match in an address mapping table.

analog Pertaining to or being a device or signal that is continuously varying in strength or quantity, such as voltage or audio, rather than based on discrete units, such as the binary digits 1 and 0. A lighting dimmer switch is an analog device because it is not based on absolute settings.

ANSI 1. Acronym for American National Standards Institute. A voluntary, nonprofit organization of business and industry groups formed in 1918 for the development and adoption of trade and communication standards in the United States. ANSI is the American representative of ISO (the International Organization for Standardization). Among its many concerns, ANSI has developed recommendations for the use of programming languages including FORTRAN, C, and COBOL, and various networking technologies. 2. The Microsoft Windows ANSI character set. This set is includes ISO 8859/x plus additional characters. This set was originally based on an ANSI draft standard. The MS-DOS operating system uses the ANSI character set if ANSI.SYS is installed.

AppleTalk An inexpensive local area network developed by Apple Computer, Inc., for Macintosh computers that can be used by Apple and non-Apple computers to communicate and share resources such as printers and file servers. Non-Apple computers must be equipped with AppleTalk hardware and suitable software. The network uses a layered set of protocols similar to the ISO/OSI reference model and transfers information in the form of packets called frames. AppleTalk supports connections to other AppleTalk networks through devices known as bridges, and it supports connections to dissimilar networks through devices called gateways.

AppleTalk Phase 2 The extended AppleTalk Internet model designed by Apple Computer, Inc., that supports multiple zones within a network and extended addressing capacity.

architecture 1. The physical construction or design of a computer system and its components. 2. The data-handling capacity of a microprocessor. 3. The design of application software incorporating protocols and the means for expansion and interfacing with other programs.

asymmetric digital subscriber line (ADSL) Technology and equipment allowing high-speed digital communication, including video signals, across an ordinary twisted-pair copper phone line, with speeds up to 8 Mbps (megabits per second) downstream (to the customer) and up to 640 Kbps (kilobits per second) upstream. ADSL access to the Internet is offered by some regional telephone companies, offering users faster connection times than those available through connections made over standard phone lines.

asynchronous communication Computer-to-computer communications in which the sending and receiving computers do not rely on timing as a means of determining where transmissions begin and end.

AutoIP Short for automatic Internet Protocol addressing. A technique used by a device to obtain a valid IP address without a DHCP server or other IP-configuration authority. With AutoIP, a device randomly chooses an IP address from a set of reserved addresses and queries the local network to determine whether another client already is using that address. The device repeats the steps of picking and verifying until an unused address is found. AutoIP, based on an Internet Engineering Task Force (IETF) Internet Draft, is used in Universal Plug and Play (UPnP) networking.

Automatic Private IP Addressing (APIPA) A feature of Windows XP TCP/IP that automatically configures a unique IP address from the range 169.254.0.1 through 169.254.255.254 and a subnet mask of 255.255.0.0 when the TCP/IP protocol is configured for dynamic addressing and Dynamic Host Configuration Protocol (DHCP) is not available.

bandwidth 1. The difference between the highest and lowest frequencies that an analog communications system can pass as measured in Hertz (Hz) or cycles per second. For example, a telephone accommodates a bandwidth of 3000 Hz: the difference between the lowest (300 Hz) and highest (3300 Hz) frequencies it can carry. 2. The data transfer capacity, or speed of transmission, of a digital communications system as measured in bits per second (bps).

baud rate The speed at which a modem can transmit data. The baud rate is the number of events, or signal changes, that occur in one second—not the number of bits per second (bps) transmitted. In high-speed digital communications, one event can actually encode more than one bit, and modems are more accurately described in terms of bits per second than baud rate. For example, a so-called 9600-baud modem actually operates at 2400 baud but transmits 9600 bits per second by encoding 4 bits per event (2400 x 4 = 9600) and thus is a 9600-bps modem.

bit Short for binary digit. The smallest unit of information handled by a computer. One bit expresses a 1 or a 0 in a binary numeral, or a true or false logical condition, and is represented physically by an element such as a high or low voltage at one point in a circuit or a small spot on a disk magnetized one way or the other. A single bit conveys little information a human would consider meaningful. A group of 8 bits, however, makes up a byte, which can be used to represent many types of information, such as a letter of the alphabet, a decimal digit, or other character.

bits per second (bps) The measure of transmission speed used in relation to networks and communication lines. Although bps represents the basic unit of measure, networks and communications devices, such as modems, are so fast that speeds are usually given in multiples of bps—Kbps (kilobits, or thousands of bits, per second), Mbps (megabits, or millions of bits, per second), and Gbps (gigabits, or billions of bits, per second). Speed in bps is not the same as the baud rate for a modem.

Bluetooth wireless technology A specification for radio links between mobile PCs, mobile phones, and other portable devices. These radio links are small-form factor, low cost, and short range.

broadband communications Of or relating to communications systems in which the medium of transmission (such as a wire or fiber-optic cable) carries multiple messages at a time, each message modulated on its own carrier frequency by means of modems. Broadband communication is found in wide area networks.

broadband connection A high-speed connection. Broadband connections are typically 256 kilobytes per second (KBps) or faster. Broadband includes DSL and cable modem service.

bus A set of hardware lines (conductors) used for data transfer among the components of a computer system. A bus is essentially a shared highway that connects different parts of the system—including the processor, disk-drive controller, memory, and input/ output ports—and enables them to transfer information. The bus consists of specialized groups of lines that carry different types of information. One group of lines carries data; another carries memory addresses (locations) where data items are to be found; yet another carries control signals. Buses are characterized by the number of bits they can transfer at a single time, equivalent to the number of wires within the bus. A computer with a 32-bit address bus and a 16-bit data bus, for example, can transfer 16 bits of data at a time from any of 232 memory locations. Most PCs contain one or more expansion slots into which additional boards can be plugged to connect them to the bus.

cable modem A modem that sends and receives data through a coaxial cable television network instead of telephone lines, as with a conventional modem. Cable modems, which have speeds of 500 kilobits per second (Kbps), can generally transmit data faster than current conventional modems. However, cable modems do not operate at the same rate upstream (when sending information) and downstream (when receiving information). Upstream rates vary from about 2 Mbps to 10 Mbps, downstream rates from about 10 Mbps to 36 Mbps.

callback A security feature used to authenticate users calling in to a network. During callback, the network validates the caller's username and password, hangs up, and then returns the call, usually to a preauthorized number. This security measure usually prevents unauthorized access to an account even if an individual's logon ID and password have been stolen.

cascading hubs A network configuration in which hubs are connected to other hubs.

Category 3 or Cat3 cable Network cable that supports frequencies up to 16 MHz and transmission speeds up to 10 Mbps (standard Ethernet). Category 3 cable has four unshielded twisted pairs (UTPs) of copper wire and RJ-45 connectors, and is used in voice and 10Base-T applications.

Category 5 or Cat5 cable Network cable that supports frequencies up to 100 MHz and transmission speeds up to 100 Mbps (using two pairs) or 1000 Mbps (using four pairs and called gigabit over copper). Category 5 cable has four unshielded twisted pairs (UTPs) of copper wire and RJ-45 connectors, and is used for 10/100/1000 Base-T, ATM, and token ring networks.

Category 5e or Cat5e cable Network cable that supports frequencies up to 100 MHz and transmission speeds up to 1000 Mbps (half-duplex mode) or 2000 Mbps (full-duplex mode). Category 5e cable has four unshielded twisted pairs (UTPs) of copper wire, RJ-45 connectors, and enhanced shielding to prevent signal degradation. Category 5e cable can be used for 10/100/1000 Base-T, ATM, and token ring networks.

CD-R Acronym for compact disc-recordable. A type of CD-ROM that can be written on a CD recorder and read on a CD-ROM drive.

CD-RW Acronym for compact disc-rewritable. The technology, equipment, software, and media used in the production of multiple-write CDs (compact discs).

CEBus Short for Consumer Electronic Bus. CEBus is an open architecture set of specification documents that define protocols for how to make products communicate through power line wires, low voltage twisted pairs, coax, infrared, RF, and fiber optics. Anyone, anywhere can get a copy of the plans and develop products that work with the CEBus standard.

client 1. In object-oriented programming, a member of a class (group) that uses the services of another class to which it is not related. 2. A process, such as a program or task, that requests a service provided by another program—for example, a word processor that calls on a sort routine built into another program. The client process uses the requested service without having to "know" any working details about the other program or the service itself. 3. On a local area network or the Internet, a computer that accesses shared network resources provided by another computer (called a server).

cluster 1. An aggregation, such as a group of data points on a graph. 2. A communications computer and its associated terminals. 3. In data storage, a disk-storage unit consisting of a fixed number of sectors (storage segments on the disk) that the operating system uses to read or write information; typically, a cluster consists of two to eight sectors, each of which holds a certain number of bytes (characters). 4. A group of independent network servers that operate—and appear to clients—as if they were a single unit. A cluster network is designed to improve network capacity by, among other things, enabling the servers within a cluster to shift work in order to balance the load. By enabling one server to take over for another, a cluster network also enhances stability and minimizes or eliminates downtime caused by application or system failure.

coaxial cable A round, flexible, two-conductor cable consisting of—from the center outwards—a copper wire, a layer of protective insulation, a braided metal mesh sleeve, and an outer shield, or jacket of PVC or fire-resistant material. The shield prevents signals transmitted on the center wire from affecting nearby components and prevents external interference from affecting the signal carried on the center wire. Coaxial cable is widely used in networks. It is the same type of wiring as that used for cable television.

communication port A port on a computer that allows asynchronous communication of one byte at a time. *Also called:* serial port

communication settings Operating parameters, such as bits per second (bps) and modem type, that apply to serial ports on a computer.

credentials A set of information that includes identification and proof of identification that is used to gain access to local and network resources. Examples of credentials are user names and passwords, smart cards, and certificates.

crossover cable A cable used to connect two computers together for file sharing and personal networking. Crossover cables may be connected to Ethernet or FireWire ports.

default gateway A configuration item for the TCP/IP protocol that is the IP address of a directly reachable IP router. Configuring a default gateway creates a default route in the IP routing table.

device A generic term for a computer subsystem. Printers, serial ports, and disk drives are often referred to as devices; such subsystems frequently require their own controlling software, called device drivers.

device driver A software component that permits a computer system to communicate with a device. In most cases, the driver also manipulates the hardware in order to transmit the data to the device. However, device drivers associated with application packages typically perform only the data translation; these higher-level drivers then rely on lower-level drivers to actually send the data to the device. Many devices, especially video adapters on PC-compatible computers, will not work properly—if at all—without the correct device drivers installed in the system.

DHCP Acronym for Dynamic Host Configuration Protocol. A TCP/IP protocol that enables a network connected to the Internet to assign a temporary IP address to a host automatically when the host connects to the network.

dial-up networking Connection to a remote network through use of a modem. Dial-up networking is typically used in reference to telecommuting, although the term is equally applicable to connecting to the Internet.

digital video disc (DVD) The next generation of optical disc storage technology. With digital video disc technology, video, audio, and computer data can be encoded onto a compact disc (CD). A digital video disc can store greater amounts of data than a traditional CD. A standard single-layer, single-sided digital video disc can store 4.7 GB of data; a two-layer standard increases the single-sided disc capacity to 8.5 GB. Digital video discs can be double-sided with a maximum storage of 17 GB per disc. A digital video disc player is needed to read digital video discs; this player is equipped to read older optical storage technologies. Advocates of the digital video disc intend to replace current digital storage formats, such as laser disc, CD-ROM, and audio CD, with the single digital format of the digital video disc.

direct cable connection A link between the I/O ports of two computers that uses a single cable rather than a modem or other active interface device. In most cases, a direct cable connection requires a null modem cable.

directory service A service on a network that returns mail addresses of other users or enables a user to locate hosts and services.

DNS Acronym for Domain Name System. The hierarchical system by which hosts on the Internet have both domain name addresses (such as bluestem.prairienet.org) and IP addresses (such as 192.17.3.4). The domain name address is used by human users and is automatically translated into the numerical IP address, which is used by the packet-routing software. DNS names consist of a top-level domain (such as .com, .org, and .net), a second-level domain (the site name of a business, an organization, or an individual), and possibly one or more subdomains (servers within a second-level domain).

DNS server Short for Domain Name System server, a computer that can answer Domain Name System (DNS) queries. The DNS server keeps a database of host computers and their corresponding IP addresses. Presented with the name apex.com, for example, the DNS server would return the IP address of the hypothetical company Apex. *Also called:* name server

DNS suffix For DNS, a character string that represents a domain name. The DNS suffix shows where a host is located relative to the DNS root, specifying a host's location in the DNS hierarchy. Usually, DNS suffix describes the latter portion of a DNS name, following one or more of the first labels of a DNS name.

domain 1. In database design and management, the set of valid values for a given attribute. For example, the domain for the attribute AREA-CODE might be the list of all valid three-digit numeric telephone area codes in the United States. 2. For Windows NT Advanced Server, a collection of computers that share a common domain database and security policy. Each domain has a unique name. 3. In the Internet and other networks, the highest subdivision of a domain name in a network address, which identifies the type of entity owning the address (for example, .com for commercial users or .edu for educational institutions) or the geographical location of the address (for example, .fr for France or .sg for Singapore). The domain is the last part of the address (for example, www.acm.org).

domain controller In Windows NT, the master server that holds the directory services database that identifies all network users and resources.

DSL Acronym for Digital Subscriber Line, a recently developed (late 1990s) digital communications technology that can provide high-speed transmissions over standard copper telephone wiring. DSL is often referred to as xDSL, where the x stands for one or two characters that define variations of the basic DSL technology. Currently, ADSL (Asymmetric DSL) is the form most likely to be provided, but even it is, as yet, available only to limited groups of subscribers.

DVD decoder A hardware or software component that allows a digital video disc (DVD) drive to display movies on your computer screen.

Ethernet 1. The IEEE 802.3 standard for contention networks. Ethernet uses a bus or star topology and relies on the form of access known as Carrier Sense Multiple Access with Collision Detection (CSMA/CD) to regulate communication line traffic. Network nodes are linked by coaxial cable, by fiberoptic cable, or by twisted-pair wiring. Data is transmitted in variable-length frames containing delivery and control information and up to 1500 bytes of data. The Ethernet standard provides for baseband transmission at 10 megabits (10 million bits) per second and is available in various forms, including those known as Thin Ethernet, Thick Ethernet, 10Base2, 10Base5, 10Base-F, and 10Base-T. The IEEE standard dubbed 802.3z, or Gigabit Ethernet, operates at 10 times 100 Mbps speed. 2. A widely used local area network system developed by Xerox in 1976, from which the IEEE 802.3 standard was developed.

expansion slot A socket in a computer, designed to hold expansion boards and connect them to the system bus (data pathway). Expansion slots are a means of adding or enhancing the computer's features and capabilities. In laptop and other portable computers, expansion slots come in the form of PCMCIA slots designed to accept PC Cards.

Extensible Markup Language (XML) A condensed form of SGML (Standard Generalized Markup Language). XML lets Web developers and designers create customized tags that offer greater flexibility in organizing and presenting information than is possible with the older HTML document coding system. XML is defined as a language standard published by the W3C and supported by the industry.

Fast Ethernet Descriptor used for any of three forms of 100 Mbps Ethernet networks: 100Base-T4, 100Base-TX, or 100Base-FX.

fiberoptic cable A form of cable used in networks that transmits signals optically, rather than electrically as do coaxial and twisted-pair cable. The light-conducting heart of a fiberoptic cable is a fine glass or plastic fiber called the core. This core is surrounded by a refractive layer called the cladding that effectively traps the light and keeps it bouncing along the central fiber. Outside both the core and the cladding is a final layer of plastic or plastic-like material called the coat, or jacket. Fiberoptic cable can transmit clean signals at speeds as high as 2 Gbps. Because it transmits light, not electricity, it is also immune to eavesdropping.

file sharing The use of computer files on networks, wherein files are stored on a central computer or a server and are requested, reviewed, and modified by more than one individual. When a file is used with different programs or different computers, file sharing can require conversion to a mutually acceptable format. When a single file is shared by many people, access can be regulated through such means as password protection, security clearances, or file locking to prohibit changes to a file by more than one person at a time.

firewall A security system intended to protect an organization's network against external threats, such as hackers, coming from another network, such as the Internet. Usually a combination of hardware and software, a firewall prevents computers in the organization's network from communicating directly with computers external to the network and vice versa. Instead, all communication is routed through a proxy server outside of the organization's network, and the proxy server decides whether it is safe to let a particular message or file pass through to the organization's network.

gateway A device that connects networks using different communications protocols so that information can be passed from one to the other. A gateway both transfers information and converts it to a form compatible with the protocols used by the receiving network.

Gigabit Ethernet The IEEE standard dubbed 802.3z, which includes support for transmission rates of 1 Gbps (gigabit per second)—1000 Mbps (megabits per second)—over an Ethernet network. The usual Ethernet standard (802.3) supports only up to 100 Mbps.

home network 1. A communications network in a home or building used for home automation. Home networks can use wiring (existing or new) or wireless connections. 2. Two or more computers in a home that are interconnected to form a local area network (LAN).

HomePNA Short for Home Phoneline Networking Alliance. An association of more than 100 companies working toward the adoption of a unified technology for setting up home networks over existing telephone wiring. Phoneline networking allows multiple PCs, printers, and peripheral devices to be connected for such purposes as multiplayer gaming, sharing printers and other peripherals, and rapid downloads over the Internet. The alliance was founded by a number of companies including IBM, Intel, AT&T, and Lucent Technologies.

HomeRF Acronym for Home Radio Frequency. A wireless home-networking specification that uses the 2.4-GHz frequency band to communicate between computers, peripherals, cordless phones, and other devices. HomeRF is supported by Siemens, Compaq, Motorola, National Semiconductor, Proxim, and other companies.

host 1. The main computer in a mainframe or minicomputer environment—that is, the computer to which terminals are connected. 2. In PC-based networks, a computer that provides access to other computers. 3. On the Internet or other large networks, a server computer that has access to other computers on the network. A host computer provides services, such as news, mail, or data, to computers that connect to it.

host name The name of a specific server on a specific network within the Internet, leftmost in the complete host specification. For example, www.microsoft.com indicates the server called "www" within the network at Microsoft Corporation.

hub In a network, a device joining communication lines at a central location, providing a common connection to all devices on the network. The term is an analogy to the hub of a wheel.

ICS *See* Internet Connection Sharing.

ICS client A computer in a home or small office network that connects the Internet through the ICS host computer.

ICS host A computer in a home or small office network that connects directly to the Internet and shares its connection with the rest of the computers on the network.

IEEE Acronym for Institute of Electrical and Electronics Engineers. A society of engineering and electronics professionals based in the United States but boasting membership from numerous other countries. The IEEE (pronounced "eye triple ee") focuses on electrical, electronics, computer engineering, and science-related matters.

IEEE 1394 A nonproprietary, high-speed, serial bus input/output standard. IEEE 1394 provides a means of connecting digital devices, including personal computers and consumer electronics hardware. It is platform-independent, scalable (expandable), and flexible in supporting peer-to-peer (roughly, device-to-device) connections. IEEE 1394 preserves data integrity by eliminating the need to convert digital signals into analog signals. Created for desktop networks by Apple Computer and later developed by the IEEE 1394 working group, it is considered a low-cost interface for devices such as digital cameras, camcorders, and multimedia devices and is seen as a means of integrating personal computers and home electronics equipment. FireWire is the proprietary implementation of the standard by Apple Computer.

IEEE 1394 connector A type of connector that enables you to connect and disconnect high-speed serial devices. An IEEE 1394 connector is usually on the back of your computer near the serial port or the parallel port. The IEEE 1394 bus is used primarily to connect high-end digital video and audio devices to your computer; however, some hard disks, printers, scanners, and DVD drives can also be connected to your computer using the IEEE 1394 connector.

IEEE 1394 port A 4- or 6-pin port that supports the IEEE 1394 standard and can provide direct connections between digital consumer electronics and computers.

IEEE 802.11 The Institute of Electrical and Electronics Engineers' (IEEE) specifications for wireless networking. These specifications, which include 802.11, 802.11a, 802.11b, and 802.11g, allow computers, printers, and other devices to communicate over a wireless local area network (LAN).

infrared (IR) Having a frequency in the electromagnetic spectrum in the range just below that of red light. Objects radiate infrared in proportion to their temperature. Infrared radiation is traditionally divided into four somewhat arbitrary categories based on its wavelength.

infrared device A computer, or a computer peripheral such as a printer, that can communicate by using infrared light.

infrared file transfer Wireless file transfer between a computer and another computer or device using infrared light.

infrared network connection A direct or incoming network connection to a remote access server using an infrared port.

infrared port An optical port on a computer for interfacing with an infrared-capable device. Communication is achieved without physical connection through cables. Infrared ports can be found on some laptops, notebooks, and printers.

input/output (I/O) port An interface through which data is transferred between a computer and other devices (such as a printer, mouse, keyboard, or monitor), a network, or a direct connection to another computer. The port appears to the CPU as one or more memory addresses that it can use to send or receive data. Specialized hardware, such as in an add-on circuit board, places data from the device in the memory addresses and sends data from the memory addresses to the device. Ports may also be dedicated solely to input or to output. Ports typically accept a particular type of plug used for a specific purpose. For example, a serial data port, a keyboard, and a high-speed network port all use different connectors, so it's not possible to plug a cable into the wrong port.

Integrated Services Digital Network *See* ISDN

Internet Connection Firewall Firewall software that is used to set restrictions on what information is communicated from your home or small office network to and from the Internet to your network.

Internet Connection Sharing (ICS) A feature in Windows XP that connects home or small office network computers to the Internet using a single Internet connection.

Internet gateway A device that provides the connection between the Internet backbone and another network, such as a LAN (local area network). Usually the device is a computer dedicated to the task or a router. The gateway generally performs protocol conversion between the Internet backbone and the network, data translation or conversion, and message handling. A gateway is considered a node on the Internet.

Internet Protocol (IP) The protocol within TCP/IP that governs the breakup of data messages into packets, the routing of the packets from sender to destination network and station, and the reassembly of the packets into the original data messages at the destination. IP runs at the internetwork layer in the TCP/IP model—equivalent to the network layer in the ISO/OSI reference model.

intranet A private network based on Internet protocols such as TCP/IP but designed for information management within a company or organization. Its uses include such services as document distribution, software distribution, access to databases, and training. An intranet is so called because it looks like a World Wide Web site and is based on the same technologies, yet is strictly internal to the organization and is not connected to the Internet proper. Some intranets also offer access to the Internet, but such connections are directed through a firewall that protects the internal network from the external Web.

IP address Short for Internet Protocol address. A 32-bit (4-byte) binary number that uniquely identifies a host (computer) connected to the Internet to other Internet hosts, for the purposes of communication through the transfer of packets. An IP address is expressed in "dotted quad" format, consisting of the decimal values of its 4 bytes, separated with periods; for example, 127.0.0.1. The first 1, 2, or 3 bytes of the IP address identify the network the host is connected to; the remaining bits identify the host itself. The 32 bits of all 4 bytes together can signify almost 232, or roughly 4 billion, hosts. (A few small ranges within that set of numbers are not used.) *Also called:* Internet Protocol number; IP number

IP telephony Telephone service including voice and fax, provided through an Internet or network connection. IP telephony requires two steps: conversion of analog voice to digital format by a coding/uncoding device (codec) and conversion of the digitized information to packets for IP transmission. *Also called:* Internet telephony; Voice over IP (VoIP)

IrDA Acronym for Infrared Data Association. The industry organization of computer, component, and telecommunications vendors who have established the standards for infrared communication between computers and peripheral devices such as printers.

ISA Acronym for Industry Standard Architecture. A bus design specification that allows components to be added as cards plugged into standard expansion slots in IBM Personal Computers and compatibles. Originally introduced in the IBM PC/XT with an 8-bit data path, ISA was expanded in 1984, when IBM introduced the PC/AT, to permit a 16-bit data path. A 16-bit ISA slot actually consists of two separate 8-bit slots mounted end-to-end so that a single 16-bit card plugs into both slots. An 8-bit expansion card can be inserted and used in a 16-bit slot (it occupies only one of the two slots), but a 16-bit expansion card cannot be used in an 8-bit slot.

ISDN Acronym for Integrated Services Digital Network. A high-speed digital communications network evolving from existing telephone services. The goal in developing ISDN was to replace the current telephone network, which requires digital-to-analog conversions, with facilities totally devoted to digital switching and transmission, yet advanced enough to replace traditionally analog forms of data, ranging from voice to computer transmissions, music, and video. ISDN is available in two forms, known as BRI (Basic Rate Interface) and PRI (Primary Rate Interface). BRI consists of two B (bearer) channels that carry data at 64 Kbps and one D (data) channel that carries control and signal information at 16 Kbps. In North America and Japan, PRI consists of 23 B channels and 1 D channel, all operating at 64 Kbps; elsewhere in the world, PRI consists of 30 B channels and 1 D channel. Computers and other devices connect to ISDN lines through simple, standardized interfaces.

ISP Acronym for Internet service provider. A business that supplies Internet connectivity services to individuals, businesses, and other organizations. Some ISPs are large national or multinational corporations that offer access in many locations, while others are limited to a single city or region. *Also called:* access provider; service provider

L2TP Short for Layer Two Tunneling Protocol. An industry-standard Internet tunneling protocol that provides encapsulation for sending Point-to-Point Protocol (PPP) frames across packet-oriented media. For IP networks, Layer Two Tunneling Protocol traffic is sent as User Datagram Protocol (UDP) messages. In Microsoft operating systems, this protocol is used in conjunction with Internet Protocol security (IPSec) as a virtual private network (VPN) technology to provide remote access or router-to-router VPN connections. Layer Two Tunneling Protocol is described in RFC 2661.

LAN Acronym for local area network. A group of computers and other devices dispersed over a relatively limited area and connected by a communications link that enables any device to interact with any other on the network. LANs commonly include PCs and shared resources such as laser printers and large hard disks. The devices on a LAN are known as nodes, and the nodes are connected by cables through which messages are transmitted.

Mbps Short for mega bits per second. One million bits per second.

media The physical material, such as paper, disk, and tape, used for storing computer-based information. Media is plural; medium is singular.

Microsoft .NET The set of Microsoft technologies that provides tools for connecting information, people, systems, and devices. The technologies provide individuals and organizations with the ability to build, host, deploy, and use XML Web service connected solutions.

modem 1. Short for modulator/demodulator. A communications device that converts between digital data from a computer or terminal and analog audio signals that can pass through a standard telephone line. Because the telephone system was designed to handle voice and other audio signals and a computer processes signals as discrete units of digital information, a modem is necessary at both ends of the telephone line to exchange data between computers. At the transmit end, the modem converts from digital to analog audio; at the receiving end, a second modem converts the analog audio back to its original digital form. In order to move a high volume of data, high-speed modems rely on sophisticated methods for "loading" information onto the audio carrier—for example, they may combine frequency shift keying, phase modulation, and amplitude modulation to enable a single change in the carrier's state to represent multiple bits of data. In addition to the basic modulation and demodulation functions, most modems also include firmware that allows them to originate and answer telephone calls. International standards for modems are specified by the International Telecommunications Union, or ITU. Despite their capabilities, modems do require communications software in order to function. 2. Any communications device that acts as an interface between a computer or terminal and a communications channel. Although such a device may not actually modulate or demodulate analog signals, it may be described as a modem because a modem is perceived by many users to be a black box that connects a computer to a communications line (such as a high-speed network or a cable TV system).

MP3 Acronym for MPEG Audio Layer-3. A digital audio coding scheme used in distributing recorded music over the Internet. MP3 shrinks the size of an audio file by a factor of 10 to 12 without seriously degrading the quality (CD-recording level) of the sound. MP3 files are given the file extension .mp3. Although MP3 is part of the MPEG family, it is audio-only and is not the same as the now-defunct MPEG-3 standard.

MPEG 1. Acronym for Moving Picture Experts Group. A set of standards for audio and video compression established by the Joint ISO/IEC Technical Committee on Information Technology. The MPEG standard has different types that have been designed to work in different situations. 2. A video/audio file in the MPEG format. Such files generally have the extension .mpg.

multicasting The process of sending a message simultaneously to more than one destination on a network.

multihoming 1. In Mac OS X, an automatic network selection feature that allows one computer to maintain multiple network addresses. Multihoming may be used with a computer that is used from multiple locations, such as home and office, or to create special connection settings, such as separate systems for communication inside and outside of an intranet. 2. The use of multiple addresses and/or multiple interfaces for a single node. A multihomed host has either multiple network interfaces connected to two or more networks, or a single network interface that has been assigned multiple IP addresses. Multihoming can be used to provide redundancy to achieve quality of service.

Musical Instrument Digital Interface (MIDI) A serial interface standard that allows for the connection of music synthesizers, musical instruments, and computers. The MIDI standard is based partly on hardware and partly on a description of the way in which music and sound are encoded and communicated between MIDI devices. The information transmitted between MIDI devices is in a form called a MIDI message, which encodes aspects of sound such as pitch and volume as 8-bit bytes of digital information. MIDI devices can be used for creating, recording, and playing back music. Using MIDI, computers, synthesizers, and sequencers can communicate with each other, either keeping time or actually controlling the music created by other connected equipment.

name resolution The process of having software translate between names that are easy for users to work with and numerical IP addresses, which are difficult for users but necessary for TCP/IP communications. Name resolution can be provided by software components such as DNS or WINS.

NAT Acronym for Network Address Translation. The process of converting between IP addresses used within an intranet or other private network and Internet IP addresses. This approach makes it possible to use a large number of addresses within the private network without depleting the limited number of available numeric Internet IP addresses. Variations of NAT displaying similar functions include IP aliasing, IP masquerading, and Port Address Translation.

network A group of computers and associated devices that are connected by communications facilities. A network can involve permanent connections, such as cables, or temporary connections made through telephone or other communication links. A network can be as small as a LAN (local area network) consisting of a few computers, printers, and other devices, or it can consist of many small and large computers distributed over a vast geographic area (WAN, or wide area network).

network adapter A device that connects your computer to a network. This device is sometimes called an adapter card or network interface card (NIC).

network administrator The person in charge of operations on a computer network. The duties of a network administrator can be broad and might include such tasks as installing new workstations and other devices, adding and removing individuals from the list of authorized users, archiving files, overseeing password protection and other security measures, monitoring usage of shared resources, and handling malfunctioning equipment.

network bridge A device that connects networks using the same communications protocols so that information can be passed from one to the other. Also, a device that connects two local area networks, whether or not they use the same protocols. A network bridge operates at the ISO/OSI data-link layer.

Network Connections A component you can use to gain access to network resources and functionality, whether you are physically at the network location or in a remote location. By using the Network Connections folder you can create, configure, store, and monitor connections

network interface card (NIC) An expansion card or other device used to provide network access to a computer or other device, such as a printer. Network interface cards mediate between the computer and the physical media, such as cabling, over which transmissions travel. *Also called:* network adapter; network card

network services 1. In a corporate environment, the division that maintains the network and the computers. 2. In a Windows environment, extensions to the operating system that allow it to perform network functions such as network printing and file sharing.

New Connection Wizard A software tool within Windows XP that helps users create Internet, dial-up, virtual private networking (VPN), incoming, and direct connections. In earlier versions of Windows, this tool was known as the Internet Connection Wizard.

node 1. A junction of some type. 2. In networking, a device, such as a client computer, a server, or a shared printer, that is connected to the network and is capable of communicating with other network devices. 3. In tree structures, a location on the tree that can have links to one or more nodes below it. Some authors make a distinction between node and element, with an element being a given data type and a node comprising one or more elements as well as any supporting data structures.

offline 1. In reference to a computing device or a program, unable to communicate with or be controlled by a computer. 2. In reference to one or more computers, being disconnected from a network. 3. Colloquially, a reference to moving a discussion between interested parties to a later, more appropriate, time. For example, "We can talk about this offline. Let's get back on topic now."

online 1. In reference to a computing device or a program, activated and ready for operation; capable of communicating with or being controlled by a computer. 2. In reference to one or more computers, connected to a network. 3. In reference to a user, currently connected to the Internet, an online service, or a BBS or using a modem to connect to another modem. 4. In reference to a user, being able to connect to the Internet, an online service, or a BBS by virtue of having an account that gives one access.

parallel port An input/output connector that sends and receives data 8 bits at a time, in parallel, between a computer and a peripheral device such as a printer, scanner, CD-ROM, or other storage device. The parallel port, often called a Centronics interface after the original design standard, uses a 25-pin connector called a DB-25 connector that includes three groups of lines: four for control signals, five for status signals, and eight for data.

PC Card An add-in card that conforms to the PCMCIA specification. A PC Card is a removable device, approximately the same size as a credit card, that is designed to plug into a PCMCIA slot. Release 1 of the PCMCIA specification, introduced in June 1990, specified a Type I card that is 3.3 millimeters thick and is intended to be used primarily as a memory-related peripheral. Release 2 of the PCMCIA specification, introduced in September 1991, specifies both a 5-millimeter-thick Type II card and a 10.5-millimeter-thick Type III card. Type II cards accommodate devices such as modem, fax, and network cards. Type III cards accommodate devices that require more space, such as wireless communications devices and rotating storage media (such as hard disks).

PCI expansion slot A connection socket for a peripheral designed for the Peripheral Component Interconnect (PCI) local bus on a computer motherboard.

PCI local bus Short for Peripheral Component Interconnect local bus. A specification introduced by Intel Corporation that defines a local bus system that allows up to 10 PCI-compliant expansion cards to be installed in the computer. A PCI local bus system requires the presence of a PCI controller card, which must be installed in one of the PCI-compliant slots. Optionally, an expansion bus controller for the system's ISA, EISA, or Micro Channel Architecture slots can be installed as well, providing increased synchronization over all the system's bus-installed resources. The PCI controller can exchange data with the system's CPU either 32 bits or 64 bits at a time, depending on the implementation, and it allows intelligent, PCI-compliant adapters to perform tasks concurrently with the CPU using a technique called bus mastering. The PCI specification allows for multiplexing, a technique that permits more than one electrical signal to be present on the bus at one time.

PDA Acronym for Personal Digital Assistant. A lightweight palmtop computer designed to provide specific functions like personal organization (calendar, note taking, database, calculator, and so on) as well as communications. More advanced models also offer multimedia features. Many PDA devices rely on a pen or other pointing device for input instead of a keyboard or mouse, although some offer a keyboard too small for touch typing to use in conjunction with a pen or pointing device. For data storage, a PDA relies on flash memory instead of power-hungry disk drives.

peer Any of the devices on a layered communications network that operate on the same protocol level.

peer-to-peer architecture A network of two or more computers that use the same program or type of program to communicate and share data. Each computer, or peer, is considered equal in terms of responsibilities and each acts as a server to the others in the network. Unlike a client/server architecture, a dedicated file server is not required. However, network performance is generally not as good as under client/server, especially under heavy loads. *Also called:* peer-to-peer network

peripheral In computing, a device, such as a disk drive, printer, modem, or joystick, that is connected to a computer and is controlled by the computer's microprocessor. *Also called:* peripheral device

plastic optical fiber *See* fiberoptic cable

plug and play (PnP) 1. Generally, a reference to the ability of a computer system to automatically configure a device added to it. Plug and play capability exists in Macintoshes based on the NuBus and, since Windows 95, on PC-compatible computers. 2. When capitalized and, especially, when abbreviated PnP, a set of specifications developed by Intel and Microsoft that allows a PC to configure itself automatically to work with peripherals such as monitors, modems, and printers. A user can plug in a peripheral and "play" it without manually configuring the system. A Plug and Play PC requires both a BIOS that supports Plug and Play and a Plug and Play expansion card.

Point-to-Point Protocol (PPP) A widely used data link protocol for transmitting TCP/IP packets over dial-up telephone connections, such as between a computer and the Internet. PPP, which supports dynamic allocation of IP addresses, provides greater protection for data integrity and security and is easier to use than SLIP, at a cost of greater overhead. PPP itself is based on a Link Control Protocol (LCP) responsible for setting up a computer-to-computer link over telephone lines and a Network Control Protocol (NCP) responsible for negotiating network-layer details related to the transmission. It was developed by the Internet Engineering Task Force in 1991.

Point-to-Point Tunneling Protocol (PPTP) An extension of the Point-to-Point Protocol used for communications on the Internet. PPTP was developed by Microsoft to support virtual private networks (VPNs), which allow individuals and organizations to use the Internet as a secure means of communication. PPTP supports encapsulation of encrypted packets in secure wrappers that can be transmitted over a TCP/IP connection.

port 1. An interface through which data is transferred between a computer and other devices (such as a printer, mouse, keyboard, or monitor), a network, or a direct connection to another computer. The port appears to the CPU as one or more memory addresses that it can use to send or receive data. Specialized hardware, such as in an add-on circuit board, places data from the device in the memory addresses and sends data from the memory addresses to the device. Ports may also be dedicated solely to input or to output. Ports typically accept a particular type of plug used for a specific purpose. For example, a serial data port, a keyboard, and a high-speed network port all use different connectors, so it's not possible to plug a cable into the wrong port. *Also called:* input/output port. 2. port number.

print sharing The ability for computers on a network to share access to a printer.

protocols A set of rules or standards designed to enable computers to connect with one another and to exchange information with as little error as possible. The protocol generally accepted for standardizing overall computer communications is a seven-layer set of hardware and software guidelines known as the OSI (Open Systems Interconnection) model. A somewhat different standard, widely used before the OSI model was developed, is IBM's SNA (Systems Network Architecture). The word protocol is often used, sometimes confusingly, in reference to a multitude of standards affecting different aspects of communication, such as file transfer (for example, XMODEM and ZMODEM), handshaking (for example, XON/XOFF), and network transmissions (for example, CSMA/CD).

proxy server A firewall component that manages Internet traffic to and from a local area network (LAN) and can provide other features, such as document caching and access control. A proxy server can improve performance by supplying frequently requested data, such as a popular Web page, and can filter and discard requests that the owner does not consider appropriate, such as requests for unauthorized access to proprietary files.

quality of service (QoS) 1. Generally, the handling capacity of a system or service; the time interval between request and delivery of a product or service to the client or customer. 2. In computer technology, the guaranteed throughput (data transfer rate) level.

radio frequency (RF) The portion of the electromagnetic spectrum with frequencies between 3 kilohertz and 300 gigahertz. This corresponds to wavelengths between 30 kilometers and 0.3 millimeter.

remote access The use of a remote computer.

remote access server (RAS) A host on a LAN (local area network) that is equipped with modems to enable users to connect to the network over telephone lines.

resource 1. Any part of a computer system or a network, such as a disk drive, printer, or memory, that can be allotted to a program or a process while it is running. 2. An item of data or code that can be used by more than one program or in more than one place in a program, such as a dialog box, a sound effect, or a font in a windowing environment. Many features in a program can be altered by adding or replacing resources without the necessity of recompiling the program from source code. Resources can also be copied and pasted from one program into another, typically by a specialized utility program called a resource editor. 3. Any nonexecutable data that is logically deployed with an application. A resource might be displayed in an application as error messages or as part of the user interface. Resources can contain data in a number of forms, including strings, images, and persisted objects.

RJ-11 connector An attachment used to join a telephone line to a device such as a modem.

RJ-45 connector Short for Registered Jack-45 connector. An eight-wire connector used to attach devices to cables. The eight wires are encased in a plastic sheath and color-coded to match corresponding slots in jacks. RJ-45 jacks are used to connect computers to LANs (local area networks) and to link ISDN (Integrated Services Digital Network) devices to NT-1 (Network Terminator 1) devices. *Also called:* RJ-45 jack

RS-232-C standard An accepted industry standard for serial communications connections. Adopted by the Electrical Industries Association, this Recommended Standard (RS) defines the specific lines and signal characteristics used by serial communications controllers to standardize the transmission of serial data between devices. The letter C denotes that the current version of the standard is the third in a series.

security The technologies used to make a service resistant to unauthorized access to the data that it holds or for which it is responsible. A major focus of computer security, especially on systems that are accessed by many people or through communications lines, is the prevention of system access by unauthorized individuals.

SerialKey device Enables you to attach an alternative input device (*Also called:* an augmentative communication device) to your computer's serial port. This feature is designed for people who are unable to use the computer's standard keyboard and mouse.

serial port An input/output location (channel) that sends and receives data to and from a computer's central processing unit or a communications device one bit at a time. Serial ports are used for serial data communication and as interfaces with some peripheral devices, such as mice and printers.

server 1. On a local area network (LAN), a computer running administrative software that controls access to the network and its resources, such as printers and disk drives, and provides resources to computers functioning as workstations on the network. 2. On the Internet or other network, a computer or program that responds to commands from a client. For example, a file server may contain an archive of data or program files; when a client submits a request for a file, the server transfers a copy of the file to the client.

share To make files, directories, or folders accessible to other users over a network.

shared folder On a Macintosh computer connected to a network and running System 6.0 or higher, a folder that a user has made available to others on the network. A shared folder is analogous to a network directory on a PC.

shared folder permissions Permissions that restrict a shared resource's availability over the network to only certain users.

shared printer A printer that receives input from more than one computer.

shared resource 1. Any device, data, or program used by more than one device or program. 2. On a network, any resource made available to network users, such as directories, files, and printers.

share name A name that refers to a shared resource on a server. Each shared folder on a server has a share name used by personal computer users to refer to the folder. Users of Macintosh computers use the name of the Macintosh-accessible volume that corresponds to a folder, which may be the same as the share name.

smart device An electronic device capable of being networked and remotely controlled in a smart home. Smart devices can include appliances, lighting, heating and cooling systems, entertainment systems, and security systems.

synchronization 1. In networking, a communications transmission in which multibyte packets of data are sent and received at a fixed rate. 2. In networking, the matching of timing between computers on the network. All of the computers are generally assigned identical times to facilitate and coordinate communications. 3. In a computer, the matching of timing between components of the computer so that all are coordinated. For instance, operations performed by the operating system are generally synchronized with the signals of the machine's internal clock. 4. In application or database files, version comparisons of copies of the files to ensure they contain the same data. 5. In multimedia, precise real-time processing. Audio and video are transmitted over a network in synchronization so that they can be played back together without delayed responses. 6. In handheld computing, the process of updating or backing up the data on a handheld computer to the linked software applications on a desktop computer. Data changes made on the desktop computer may also be copied to the handheld during synchronization.

synchronize To cause to occur at the same time.

TCP Acronym for Transmission Control Protocol. The protocol within TCP/IP that governs the breakup of data messages into packets to be sent via IP (Internet Protocol), and the reassembly and verification of the complete messages from packets received by IP. A connection-oriented, reliable protocol (reliable in the sense of ensuring error-free delivery), TCP corresponds to the transport layer in the ISO/OSI reference model.

TCP/IP Acronym for Transmission Control Protocol/Internet Protocol. A protocol suite (or set of protocols) developed by the U.S. Department of Defense for communications over interconnected, sometimes dissimilar, networks. It is built into the UNIX system and has become the de facto standard for data transmission over networks, including the Internet.

telephony Telephone technology—voice, fax, or modem transmissions based on either the conversion of sound into electrical signals or wireless communication via radio waves.

tunnel To encapsulate or wrap a packet or a message from one protocol in the packet for another. The wrapped packet is then transmitted over a network via the protocol of the wrapper. This method of packet transmission is used to avoid protocol restrictions.

tunnel server A server or router that terminates tunnels and forwards traffic to the hosts on the target network.

twisted-pair cable A cable made of two separately insulated strands of wire twisted together. It is used to reduce signal interference introduced by a strong radio source such as a nearby cable. One of the wires in the pair carries the sensitive signal, and the other wire is grounded.

Universal Plug and Play (UPnP) A Microsoft initiative which prompted the creation of the UPnP Forum for interconnecting computers, appliances, networks, and services. UPnP extends conventional Plug and Play to include devices connected to networks. It allows peripheral devices to discover and connect to other devices and to enumerate the characteristics of those devices. UPnP is intended to be an element of home networking, in which PCs, appliances, and the services they provide are linked together.

universal serial bus (USB) A serial bus with a data transfer rate of 12 megabits per second (Mbps) for connecting peripherals to a microcomputer. USB can connect up to 127 peripherals, such as external CD-ROM drives, printers, modems, mice, and keyboards, to the system through a single, general-purpose port. This is accomplished by daisy chaining peripherals together. USB is designed to support the ability to automatically add and configure new devices and the ability to add such devices without having to shut down and restart the system (hot plugging). USB was developed by Intel, Compaq, DEC, IBM, Microsoft, NEC, and Northern Telecom. It competes with DEC's ACCESS.bus for lower-speed applications.

USB port An interface on the computer that enables you to connect a Universal Serial Bus (USB) device. USB is an external bus standard that enables data transfer rates of 12 Mbps (12 million bits per second). USB ports support a plug that is approximately 7 mm x 1 mm.

virtual private network (VPN) 1. Nodes on a public network such as the Internet that communicate among themselves using encryption technology so that their messages are as safe from being intercepted and understood by unauthorized users as if the nodes were connected by private lines. 2. A WAN (wide area network) formed of permanent virtual circuits (PVCs) on another network, especially a network using technologies such as ATM or frame relay.

Voice over Internet Protocol (VoIP) The use of the Internet Protocol (IP) for transmitting voice communications. VoIP delivers digitized audio in packet form and can be used for transmitting over intranets, extranets, and the Internet. It is essentially an inexpensive alternative to traditional telephone communication over the circuit-switched Public Switched Telephone Network (PSTN). VoIP covers computer-to-computer, computer-to-telephone, and telephone-based communications. For the sake of compatibility and interoperability, a group called the VoIP Forum promotes product development based on the ITU-T H.323 standard for transmission of multimedia over the Internet.

WAN Acronym for wide area network. A geographically widespread network, one that relies on communications capabilities to link the various network segments. A WAN can be one large network, or it can consist of a number of linked LANs (local area networks).

Web phone Point-to-point voice communication that uses the Internet instead of the public-switched telecommunications network to connect the calling and called parties. Both the sending and the receiving party need a computer, a modem, an Internet connection, and an Internet telephone software package to make and receive calls.

Wi-Fi Short for wireless fidelity, a standard approved by the Institute of Electrical and Electronics Engineers (IEEE) for wireless networking. Also known as 802.11b.

wireless Of, pertaining to, or characteristic of communications that take place without the use of interconnecting wires or cables, such as by radio, microwave, or infrared light.

wizard 1. Someone who is adept at making computers perform their "magic." A wizard is an outstanding and creative programmer or a power user. 2. A participant in a multiuser dungeon (MUD) who has permission to control the domain, even to delete other players' characters. 3. An interactive help utility within an application that guides the user through each step of a particular task, such as starting up a word processing document in the correct format for a business letter.

workgroup A group of users working on a common project and sharing computer files, typically over a LAN (local area network).

writeable CD A recordable compact disc (CD-R) or rewritable compact disc (CD-RW). Data can be copied to the CD on more than one occasion. Rewritable compact discs can also be erased.

xDSL An umbrella term for all of the digital subscriber line (DSL) technologies, which use a variety of modulation schemes to pack data onto copper wires. The x is a placeholder for the first or first two letters of a member technology, which might be ADSL, HDSL, IDSL, RADSL, or SDSL.

XML Acronym for eXtensible Markup Language, a condensed form of SGML (Standard Generalized Markup Language). XML lets Web developers and designers create customized tags that offer greater flexibility in organizing and presenting information than is possible with the older HTML document coding system. XML is defined as a language standard published by the W3C and supported by the industry

Index

Numbers and Symbols

A

B

C

D

H

I

J

K

L

M

N

T

U

V

W

Curtis Frye

Curtis Frye is a writer specializing in Internet technologies, Web commerce, and Microsoft Office. He has written ten books, authored three online training courses, and is the editor and lead reviewer for *Technology & Society Book Reviews*.

The manuscript for this book was prepared and submitted to Microsoft Press in electronic form. The pages were composed by nSight, Inc., using Adobe FrameMaker+SGML for Windows, with text in Garamond and display text in ITC Franklin Gothic Condensed. Composed pages were delivered to the printer as electronic pre-press files.

Cover Designer:	Tim Girvin Design
Interior Graphic Designer:	James D. Kramer
Compositor:	Patty Fagan
Project Manager:	Tempe Goodhue
Copy Editor:	Lisa Wehrle
Technical Editor:	Christopher M. Russo
Proofreaders:	Janice O'Leary, Robert Saley
Indexer:	Jack Lewis

Get a **Free**

e-mail newsletter, updates, special offers, links to related books, and more when you

register on line!

Register your Microsoft Press® title on our Web site and you'll get a FREE subscription to our e-mail newsletter, *Microsoft Press Book Connections.* You'll find out about newly released and upcoming books and learning tools, online events, software downloads, special offers and coupons for Microsoft Press customers, and information about major Microsoft® product releases. You can also read useful additional information about all the titles we publish, such as detailed book descriptions, tables of contents and indexes, sample chapters, links to related books and book series, author biographies, and reviews by other customers.

Registration is easy. Just visit this Web page and fill in your information:

http://www.microsoft.com/mspress/register

Microsoft®

Proof of Purchase

Use this page as proof of purchase if participating in a promotion or rebate offer on this title. Proof of purchase must be used in conjunction with other proof(s) of payment such as your dated sales receipt—see offer details.

Faster Smarter Home Networking

0-7356-1869-0

CUSTOMER NAME

Microsoft Press, PO Box 97017, Redmond, WA 98073-9830